D1377978

HERESY,
Yes
CONSPIRACY,
No

HERESY,
Yes
CONSPIRACY,
No

Sidney Hook

PROFESSOR OF PHILOSOPHY

NEW YORK UNIVERSITY

THE JOHN DAY COMPANY

NEW YORK

Copyright, 1953, by Sidney Hook

Manufactured in the United States of America

Library of Congress Catalog Card Number: 53-6587

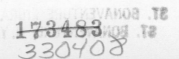

To
NORMAN THOMAS
AMERICAN HERETIC AND DEMOCRAT
AND TO
HORACE M. KALLEN
AMERICAN INDIVIDUALIST—CULTURAL PLURALIST

CONTENTS

INTRODUCTION

Any sober assessment of the state of cultural freedom in this country is bound to displease two articulate groups whose influence is out of all proportion to their numbers.

The first group, legitimately appalled by the growth of communism as a world power and by the evidence of its penetration into many places in American life, has exaggerated the threat of communism as a domestic danger. It has interpreted innocence, ignorance and naiveté in combating communism, because of the gravity of their effects, as morally indistinguishable from treason. It has attacked as a menace to American freedom and security men and ideas that are not only non-Communist but sometimes anti-Communist. Drawn by the turbid water its threshing has produced, a considerable number of hate-obsessed individuals has been attracted to its side. These men and women regard the anti-Communist mood in the country as a heaven-sent opportunity to discredit opponents of their pet aversion or panacea, whether it be high taxation, progressive education, public housing or separation of church and state. The most popular technique by which this is accomplished is to suggest that such opposition is incompatible with anti-Communism, or to show that the Communists, too, are arrayed in opposition, and thus to insinuate, by the commonest fallacy in human life, (which the text-books characterize as the fallacy of the undistributed middle term), that their opponents are Communists.

9

Introduction

The second group, aware of the excesses and foolishness of those who under the guise of anti-communism attack many good causes, have tended to dismiss too lightly the conspiratorial character of the Communist movement. What is even worse, they have cried havoc and made such fearful lament, that one would think in consequence of episodic injustices here and there or an ill-considered piece of legislation that the whole structure of American freedom has been eroded. Carried away by legitimate resentment against injustice, they have with a good conscience, sometimes with a sense of righteous indignation, invented malicious legends about the state of political freedom in this country which fits the Communist picture of a nation under the iron heel of terror. If they have not declared outright that we are living under an American version of "fascism," their exaggerations have been cited as conclusive evidence by those who have made such declarations. This has been particularly true abroad where the influence of this group has proved most mischievous.

All this confusion has been compounded by a government policy whose chief architects have undoubtedly been men of moral integrity and patriotism but either of mediocre intelligence or the most extraordinary ignorance of the nature of the international Communist movement—an ignorance, sad to say, accentuated by stubbornness in refusing to admit that any errors have been made. This policy laid down a Truman doctrine to contain communism in Western Europe and sent an official emissary to urge Chiang-kai-shek to take the Chinese Communist Party into his regime. The chief executive of the nation almost at one and the same time dismissed the Hiss case as a "red herring" and instituted a most sweeping and indiscriminate loyalty program. He properly warned against inflation as a menace to a free culture and then with the spectacle of a free Britain before him referred to price controls as a sign of a police state.

The aberrations in official American policy have contributed in different ways to strengthening the influence of the two groups distinguished above and whom I have characterized respectively as "cultural vigilantes" and "ritualistic liberals." Both groups flourish on each other's misapprehension and their outcries have drowned out the voice of intelligence. The first group is institutionally stronger and far more dangerous because in a position to commit excesses. The second group has prevented the emergence of a unified liberal movement which can contain reaction at home and give leadership to the struggle against communism abroad.

As I read the cultural scene matters are growing worse. As the Kremlin continues to deploy its force in both hemispheres to undermine the United States, its chief remaining obstacle to world domination, and as American costs and casualties in the cold war mount, a mood of impatience is sure to grow with those who wish to examine whether the latest measures to protect Americans from Communism may not be more productive of harm than good. Unless carefully checked this impatience may equate difference with disloyalty and choke off the vigorous criticism and loyal opposition which generate the anti-bodies essential to democratic health. The calamity howlers and hysteria-mongers on both sides in virtue of their shrill exaggerations today may very well contribute to bring about tomorrow the state of affairs they deplore, and therewith help in the eclipse of liberalism in our generation.

Who are the leaders of the "cultural vigilantes"? They are the political demagogues in *both* political parties, religious fundamentalists in both Catholic and Protestant denominations, and some zealots and marginal types in some patriotic organizations. To these must be added certain lobbyists and advertisers who wish to discount the principles of democratic socialism, the New Deal, the Welfare State—the strongest enemies of communism— because the economic and social interests they represent would be adversely affected were these principles widely carried out.

Who are the leaders of the ritualistic liberals? They are some "professional" liberals, who are more hostile to anti-Communists than to communists, some inhumanists who call themselves Humanists, some irrationalists who think of themselves as Rationalists, some who have actively cooperated with Communist front organizations and who still regard communism as a kind of left wing liberalism, some absolute pacifists and that extreme wing of the Quakers which believes in peace at any price—even the price of freedom. The habitat of this group is in the main in the colleges and universities but they are also found in strategic places in the media which influence public opinion. They consist, with the exception of a few fellow travelers of the Communist Party who have changed their strategy of infiltration, of men and women full of the milk of human kindness. Unfortunately they carry it in their head instead of their breast.

The underlying premise of this book is that American institutions have a vitality and viability which, with a little gumption and intelligence, can effectively meet the threat of totalitarianism from abroad and at home without the loss of our own essential freedoms. Having when young experienced the years of the Palmer raids, massed physical assaults on peaceful meetings, systematic violations of due process of law by courts and police in relation to the rights of citizens, I regard the period since then, on the whole, as a progressive improvement with some serious but transitory setbacks like the forcible relocation of the Japanese during World War II. There is always the danger that an all out conflict with the Soviet Union may develop the psychology, if not the institutions, of a garrison state but the likelihood that this can be avoided may largely depend upon our ability to distinguish between relative degrees of danger. Those who shout that Fascism is here today, even when this does not echo the Communist Party line, can produce nothing but wearied resignation before the real thing. Preachers desperate for a text may lament the universal fear which silences everyone but themselves and a hundred million others from complaining. College presidents at a loss for a theme for a commencement address may deplore the threat to academic freedom somewhere or other but never at their own institution. They should begin to test their generalizations by reference to what they know best.

Introduction

The specific repressions and evils which are prevalent today are grave enough even if they do not prove that our democracy is lost. Exaggeration really induces complacency. If one believes that our democracy is on its way to disappearing he is not likely to bother protesting specific outrages, or to protest vigorously if he does.

The chapters which follow, written at different times but now revised and integrated with each other, revolve around the key distinction between heresy and conspiracy. The most important practical application of this distinction is to the question of academic freedom to which the second part of the book is devoted. It is safe to predict that the questions of academic freedom will grow in importance as the struggle between the West and Communist East becomes more intense. But it is a theme of perennial significance and one attended by all sorts of confusions. There is more sloppy rhetoric poured out per page about academic freedom both by those who believe that they are supporting, and those intent on criticizing it, than on any other theme with the possible exception of democracy. But whatever the character of the discussion, it is the teachers themselves who must formulate and administer the proper standards of academic freedom, not congressional committees or other agencies of the State.

The reader is asked to judge this book as a whole since different aspects of a problem are sometimes considered in different chapters. I am indebted to the *New York Times, Commentary, The Journal of Philosophy,* the *Journal of Higher Education, American Mercury, School and Society, The Saturday Evening Post,* and the *New Leader* for permission to reprint material which originally appeared in their pages.

SIDNEY HOOK

South Wardsboro, Vermont.
January 1, 1953

Part One

HERESY AND CONSPIRACY

Men of Athens: I honor and love you; but I shall obey God rather than you, and while I have life and strength I shall never cease from the practice and teaching of philosophy . . .

Some one will say: yes, Socrates, but cannot you hold your tongue, and then you may go into a foreign city, and no one will interfere with you? Now I have great difficulty in making you understand my answer to this. For if I tell you that to do as you say would be a disobedience to the God, and that therefore I cannot hold my tongue, you will not believe I am serious; and if I say again that daily discourse about virtue, and of those other things about which you hear me examining myself and others, is the greatest good of man and that the unexamined life is not worth living, you are still less likely to believe me. Yet I say what is true. . . .

—Socrates

The democratic idea of freedom is not the right of each individual to *do* as he pleases, even if it be qualified by adding "provided he does not interfere with the same freedom on the part of others." While the idea is not always, not often enough, expressed in words, the basic freedom is that of freedom of *mind* and of whatever degree of freedom of action and experience is necessary to produce freedom of intelligence. . . .

—John Dewey

Chapter 1

HERESY AND CONSPIRACY

The "hot war" in Korea makes it even more urgent that we clarify our thinking on the "cold war" of ideologies. At the heart of the matter are basic philosophical issues which in more settled times would have been dismissed as of no practical concern. One of them is the meaning of "liberalism." Subject of innumerable conferences, books and articles, it is also a recurrent theme of court decisions and even some current state papers.

Judging by public discussion, there are few Americans who do not regard themselves as "liberals." Legislation is often defended or criticized not in terms of its reasonably anticipated consequences but because it seems to be in accordance with, or opposed to, the "principles" of liberalism. Sometimes those who profess liberalism will line up on opposite sides of the fence in respect to an identical legislative measure, even when they agree on the facts of the case. This suggests, that like all large words in human affairs—for example, "freedom," "love" and "experience"—the term "liberalism" is multiply ambiguous. In different periods, liberalism has meant different things, especially when it became the fighting slogan of particular groups with a special program. But there is a certain nucleus of meaning which has remained an historical constant in all movements that have called themselves liberal despite their differences on specific issues, and which is reflected in common usage. In this sense, no party has a monopoly of the term. Liberal men and ideas may sometimes be found in quarters that bear other labels.

What makes analysis of the meaning of liberalism more than an academic exercise is the challenge of the Communist movement, which invokes the freedoms that prevail in a liberal society in order to destroy it. Many proposals have been made to cope with this problem. All of them must face the question of whether, in advocating such measures, the principles of liberalism are themselves being consistently applied or compromised.

It is easier to say what liberalism is not than what it is. It is not identical with the belief in laissez faire or free enterprise in economics. For it is found among thinkers who anteceded the rise of capitalism. The temper of Great Britain has remained liberal despite the shifting economic programs and institutions of the last century, which have ranged from an unregulated private profit economy and great extremes in wealth and income to a moderate socialism and moderate differences in standards of life. Those who regard themselves as liberals today recognize that property is a form of power, and, like all power of man over man, must be responsible, and therefore limited. There is no agreement among liberals about the precise form social control must take. But in contradiction to some of their historical ancestors, they no longer regard all government action to further social welfare as unmitigated evil.

Nor is liberalism the philosophy of invariable compromise, nor the comforting notion that it is always possible to find a middle ground. No liberal who understands the nature of Fascism can say: "I am neither a Fascist nor an anti-Fascist." Neither can he say, if he understands the nature of communism, what Thomas Mann has repeatedly said: "I am neither a Communist nor an anti-Communist." Although prepared, even eager, to negotiate the conflict of legitimate claims even when they are extreme, in

Heresy and Conspiracy

order to avoid civil strife, he knows that not all claims are legitimate and that some causes cannot be compromised. If a man demands my purse, to grant him half of it is not a liberal solution. Were the U.S.S.R. to demand the cession of Alaska on the ground that the Tsar had no authority to sell it, it would not necessarily be a liberal policy to settle for half the territory.

From this it follows that although liberalism is naturally pacific, it is not pacifist. It does not make a fetish of "sweet reasonableness" in the face of aggression, and it is aware that appeasement may be a greater provocation to armed conflict than a judicious show of force as an index of ability to resist. The history of Allied relations with Hitler is indisputable evidence on this point.

Finally, liberalism cannot be identified with the traditional belief in specific, absolute or inalienable rights, since every such right is in fact evaluated in terms of its conseqences for society and is therefore subject to modification. One right limits another, and the final adjudication of the conflict of rights is made in the reflective light of the total situation, or of that set of rationally preferred freedoms whose existence may entail the temporary abridgement of any one freedom. To say that we cannot preserve our freedoms by sacrificing them is an empty piece of rhetoric, because a *particular* freedom must sometimes be sacrificed to preserve other freedoms.

The most comprehensive and adequate definition in positive terms of the meaning of liberalism, from Socrates to John Dewey, is suggested by the memorable words of Justice Holmes. It is the belief "in the free trade of ideas—that the test of truth is the power of thought to get itself accepted in the competition of the market." This is not a program of action nor a philosophical theory of truth, but an attitude or temper of mind towards all programs. Liberals may disagree among themselves about everything else; but all of them have this faith in common. It is a faith which marks off liberal from totalitarian culture. Any action which restricts the freedom of ideas to develop or circulate is illiberal.

There are at least two presuppositions of this belief in the free market of ideas. One of them is explicitly drawn by Justice Holmes and already recognized by Jefferson; the other is implicit and perhaps more important, for around it center most of our present difficulties.

The first is that the free expression and circulation of ideas may be checked wherever their likely effects constitute a clear and present danger to public peace or the security of the country. This is a specific application of the principle that no right is absolute when it endangers rights of equal or greater validity. In ordinary affairs, this is a commonplace. The right to inquire is innocent, but not when it leads someone to experiment on a human being to determine how long he can survive torture. The right to free speech is precious, but not when it blasts a reputation by libelous accusation. Truth is sacred, but a person who revealed it knowing that it would be used to destroy his country is a traitor. Freedom to worship God according to one's conscience is one of the historical cornerstones of the structure of American liberties, but it cannot be invoked to protect rituals which require human sacrifice or practices like plural marriages or refusal to submit to vaccination against plagues.

In the context of public affairs, however, there is a certain ambiguity involved in the conception of clear and present danger. Clear to whom? To the public enforcement agencies, to Congress, to the Justices of the Supreme Court (who are notoriously at odds with each other and who, on matters of fact, are less well informed than many laymen)? And how present must a "present danger" be? Must a riot be in progress before an anti-Semitic orator ranting about the forged *Protocols of Zion* is stopped from speaking? Must we await the actual delivery of an atomic bomb by a foreign power, or a formal declaration of war, before the incitements to treason by its fifth columnists in this country are curbed? These are some of the difficulties that attend the clear

Heresy and Conspiracy

and present danger formula. They cannot be solved by fiat. In all such questions of "proximity and degree," good judgment is required. The most we can expect is that those who make the judgment will be competently informed and ultimately responsible to the community at large. According to our practice, a clear and present danger exists in the United States when a majority of the Supreme Court says it does; in England, when Parliament says it does.

The second presupposition of the liberal's faith in the free market of ideas is that the competition will be honestly and openly conducted. For unless there are certain rules, so to speak, of honest competition, analogous to those which hold in other domains of testing and inquiry, freedom of choice is an illusion. If the market is rigged by money, power or fraud, what gets accepted is anything but the truth. If ability to withstand honest competition is not a sufficient condition of truth it is at least a necessary one. From the point of view of the liberal, it is not doctrines "fraught with death" which he fears, for his faith in intelligence is such that he is confident that in the open and honest exchange of opinion the majority of men will choose life, not death, and that if they choose death they deserve their fate. Men cannot be compelled to remain free, any more than they can be compelled to love one another. What the liberal fears is the systematic corruption of the free market of ideas by activities which make intelligent choice impossible. In short, what he fears is not heresy but conspiracy.

The failure to recognize the distinction between heresy and conspiracy is fatal to a liberal civilization, for the inescapable consequence of their identification is either self-destruction, when heresies are punished as conspiracies, or destruction at the hands of their enemies, when conspiracies are tolerated as heresies.

A heresy is a set of unpopular ideas or opinions on matters of grave concern to the community. The right to profess publicly a heresy of any character, on any theme, is an essential element of a liberal society. The liberal stands ready to defend the honest heretic no matter what his views against any attempt to curb him. It is enough that the heretic pays the price of unpopularity which he cannot avoid. In some respects each of us is a heretic, but a liberal society can impose no official orthodoxies of *belief*, disagreement with which entails loss of liberty or life.

A conspiracy, as distinct from a heresy, is a secret or underground movement which seeks to attain its ends not by normal political or educational processes but by playing outside the rules of the game. Because it undermines the conditions which are required in order that doctrines may freely compete for acceptance, because where successful it ruthlessly destroys all heretics and dissenters, a conspiracy cannot be tolerated without self-stultification in a liberal society.

A heresy does not shrink from publicity. It welcomes it. Not so a conspiracy. The signs of a conspiracy are secrecy, anonymity, the use of false names and labels, and the calculated lie. It does not offer its wares openly but by systematic infiltration into all organizations of cultural life, it seeks to capture strategic posts to carry out a policy alien to the purposes of the organization. There is political conspiracy, which is the concern of the state; but there may also be a conspiracy against a labor union, a cultural or professional association, or an educational institution which is not primarily the concern of the state but of its own members. In general, whoever subverts the rules of a democratic organization and seeks to win by chicanery what cannot be fairly won in the process of free discussion is a conspirator.

Communist *ideas* are heresies, and liberals need have no fear of them where they are freely and openly expressed. They should be studied and evaluated in the light of all the relevant evidence. No one should be punished because he holds them. The Communist *movement*, however, is something quite different from a mere heresy, for wherever it exists it operates along the lines laid down by Lenin as guides to Communists of all countries, and perfected in great detail since then.

Heresy and Conspiracy

It is necessary [so Lenin instructs all Communists] . . . to agree to any and every sacrifice and even—if need be—resort to all sorts of stratagems, manoeuvres, and illegal methods, to evasions and subterfuges . . . in order to carry on Communist work in them [trade unions] at all costs.

Selected Works, English translation, Vol. X, p. 95.

Further:

In all organizations without exception . . . (political, industrial, military, cooperative, educational, sports), groups or nuclei of Communists should be formed . . . mainly open groups but also secret groups.

Op. cit., p. 169.

There are no exceptions:

In all countries, even the freest, "legal" and "peaceful" in the sense that the class struggle is least acute in them, the time has fully matured when it is absolutely necessary for every Communist Party systematically to combine legal with illegal work, legal and illegal organizations. . . . Illegal work is particularly necessary in the army, the navy, and police.

pp. 172-3.

Under present conditions of political and military warfare, it is not hard to see what immense dangers to the security of liberal institutions is implicit in this strategy of infiltration and deceit. Even a few men in sensitive posts can do incalculable harm. These instructions—and there are many more detailed ones, combined with explicit directives to Communists to transform any war in which their country is involved, except one approved by the Soviet Union, into a civil war against their own government—indicate that members of the Communist party are not so much heretics as conspirators and in actual practice regard themselves as such.

There may be some justification for conspiratorial activity in undemocratic countries where heresies are proscribed, but Lenin,

23

as we have seen, makes no exceptions. Since 1917, he maintains, in no country of the world can the revolution be peacefully achieved. "Today, both in England and America, the 'essential' thing for 'every real people's revolution' is the *smashing,* the *destruction* of the 'ready-made state machinery'. . . ." (*Op. cit.* Vol. VII, p. 37, italics in original.)

How faithfully the Communist movement pursues the pattern laid down by its authoritative leaders in the political sphere is a matter of historical record. But unfortunately for the peace of mind of liberals, the same tactics are followed in other areas of social and cultural life. The history of American labor is replete with illustrations.

Every large labor organization in the United States has been compelled to take administrative action against Communist party elements not because of their beliefs—their heresies—but because their pattern of conduct made the Communist party, and ultimately the Kremlin, the decisive power in the life of the union, and not the needs and wishes of the membership. President Philip Murray of the CIO exposed the technique in detail when his organization ousted the Mine, Mill and Smelter Workers Union. In all these situations, it is not fear of Communist ideas which has led to disciplinary action. The charge against the Communists is that it is *they* who fear the open and honest confrontation of ideas. They operate through "fronts," the charge continues, because they fear that, given a free choice of honestly labeled alternatives, they will be rejected; once they slip into power, they consolidate their position by terror.

Under existing law punishment is provided for criminal conspiracy, whether this be conspiracy in restraint of trade or conspiracy to overthrow the government by insurrection or to advocate such overthrow in time of clear and present danger. But there are noncriminal conspiracies in sectors of life which are not affected by legislative power. These sectors of life are social and cultural and are regulated by tradition, common standards of propriety or decency in personal relations, and sometimes by explicit rules. The transfer of some of the techniques by which conspirators in the past have seized the state to capturing control of benevolent associations, social, chess, and athletic clubs, literary societies, research groups, professional and trade unions, even philanthropic agencies is unique to modern totalitarian movements. In the past, it was here if anywhere, that honest opposition openly declared itself. The elaborate devices adopted by Communists to disguise the nature of their opposition and to prevent others from functioning in opposition to them when they seize control may have been anticipated in earlier times by other groups but they never were previously employed with such fanaticism, rationalized by such body of doctrine, and executed with such lack of scruple.

By now it should be apparent that liberals in the twentieth century are confronted by a situation quite unfamiliar to their forbears. For they must contend not with fearless heretics, indigenous elements of the community who, like the abolitionists and revolutionists of old, scorn concealment, and who make no bones about their hostility to the principles of liberalism. They find themselves in the unique historical predicament of having to deal with native elements who, by secrecy and stratagem, serve the interests of a foreign power which believes itself entitled to speak for all mankind, and whose victory spells the end of all liberal civilization and with it the right to heresy. It is now plain that the Communist regimes of the world have turned out to be the greatest and cruelest heresy-hunters in history, not merely in politics but in every branch of theory and practice. They have even abolished the right to be silent, for on any matter on which the Central Committee of any Communist party has laid down the law, silence is construed as treason.

It is a great pity and a source of much confusion that present-day Communists are often referred to as Marxists, without further qualification. For this overlooks the radical departure from Marx's own position initiated by Lenin and Stalin on the question of conspiracy. Marx was an unconcealed heretic. Even

25

when writing in nondemocratic countries, subject to repression and imprisonment, he scorned the use of conspiratorial techniques and excoriated Bakunin and others for adopting them. The concluding sentence of the *Communist Manifesto* frankly tells the rulers of the nondemocratic countries of Europe: "The Communists disdain to conceal their views and aims. They openly declare that their ends can be attained only by the forcible overthrow of all existing social conditions."

Contrast with this the instructions given to Communists by the Kremlin in democratic countries, to adopt para-military organizational forms, to work underground even when legal work is permitted, and to develop systematic techniques of deception, and we can see the difference between honest and open revolutionists and underground conspirators.

The problems which underground conspiracy creates for a liberal society are of tremendous magnitude. They cannot be dismissed by a quotation from Jefferson. Nor can they be solved by indiscriminately placing the Communist movement and its entire periphery outside the law by special legislation. They require constructive intelligence, the discovery and application of techniques in each field which will meet conspiratorial threats to the proper functioning of liberal institutions without creating still greater ones. Legal outlawry of the Communist Party will not prevent it from reappearing under different names.

Failure to take this approach is characteristic of some current wholesale responses to the problem. The first is that of frightened reactionaries who cannot distinguish between heresy and conspiracy, and identify communism with any decent thing they wish to destroy. By making reckless charges of conspiracy where there is only honest heresy, they prevent intelligent choice. And by labeling all progressive ideas as Communist heresies, they help Communist strategy. For the Communist strategy is to make it appear that Communists are an integral part of the indigenous progressive movement, instead of a cancerous growth upon it, and that any legitimate measures directed against them is actually an attack upon all progressives, and indeed upon the philosophy of liberalism itself. There is nothing new about this unreasoning reaction. It emanates from the same quarters which called the Taft-Ellender Housing Bill "Communist," and plans for national health insurance "un-American."

A second response is made by a small but influential group of men who believe that they can check Communist conspiracy merely by passing laws against it, and that they can protect institutions from subversives by requiring all individuals, particularly teachers, to take loyalty oaths. As if any member of the Communist party regarded any oaths except one to the Communist party and the Soviet Union as binding! This results in foolish legislation like the Feinberg Law in New York and the Ober Law in Maryland, which are potentially dangerous in that they fail to make proper distinctions between conspirators and heretics.

A third group consists of those whom we may call ritualistic, as distinct from realistic, liberals. They ignore or blithely dismiss as comparatively insignificant the mass of evidence concerning the conspiratorial character of the Communist movement in all institutions in which it is active. They regard communism merely as an unpleasant heresy just a little worse than a crotchety theory of disease or finance. They sometimes characterize prosecution of a conspirator for espionage or perjury as persecution of a heretic. Or they condemn as "witch hunting," measures taken to deny access to sensitive posts in government or social institutions to members of the Communist party, who are under explicit instructions to sabotage the purposes of these organizations. The ritualistic liberals would wait until the sabotage has been carried out before proceeding against Communists. This gives a new lease of life to the reactionaries, who now tend to regard the ritualistic liberals as the dupes or accomplices of the Communists, thus confirming the illusions of the ritualistic liberals that there really is no problem of Communist conspiracy.

One of the most ambiguous phrases in current use among ritualistic liberals is "guilt by association." I shall analyze the meaning of this phrase at length in Chapter IV. A few preliminary observations are sufficient here.

American tradition is opposed to the doctrine of *legal* guilt by association. But common sense has always recognized that there may be moral guilt by continuous association with disreputable persons, as when a city official is condemned because the intimate cronies with whom he "associates" may be gangsters or racketeers. Sometimes a man's fitness for a post of trust is determined by his associations. It all depends upon the specific character of the associations.

Professor Arthur Lovejoy has pointed out in a brilliant note that the very term "association" is highly equivocal and is systematically employed to blur the truth about Communists. It covers innocent social gatherings and chance contacts as well as active collaboration. "One may 'associate' with Communist Party members (as I myself have done)," he writes, "in the hope of convincing them of their errors."

Those who argue that to judge a man by his membership in the Communist Party is to judge him "guilty by association" overlook the verifiable fact that membership in the Communist Party is rigorously controlled by an iron-clad discipline which excludes those who are inactive or in disagreement with the line of the party on *any* question. They seem unaware of the existence in the Communist Party of a "Control Commission" whose task, among other things, is to check up on the activities of members and expel those who disobey instructions. Before the practice became dangerous to the Communist Party, the Central Control Commission actually published the lists of members dropped for violations of party discipline. This is frankly admitted by leaders of the American Communist Party, as in the following colloquy a few years ago between Earl Browder and members of the House Committee on Un-American Activities:

Mr. Mathews: In numerous instances we have a notation [of the Central Control Commission] that the expelled

Heresy and Conspiracy

member "refused to carry out decisions." That is in line with your explanation of the relationship between the Communist Party of the United States and the Comintern?

Mr. Browder: Exactly.

Mr. Mathews: A member must carry out all decisions of the party or be expelled from the party?

The Chairman: Is that correct?

Mr. Browder: Yes, that is correct.

Mr. Starnes: A party member does not have any latitude or discretion in the matter—he has to carry out orders?

Mr. Browder: The party [member] has to carry out orders. (Hearings before Special Committee on Un-American Activities, House of Representatives, 76th Congress, First Session on H.Res. 282, Vol. 7, p. 4417.)

The Central (or National) Control Commission of the Communist Party still exists. This was dramatically revealed in the fall of 1952 at a public session of a subcommittee of the Senate Committee on Internal Security at which a professor of Brooklyn College testified to his former connections and the methods of blackmail used to prevent him from leaving the Communist Party. Among those present was an individual, one Konstantin Radzie, recognized by committee investigators as a functionary of the Communist Party. When explicitly asked whether he was a member of the Control Commission of the Communist Party, he refused to reply on the ground that his answer would be self-incriminating and pleaded the privileges of protection under the Fifth Amendment. (Cf. *New York Times,* Sept. 26, 1952.) Subsequently Mr. Radzie was identified publicly by John Lautner, formerly a member of the National Control Commission and Chairman of the New York State Control Commission of the Communist Party, as a member of the National Control Commission. Documentary evidence that Mr. Radzie's membership was of long standing was introduced in the form of a photostatic copy of the *Daily Worker* of March 11, 1929, announcing the selection of K. Radzie to the Central Control Commission by the Central Executive Committee of the Communist Party.*

Very few individuals who have discussed the issues posed by the existence of the Communist movement have paid proper attention to the existence of the mechanisms of control by which the Communist parties in all countries purge their ranks of the inactive, the doubtful, the half-hearted, or the critical—in short of all whose conformity is less than total. Still fewer have grasped the significance of these controls and the empirical evidence they offer that membership in the Communist Party is something earned only by good behavior as tested by rigorous standards set by a group which is professionally and doctrinally suspicious. If a man has been a member of the Communist Party over a period of time one can bet one's bottom dollar that he has carried out his major instructions and duties of membership to the satisfaction of his Communist superiors. Otherwise he would be outside of the party.

It is or should be now clear that "association" by way of membership in the Communist Party is not innocent or coincidental but is *a form of active co-operation and collaboration* in carrying out the purposes of a conspiratorial organization. The Communist Party sees to it that all members are instructed about the purposes as soon as they join. Continued membership is possible only in virtue of a series of continued *acts* of obedience to instructions. Those who dub the active co-operation required of all members of the Communist Party "guilt by association" coyly suggest by that phrase the innocuous association of chance or occasional encounters with Communists in social gatherings. They simply ignore the fact that all members of the Communist Party must "associate" by active co-operation with its purposes or be expelled.

Ritualistic liberals legitimately criticize the dangerous nonsense of those who proscribe heresy. But they carry their criti-

* *Hearings Before the Subcommittee of the Committee on the Judiciary of the U. S. Senate,* October 13, 1952, pp. 248-9.

cism to a point where they give the impression that the country is in the grip of a deadly reign of terror or hysteria much more dangerous than Communist expansion from without and infiltration from within. Because someone has given a silly characterization of a subversive organization, they imply that there are no subversive organizations. The sad history of recent American liberal movements, however, shows that the instructions given to American Communists by Otto Kuusinen, as Secretary of the Communist International, bore bitter fruit for liberals. Kuusinen advised: "We must create a whole solar system of organizations and smaller committees around the Communist Party, so to speak, smaller organizations working under the influence of the Party." (*American Communist*, May 1931.)

The problem of membership in Communist front organizations which often conceal their purposes is much more difficult. Many innocent people have been ensnared by these organizations. No hard and fast rule can be laid down as a guide. The number of such organizations an individual has joined, the time he joined, his function and activities upon joining—all these, as we shall see, are highly relevant in determining the degree to which an individual is untrustworthy from the point of view of security. Only those exceptional souls who have never made a mistake or have never been fooled can shut the gates of understanding and charity against all members of such groups and pronounce a blanket judgment against them. This troublesome question should not be made a matter of legislation but of judicious administration.

Because some security regulations in government are questionable, and because some blunders have been made, ritualistic liberals intimate that no security regulations are necessary and that the existing laws against treason and criminal conspiracy are sufficient for all purposes. They do not understand that the purpose of the security program is not punishment for acts committed but prevention of acts threatened by those who are under instructions to commit them or whose behavior or habits make them dangerous risks. By artfully collecting instances of foolishness from the press and blowing up their significance, they convey a very misleading picture comparable to what an account of American business would be like if only bankruptcies were reported, or an account of public order that featured only crime stories.

David Lilienthal, a realistic not a ritualistic liberal, has warned us against the "Scare-the-dopes!" method of discussing nuclear energy. There is also a "Scare-the-dopes!" method of discussion of the problem of Communistic conspiracy. It is used by those who employ the term Communist with scandalous looseness as a synonym for any economic or political heresy, and who shout conspiracy where there is only heresy. It is also used by those who do not tell us how to meet the real dangers of Communist conspiracy but shout "Hysteria!" "Fascism!" or "Police State!" when the first faltering efforts are made to cope with dangers hitherto unprecedented in the history of American democracy.

The position of realistic liberalism in three troubled centers of American life in which overt conspiratorial activity of a criminal nature is not involved may be briefly indicated as illustrative of its attitude.

Where government service is concerned, the operating maxim for every sensitive and policy-making post should be a principle enunciated by Roger Baldwin, former head of the American Civil Liberties Union: "A superior loyalty to a foreign government disqualifies a citizen for service to our own." This is not a matter of civil rights but of common sense. Once a policy is adopted by the governing agencies of a liberal society empowered by a democratic consensus to safeguard the public welfare, it is not only its right but its duty to insure its loyal execution. It cannot wait for a major piece of sabotage or leak of information in order to act. Yet this is precisely the procedure advocated by those who urge that once an individual has been appointed and served a probationary period, he should be dismissed only if he is caught engaging in espionage or sabotage. Presumably, even if it had been known that Hiss, Fuchs, Boyer, et al. were members of the

Heresy and Conspiracy

Communist Party, once employed they should not have been dismissed until they had carried out their objectives or were on the verge of doing so.

The difficulty lies in determining what constitutes sufficient evidence to warrant the inference that a particular individual is unsafe, for in some cases even past membership in subversive organizations is not conclusive. On the other hand, notoriously bad judgment might bar someone from an important post whose loyalty is not impugned. A fool may sometimes be as dangerous as a rogue. Nor can the principles that apply in a courtroom in determination of *criminal* guilt be applied in these situations. The criteria for establishing "unreliability" must obviously be less stringent than those which lead us to deprive an individual of his life or freedom.

It is not impossible to find knowledgeable individuals who can supervise such a program. Where certain procedural safeguards are adopted and individuals allowed in doubtful cases to resign quietly without prejudice when they do not wish to accept posts in nonsensitive sectors, the likelihood of injustice diminishes. The more fanfare and publicity, however, the greater are the chances of error and injury to reputation. Ritualistic liberals who insist that everything be decided in the public eye, and that a case be made out that can stick in a court of law before an individual is dropped as a security risk, are inviting political circuses and a reaction that will sweep away all administrative safeguards against arbitrary dismissal. It cannot be emphasized too often that there is a difference between legal rules of evidence absolutely essential to our tradition where a man's life or liberty is at stake and rules of evidence that bear only on an individual's qualifications for a position of trust. There is certainly room for criticism of present procedures, but whoever speaks up will be more persuasive if he presents alternative positive proposals which show that he at least recognizes the problem.

In labor organizations, the existence of Communist leaders is extremely dangerous because of their unfailing use of the strike

33

as a political instrument at the behest of the Kremlin. The history of Communist-led trade unions here and abroad is instructive enough. The most effective way of meeting this situation, however, is not by requiring non-Communist oaths on the part of union officers; for this can be circumvented by delegating office to individuals who are faithful but non-cardholding Communists. The most intelligent procedure for labor here is to let labor clean its own house. Free and independent trade unions, which are essential to a democracy, cannot be liberated from the organizational stranglehold of the Communist Party by government intervention. Only an aroused membership together with other labor organizations can do the job.

The question of freedom and responsibility in the schools will be discussed at length further along in this book. But in a preliminary way I wish to point out that the question is not primarily political. It does not involve civil rights so much as the ethics of professional conduct. Heresy in the schools—whether in science, economics, or politics—must be protected against any agency which seeks to impose orthodoxy. For the scholar there is no subversive doctrine, but only that which is valid or invalid or not proven in the light of evidence. The primary commitment of the teacher is to the ethics and logic of inquiry. It is not his beliefs, right or wrong—it is not his heresies—which disqualify the Communist party teacher, but his declaration of intention, as evidenced by official statements, to practice educational fraud. Must one catch him in the act before dismissing him? Not necessarily; any more than we must catch a judge who is a *present* and *active* member of the Ku Klux Klan in the act of discriminating against Negroes or Jews before concluding he is unfit for judicial office. It is amazing to hear from ritualistic liberals that it is a violation of academic freedom to prevent a man from carrying out the professional misconduct which he has pledged himself to engage in by virtue of his membership in an organization whose publicly professed aim is to indoctrinate for the Communist Party in classrooms, enroll students in Communist Youth organizations, rewrite textbooks from the Communist point of view, build cells on campuses, capture departments, and inculcate the Communist Party line that in case of war students should turn their arms against their own government.

This is a matter of ethical hygiene, not of political heresy or of persecution. And because it is, the enforcement of the proper professional standards should rest with the teachers themselves, and not with the state or regents or even boards of trustees. The actual techniques of handling such issues must be worked out, but the problem cannot be confused with the issue of heresy. If the conspiratorial purposes of Communist Party teachers is glossed over by ritualistic liberals as merely a manifestation of heresy, then all heresy comes under fire. This does not mean that faculties must engage in a hue and cry to rout out the few unfaithful members of the profession who are betraying their trust. But they must not refuse to act whenever evidence of such unfitness is established thus making clear that "not everything gives." What this involves will be spelled out in greater detail in Part II.

Liberalism in the twentieth century must toughen its fibre, for it is engaged in a fight on many different fronts. It must defend the free market in ideas against the racists, the professional patrioteers, and those spokesmen of the status quo who would freeze the existing inequalities of opportunity and economic power by choking off criticism. It must also be defended against those agents and apologists of Communist totalitarianism who, instead of honestly defending their heresies, resort to conspiratorial methods of anonymity and other techniques of fifth columnists. It will not be taken in by labels like "left" and "right." These terms came into use after the French Revolution, but the legacy of the men who then called themselves "left"—the strategic freedoms of the Bill of Rights—is today everywhere repudiated by those who are euphemistically referred to as "leftists" but who are actually Communists more reactionary than many of those who are conventionally called "rightists."

Heresy, Yes — Conspiracy, No

There is always a danger of excesses being committed when exposure of Communist conspiracy is left to the leadership of reactionaries. When this happens, it testifies to the fact that the liberals have failed to do the necessary job of moral education which is implicit in their dedication to the "free market in ideas." Similarly, they lose by default when, instead of taking the leadership in the struggle against "Know-Nothingism," racial persecution, and cultural repression, they permit Communists to exploit for their own political purposes the idealism of youth and the just resentments of the underprivileged.

Realistic liberalism recognizes that to survive we must solve many hard problems, and that they can be solved only by intelligence, and not by pious rhetoric. Our greatest danger is not fear of ideas but *absence* of ideas—specific ideas, addressed to concrete problems, here and now, problems of such complexity that only the ignorant can claim to know all the answers to them.

Finally, liberalism today conceives life not in terms of bare survival or of peace at any price, but in the light of ideas and ideals without which a life worthy of man cannot be attained. Among them are the strategic freedoms of those American traditions which make the continuous use of intelligence possible.

Unfortunately the use of intelligence has been made more difficult by the rise of a mood of cultural vigilantism in American life, to a consideration of which we now turn.

Chapter 2

CULTURAL VIGILANTISM

Letters, periodicals and visitors from foreign countries provide convergent evidence that a strange picture of American life and culture is being etched in acid abroad. Even in non-Communist circles in Europe and Asia the view is sedulously being cultivated that the United States, posing as the chief defender of Western values of freedom, tolerance and respect for individual differences, is actually in the grip of an epidemic hysteria of witch hunting, Communist baiting, and character lynching. It is sometimes alleged that a cultural and political reign of terror is rampant in this country differing in degree but not in moral kind from the ruthless suppressions of the Iron Curtain countries.

Similar assertions are growing in volume even on this side of the Atlantic. On the basis of one or another deplorable incident, loud outcries have been raised in the press and on the platform that we are on the verge of fascism. Orators with greater eloquence than discriminating judgment announce that we are already living in a police or garrison state, and that our traditional Bill of Rights functions only as a deceptive ritual to conceal the ugly facts of repression. Predictions have been freely made that before long we will be officially burning books in the street. On the strength of the Supreme Court decision upholding the Smith Act some commentators have already composed requiems on American democracy. Not seldom, it is these tirades, picked up by neutralists abroad, which are cited as evidence that Europe and Asia must protect themselves from the two colossi of cultural intolerance—the U.S.S.R. and the U.S.A.

Such violent exaggerations are not only foolish but dangerous. They weaken the moral case of Western democracy against Communist totalitarianism. Their reiteration tends to anesthetize people to a point where, if ever a genuine threat of a police state were to arise in this country, Cassandra cries of "fascism" would leave them apathetic. This actually happened in Germany. So many pre-Hitler regimes were denounced as "Fascist" that when Hitler was proclaimed a "Fascist" too, many thought his rule would be no more onerous than previous regimes.

Most important of all, these exaggerations are harmful because they divert our attention from some powerful sources of present danger to our freedoms. *They flow not so much from the actions of our government, as foolish as some of them have been, but from the cultural vigilantism of certain pressure groups in education, religion, national and economic affairs.* With growing boldness, they seek to exploit the perfectly legitimate opposition of the American community to Communist influence and penetration, in order to make it appear that those who differ with them on subjects which have no relevance whatsoever to communism are consciously or unconsciously giving aid and comfort to subversion.

Teachers, government officials, editors and others in positions of quasi-public trust are pilloried because they do not see eye to eye with these groups on issues which would have been open, controversial questions even if Russian democracy had never been overthrown by the Bolsheviks. And let anyone disagree with them about the most effective ways of containing or combating communism, and he is forthwith portrayed in the most baleful colors as a friend or protector of Communists. Sometimes it seems as if they hated fellow Americans whose strategy of opposing communism differed from theirs, more than they hated communism.

In the American tradition, no individual or policy can claim immunity from criticism no matter how well intentioned his or its motives. But it is one thing to express criticisms on grounds germane to a specific issue, and quite another to fortify a weak case with rhetorical substitutes for reasoned inquiry. The most vociferous opponents of Communists are not always the most intelligent opponents. And nothing delights the heart of a genuine Communist or Communist fellow traveler so much as the spectacle of his liberal critics being tagged with a subversive label by mindless opponents of communism for whom the political color spectrum consists of two shades—black and red.

Let us glance at some illustrations of what I have called cultural vigilantism. Progressive education is primarily a movement resulting from the application of modern psychology to the processes of learning and teaching. There is a considerable body of experimental evidence, weighty but not conclusive, which shows that its methods are more effective than the conventional ones. Some educators who are conservative in social outlook approve of progressive techniques in education, just as some whose social philosophy is progressive frown upon "progressivism" in education. It raises all sorts of complex issues which are the first concern of the professional educator. But because it is interested in the individual growth of the child and in enriching his present experience as well as imparting common skills and a fund of common knowledge, progressive education is usually more expensive than the conventional variety.

There are some groups in the community which resent the additional tax burden which a progressive education program, when properly administered, brings with it. Some parents are impatient with the seeming slowness with which their children develop reading and writing skills. These are certainly legitimate grounds for criticism if considered in the light of alternative uses of tax money, the experimental evidence, and the total educational program. Since, however, most people consider themselves parents first and taxpayers second, and since they regard their children as their most precious possessions and are aware that children enjoy progressive schooling, the above considerations are not always persuasive. The issue is still open and alive, and should be resolved by the processes of experiment and discussion.

It is at this point, unfortunately, that some of the most vocal opponents of progressive education, unable to win their case by legitimate educational criticism, charge that progressive education is ideologically and professionally linked with communism. This is monstrously untrue. The fact is that Hitler and Stalin both have had absolutely no use for progressive education and extirpated whatever vestiges of it existed when they came to power. Further, the leaders of the progressive education movement in this country, John Dewey, William Kilpatrick, George S. Counts, John L. Childs, Horace Kallen and Boyd Bode, far from sympathizing with communism, were conducting a struggle against it long before their detractors took the field against it. In the 1930's, these men were organizers and members of the first American Committee for Cultural Freedom, dedicated to the struggle against all forms of totalitarianism, and especially communism, when many critics of progressive education slept either in peaceful ignorance of, or in friendship with, the Communists.

So manifestly unjust are some of the allegations made about progressive education that it is hard to take them at their face value. For example, progressive educators are accused of indoctrinating children with all sorts of un-American notions (unspecified), whereas if there is anything which can be called an educational sin according to progressive theory it is precisely indoctrination of ideas. There seems some reason to believe that those who attack progressive education, under the protective coloration of patriotism, are not opposed to indoctrination. What some of the critics really desire is indoctrination for the economic *status quo* and a low tax rate.

Cultural Vigilantism

A community has a right to decide whether it wishes to support a medical system or a school system. But it would be absurd to try to settle, by the pressures of the market place, what medical theories should guide medical practice or what educational theories should guide educational practice. The teaching staff, superintendents and board are professionally equipped to determine whether progressive or conventional education should be introduced. Ultimately, the community will judge the educational system by its fruits. To prejudge the issue by seeking to frighten the public with irrelevant and irresponsible accusations is, in the last analysis, to deprive the children of the community of their birthright to the best education available—whatever wisdom and experience decide it to be.

The same cloudy and irresponsible thinking is apparent when political tags are affixed to fiscal or economic proposals. Recently the charge was made that a withholding tax on dividends was a sign of a police state. It is noteworthy that a group which pressed this discovery on the public did not interpret a withholding tax on wages as a subversive policy. There may be relevant arguments against any general or specific form of tax withholding, but they are of a technical economic nature and have absolutely nothing to do with a police state. Democrats may support or oppose them with an easy conscience. What is true of a withholding tax is also true of price and wage controls, rollbacks, public housing projects—all of which have been denounced by some pressure group as police-state measures.

Even when honestly motivated, such attacks confuse two things which must be carefully distinguished if our democracy is to survive—the traditional *economic* meaning of communism (or more accurately, socialism), and the current *political* meaning of communism. A measure is socialistic to the extent that it introduces community ownership or controls into economic life, thereby limiting private ownership and control. *Communism as a political movement is a conspiracy in the interests of a foreign power scheming to destroy the very process by which we freely decide whether or not to introduce socialism or anything else. Only communism as a conspiratorial political movement is incompatible with the processes of democracy.*

Whatever their merits, neither free enterprise, the New Deal, nor any other economic system is part of the American Constitution. In a democracy, socialistic measures may be wise or unwise; they are neither patriotic nor unpatriotic. When such measures, proposed for adoption by normal democratic processes are denounced as first steps in a Communist movement of *political* subversion, and their proponents smeared as conspirators or partisans of a police state, the consequences may have a far greater subversive effect upon free institutions than economic measures of any kind no matter how ill conceived.

There is a normal tendency to associate what we intensely dislike with the particular kind of evil which the community fears at any given time. A few years ago it was fashionable among some groups to accuse individuals of fascism who, irrespective of their grounds, opposed New Deal legislation. A decade or more ago, the same epithet was applied to those who believed that adequate military preparation was a more effective deterrent to totalitarian oppression than pacifism. And shortly before, it was worth one's reputation as a liberal to link Stalin and Hitler as enemies of democracy. Today, when the mortal threat of Soviet communism to Western democracy is apparent even to many former fellow travelers, the shoe is on the other foot. The easiest way to discredit an individual or cause is to link him or it in the public mind with communism. Many who used to lead the chase for scapegoats among "rotten liberals," as the classic Communist phrase went, or who signed statements castigating American democrats as "Trotskyite-Fascists," are themselves scurrying for cover protesting as they run against the method of amalgams they themselves used to employ.

Whatever poetic justice there may be in their plight, no principled democrat can take pleasure in it. To denounce an idea merely on the basis of the political past of its sponsor substitutes a blind resentment against current dangers to American security for an intelligent appraisal of the best methods of meeting them. It overlooks the fact that many who were duped or innocently used by Communist front organizations have acquired some political sophistication. It degrades the level of political discussion and substitutes a competition in flag waving for the quest of specific problems which is the mark of applied intelligence. The fact that an individual has switched and swerved with every variation in the political line of the Communist Party may indeed be relevant, in that it should cause us to look hard at the grounds or "good reasons" he advances for a position; but even when we are confident that he is intellectually dishonest, that his "real reasons" are different from his "good" ones, this should not absolve us from examining the latter carefully.

Another illustration of cultural vigilantism is provided by the plethora of needless loyalty oaths in education and other professional fields. The notorious fact is that no genuine Communist has ever been stopped from carrying on his activities by the requirement that he disavow his doctrines, intentions or actions. For one thing, he believes himself absolved from violating his pledged word by a higher authority. For another, he can make words mean whatever he pleases by the mumbo jumbo of Communist dialectic. He can convince himself that the use of force and violence as a defensive measure against those who may object to being liquidated as enemies of mankind is a genuinely democratic procedure, and thus swear to any oath with subjective sincerity. The net result of the imposition of loyalty oaths has been the punishment of non-Communists.

More vicious still is the invasion of the professional prerogatives of educators by efforts of private persons and groups not particularly qualified by training, or study, to dictate what textbooks should be used in classes, and what literature on social questions should be made available in school libraries. Actually there are few things more deadly to Communist pretensions than

43

a close study of the writings of Lenin, Stalin and the official documents of the Communist Party, whose zigzag career is determined by its absolute fanaticism of goal and unlimited opportunism of means. But no doctrine that commands the allegiance of multitudes is likely to be wholly a tissue of falsehoods. Intelligent students of communism or of anything else must be prepared to learn from it, particularly in its criticisms of the shortcomings of democratic life which are remediable not by the total cultural terror of Communist dictatorship but by more and better democracy. In contradistinction to totalitarianism, democracy can face and live with the truth about itself.

Cultural vigilantism has also reared its head in the field of the arts. Certain individuals and groups have set themselves up as guardians of the political morality of stage, screen and radio, and have sounded loud alarms about the political pasts of the performers or the content of their performances. No one can reasonably object to authentic disclosure, under proper procedural safeguards, of Communist penetration into the fields of communication and entertainment. It seems to have been systematic, well organized and one of the chief sources of financial support for Communist activities. Here the disclosure itself is sufficient to meet the evil. But any effort to usurp the judgment of professional critics and the public—if box-office appeal expresses public judgment—by antecedent condemnation of the content of plays, movies and radio can, if successful, result in the further emasculation of the popular arts. As it is, they are too much harried by the exaggerated susceptibilities of every organized group in the country.

There is, to be sure, justification for barring from positions of trust Communists who seek to put over the position of the Kremlin by stealth or outright falsification. But it is hard to see what damage anyone can do who must read lines written by others or earn his living as a fourth row fiddler in a symphony orchestra. Standards of professional conduct should be drawn up by professional associations, and violations punished on professional, not political grounds.*

A vital tradition in the arts requires freedom of criticism, even exaggerated criticism, to expose the hypocrisies and cruelties of the folkways as well as social evils and injustices. It is true that some of the novels of Sinclair and Steinbeck, plays like *Born Yesterday* and films like *The Grapes of Wrath*, have been exploited by Communist propaganda abroad. But the fact that they can be written, produced, and widely acclaimed in this country, and that they often influence public opinion to press for social reforms and remedies, can be driven home with great effect when the truths about American democracy are counterposed to Soviet lies. To silence our critical or dissenting writers, even when they seize upon the bizarre and atypical, out of fear that our enemies will pick up what they say, is not only to doom our cultural life to inanity but to deprive ourselves of stimulation, variety and possibly good counsel. The necessary correction of distortions and exaggerations can be left to the normal processes of criticism.

What was most impressive about General MacArthur's criticism of the Administration's policy was not so much what he said but that he was free to say it. Sometimes it seems as if everybody believes in criticism except of his own sacred cows.

Even more disquieting is to observe in the field of religion the same tendency to blow up disagreement over local issues into alleged disagreement over basic loyalties to democracy. The implications of the doctrine of separation of church and state, released time, and federal support for parochial schools are difficult problems to settle in the light of the secular and religious interests involved. How difficult is evidenced in some of the conflicting decisions of our courts. But no matter how they are settled, they have nothing to do with the problem of communism. This

* The most illuminating discussion of this problem as it affects the entertainment industry is Louis Berg's analysis in *Commentary*, October, 1952, pp. 315-325: "How End the Panic in Radio-TV? The Demagogic Half-Truth vs. the 'Liberal' Half-Lie."

is demonstrable in the sense that equally democratic countries have conflicting policies on each and every one of these questions, and Communist practice either crushes or supports religious schools depending upon which approach best strengthens Communist authority.

Nonetheless, in some communities movements that oppose the introduction of religious instruction into the school, or the use of school time for such a purpose, are denounced as ideological fifth columns of "atheistic communism" despite the support such movements have received from leading figures of some religious denominations.

The lengths to which these ideological amalgams can be carried is revealed in a screaming headline some time ago, on page one of a newspaper in—of all places!—John Dewey's native city, which ran! "P— SAYS DEWEY'S PHILOSOPHY LIKE HITLER'S AND CORRESPONDS TO STALIN'S." The news story was accompanied by a vigorous editorial endorsing this attack on Dewey's "Godless and baboonlike philosophy." The chief evidence cited for charging John Dewey, America's foremost philosopher and probably the leading philosopher of democracy of our time, with holding a philosophy like that of Hitler and Stalin was Dewey's denial of absolute truth, his belief that the universe is self-existing and man its evolutionary product, continuous in some respects, unique in others, with other natural creatures.

The plain intent of such wild assertions is to link an abstruse philosophical doctrine, about which democrats may amicably disagree, to the most virulent despotism in modern history in order to forego the necessity of meeting its arguments on relevant grounds. It is an attempt to lynch a philosophy instead of combating with philosophical means its alleged errors.

By the same questionable logic by which an expert on Vermont baboons seeks to assimilate Dewey's naturalistic thought to Stalin, one can argue that the supernaturalism of Franco, Salazar and Peron is responsible for their undemocratic practices. This bad logic is dangerous. It is a short step from propounding the absurdity that Dewey's philosophy is essentially like Hitler's and Stalin's to advocating the cultural atrocity of ridding our schools of progressive educators, naturalists and humanists. In some quarters, this step has been taken.

Almost every day, some incident reveals the growing pattern of cultural vigilantism which invokes the slogans of Americanism while betraying its best traditions. If it remains unchecked, it is not hard to predict the outcome—the rule of the loud shouters, the intimidation and silencing of the thoughtful. It is not controversy we must avoid—but the noisy competition in irrelevancy, the distortions of patent fact, the unsubstantiated aspersions on personalities which in time remove all characters from the political scene but the mob and the demagogue.

What are the causes of the development of cultural vigilantism? What can be done to check it?

The obvious main cause is fear of communism, and to the extent that the fear is based on knowledge it is a healthy and legitimate fear. Contributing to it is a widespread feeling that there has been bungling and blundering in high places, and that the initiative in world affairs affecting our destiny is in the hands of the Kremlin, not our own leaders.

What is overlooked, however, is important. In world affairs, American political leadership is giving some evidence that it knows the nature of the Communist danger. Domestically, we need not fear communism as a set of ideas but only as a movement of infiltration, subversion and sabotage. In the nature of the case, what is fearful about domestic communism cannot be overcome by cultural vigilantism, but by devising certain safeguards against organized infiltration whose efficacy is an inverse function of their publicity.

There are some who scoff at the whole idea of Communists constituting any menace at all to American security. Whether out of naiveté or stubborn ignorance of the ways of the Communist party, they airily dismiss the evidence of planned infiltration. "The Soviet Union has its spies and so have we," they say. It is as simple as all that! There might be a point to such remarks if the United States had organized a political party of Russian citizens in the Soviet Union, or a faction in the Communist Party to bore within the army, police, and all other government agencies, to commit sabotage and espionage, and to strike for power when a revolutionary situation or war developed. It should not be hard to see the difference between the conventional professional spy, who is rapidly becoming as extinct as the hired mercenary, and doctrinaire or ideological groups that masquerade as normal political parties and claim the rights and privileges of citizenship in order to do the work of a foreign power. Even the Kremlin makes no bones of the fact that the first and last duty of Communist Parties everywhere is to defend the Soviet Union by *all* means. Every Communist Party which has not broken with the Kremlin has proudly and publicly accepted this mission.

Sometimes it is claimed that existing laws are sufficient to punish overt acts of espionage and sabotage. The main problem, however, is to *prevent* the commission of such acts, which in part can be achieved by judicious elimination from sensitive places of those pledged to perform the kind of service for the Kremlin from which it has benefited remarkably in the past.

Pooh-poohing the danger of Communist infiltration helps create, by way of reaction, a public atmosphere in which those who wish to apply the necessary safeguards, justly, and without injury to innocent persons, are themselves suspected of coddling the enemies of the nation. To a considerable degree, demagogues who rant indiscriminately about the menace of communism in high places and make unfounded charges owe their successes to those who, instead of suggesting better ways of preventing Communist infiltration, tossed off the whole problem as a "red herring." As is usually the case, one kind of extremism provokes another. It is a safe rule to be skeptical of those who never criticize anyone but Communists or those they think are Communists.

Cultural Vigilantism

We should be even more skeptical of those who never criticize anyone except critics of communism.

Nor is it true to say that the cause of cultural vigilantism is to be found in the activities of the Government in prosecuting Communist leaders under the Smith Act. This Act has been on the statute books for more than ten years. Under its provisions, sixteen members of a Trotskyist Communist splinter group were sent to jail in 1941 to the violent applause of the Communist party and the eloquent silence of some of the most vocal critics of its present application. Whatever one thinks of the wisdom of the Act, the leaders of the Communist Party were tried in open court, with counsel of their own choice, and with the right of repeated appeal. Instead of whipping up sentiment against the domestic agents of the Kremlin, the Government had been accused by some of its critics of lagging behind the mood of the people.

It is true, however, that in some respects governmental measures have fallen short of proper standards of justice. The loyalty program should be rethought and more selectively applied. The list of subversive organizations issued by the Attorney General's office was not properly drawn up; nor were proper procedures followed in reaching decisions. Visa and passport regulations should be more intelligently administered under a thoroughly revised immigration law drafted by others than Senator McCarran. But it is emphatically not true that the Government has created the anti-Communist mood of the country or that it is prosecuting heresies rather than conspiracies. If anything, government agencies find their work hampered by the private fevers of cultural vigilantism which have arisen like a rash from the anti-Communist mood. That mood is the cumulative result of a long series of Communist actions, from the postwar usurpation of power in the satellite countries to the espionage cases and the invasion of Korea. In the face of criticisms by ritualistic liberals who scoff at the need for any security program, one can do no better than to cite the words of John Carter Vincent, a highly placed State

Department official, who had for years been the object of severe criticism as a Communist fellow traveler. His case had often been referred to as illustrating the horrible lengths to which investigations can be carried. Without discussing the ground or merits or methods of the charges against him or the decision of the State Department's Loyalty and Security Board, I quote his own statement. Coming from one who has undoubtedly suffered in the process, his words are especially significant.

> Any officer in a position of public trust should be prepared to have his record subjected to an objective examination. The security of the United States transcends consideration of personal feelings. Loyalty and security investigations are a necessity, especially as the increased danger of Soviet espionage calls for constant vigilance.
>
> *New York Times,* February 2, 1952.

One should add that constant vigilance does not require private citizens to usurp the functions of agencies entrusted with the task of detection and exposure.

What can be done to reduce the incidence of cultural vigilantism? We obviously cannot pass laws against it; nor, in a democracy, deny freedom of speech to those who use it foolishly rather than criminally. In the last analysis, the health of a democracy rests on self discipline, not on threats of sanctions. But a few suggestions may be in order.

First, those who discuss communism, whether they regard it as a threat or an airy phantom, before opening their mouths in public should spend some time studying it. Stalin's *Problems of Leninism* and his *History of the Russian Communist Party* come nearest to being the *Mein Kampf* of the international Communist movement. The leading resolutions of the World Congresses of the Communist International should be examined, including the famous twenty-one conditions of affiliation. Not only Communist doctrine, but the organizational role of the Communist party should be carefully read together with the report of the

Cultural Vigilantism

Canadian Royal Commission on Communist espionage and the works of such former agents as Krivitsky and Foote, which contain an impressive array of names, dates, places and descriptions of conspiratorial techniques. In addition to works sympathetic to the Soviets, by Anna L. Strong, Harry Ward, and the Webbs, the books of Dallin, Kravchenko and W. H. Chamberlain should be consulted together with the life stories of Elinor Lipper and Margaret Buber who spent years in Soviet concentration and forced labor camps. I predict that anyone who reads all these books will not hurl the charge of communism lightly against anybody.

Second, where present and active membership in the Communist Party constitutes a *prima facie* case of professional unfitness for a position in non-federal public and quasi-public organizations, hearings should be confidentially conducted by a board representing management and personnel. Unless a request to the contrary is received from the individual concerned, these hearings should be confidential because not everyone can survive acquittal.

Third, the Attorney General's list of subversive organizations should be published only after hearings have been conducted and the relevant evidence published, including the demurrers, if any, of the responsible officers of the organizations. The procedure should parallel that followed by the courts in such cases as that involving the charge that the International Workers Order was not a bona fide benevolent association but in reality a front for the Communist Party and its causes. The importance of re-evaluating this list becomes more urgent because of the ill-considered Feinberg Law of New York, whose constitutionality was upheld by the U.S. Supreme Court. The fundamental defect of this law is that it substitutes political criteria, which lend themselves to ambiguous interpretation, for professional criteria in determining fitness to teach. More important, it does not recognize the important difference between membership in the Communist party, which is *prima facie* evidence of professional unfitness to teach because of the nature and functioning of the party, and membership in front organizations with loose conditions of affiliation drawn to snare the unwary. Although the decisive point depends on the manner in which the Feinberg Law is carried out, its liability to abuse reinforces the wisdom of entrusting to the professional organizations of the teachers themselves the determination of standards of professional integrity.

Fourth, in a democracy no one can silence for long the man who has the moral and intellectual courage to stick by his guns. Individual temperaments differ, and many would rather hold their peace than risk open polemic. But where the issue is of sufficient importance, moral integrity as well as public responsibility require that each one take his stand independently of the spirit of faction or fanaticism, whether manifested by bigoted obscurantists to whom every liberal is a Communist *malgré lui*, or Soviet apologists to whom every critic of Communist conspiracy and terror is a faithless liberal or ally of fascism. A show of independence is contagious and more necessary than ever as society becomes more bureaucratized.

Finally, we must not lose perspective and paint the picture in colors so dark as to discourage action. We must do better; but given what is in effect an undeclared war, conditions could have been far worse. Anyone who remembers the actions of the Gegan-Brown-Scully Bomb Squad in 1920 and the Palmer raids and deportations will be as careful with the charge of hysteria as of communism. Not all citizens can participate directly in the military or defense efforts of the country. But perhaps it is not too much to say that in a world grown more perilous despite our social securities, every citizen has a post in the cultural and social life of the country more important than ever before. He must help keep freedom alive at home while we defend it abroad. To do so he must muster all his resources of courage, knowledge, human kindness and, above all, intelligence.

Dramatic failure of intelligence is manifested not only by the cultural vigilantes but by those who hysterically exaggerate both its degree and its consequences to an extent that McCarthyism becomes a danger to the survival of the nation equal to, if not greater than, Stalinism. There are two kinds of pendular rhythm in human affairs. The first is between foolishness and wisdom. The second is between one pole of foolishness and another—which brings to mind Bradley's observation that the opposite of an absurdity may be every whit as absurd. At the risk of some repetition I turn to some recent expressions of needless and hurtful exaggeration.

Chapter 3

FREEDOM IN AMERICAN CULTURE

It is now apparent except to the hopelessly doctrinaire that the basic issue underlying the international conflict between East and West is not capitalism or socialism or imperialism but whether or not a free culture is to survive. What exists in the Soviet Union and its satellite countries is not socialism; what exists in Great Britain and the United States is not capitalism as socialists traditionally understood it; and the imperialisms of yesteryear are gradually being replaced by independent national states or by a new type of Soviet exploitation more systematic and ruthless than most of the imperialisms socialists and democrats have always denounced. Economic questions still have a vast importance but they have become subordinated to questions posed by the politics of freedom. Honest socialists recognize this. "There is a lot of loose talk," Clement Atlee recently said, "about the United States from people who refer to American imperialism and similar phrases, but no country in history has ever made greater efforts to help other countries than the United States has done in the last six years." (*Time*, June 16, 1952.) These efforts have not been motivated by philanthropy alone. But neither have they been part of a strategy of imperial conquest or world domination on the Nazi and Soviet models.

Freedom in American Culture

The United States has been slow to awaken to the fact that its own existence as a free culture is threatened by the programmatic declaration of enmity on the part of the leaders of the Soviet Union and the political measures they have adopted to give it force. This enmity rests on the fanatically held conviction that their empire is not safe as long as any large nation still remains outside the orbit of Bolshevik power. The United States was even slower in grasping the extent and intensity of the Kremlin's assault on American culture in preparation for the denouement the Communist leaders consider inevitable. Very few in this country even now know the variety and complexity of the techniques of propaganda, indoctrination, infiltration, espionage and sabotage which the Kremlin has at its command, and which it has unloosed through its open and concealed fifth columns against American democracy at home and aboard. Fanciful fiction often seems pale and flat when compared with the plain truth.

Stung, however, by the espionage revelations which helped break American monopoly of atomic weapons, by the triumphs of communism in Asia, by events like the Communist coup d'état in Czechoslovakia, the blockade of West Berlin, and the invasion of South Korea, the United States slowly began to move to defend itself against the multiple attacks against its security mounted by the best propaganda machine and espionage apparatus the world has ever seen. (The truth is that it is *here* and not in its five-year plans that the Kremlin has enjoyed its greatest technological triumphs.)

This movement of defense has not only been slow, but blundering and contradictory, more productive of excited rhetoric than of intelligent practical devices to meet specific dangers. Private citizens have rushed in to remedy affairs, seemingly neglected by government agencies, with foolish and reckless proposals. What is worse, some legislators have been guilty of irresponsible denunciations, and of methods taken from the arsenal of Communist slander. Not all of Senator McCarthy's charges have been false but his indiscriminate use of the term Communist, and his insinuation that those who oppose his shotgun methods of fighting communism are themselves infected with communism, has prevented intelligent discussion and terrorized the innocent as much as the guilty. Trumanism may explain McCarthyism but it does not justify it. There is still a difference between an honest mistake or foolishness—even mule-headed foolishness—and treason.

Other citizens, reacting to this fanaticism and irresponsibility, angrily deny even that there is any occasion for special concern. They cry out against hysteria and believe that we have no more to fear from Communists than we have from witches. Indeed a whole library has been published designed to prove that it is not communism but fear of communism which threatens our democracy. Indeed, so sharply have they reacted that at the very time that the United States is striving to take the lead in the world-wide struggle of the free world, American society has itself become the object of a massed attack on the ground that it lacks freedom, that its democratic traditions are either dead or dying. Every national failing, every discrepancy between American ideals and performance, every instance of social injustice is now cited as evidence by a swelling chorus throughout the world, and even in this country, that there is really little freedom left to defend. It is merely hypocritical pretense, we often hear it declared, to regard America as a champion of the free way of life. And I am not now referring to the Kirchwey-del Vayo line imposed on the once liberal *Nation,* according to which the fumbling efforts to preserve both democracy and security spell "the rise of a new fascism."

This developing mood, unless checked, is certain to produce extremely mischievous results.

To appreciate what has taken place and its significance, it is necessary to go back a few years when American public opinion was becoming aroused by Hitler's domestic terror and threat of foreign expansion. In his efforts to justify the Nazi persecution

Freedom in American Culture

of Jews and other "non-Aryans," Goebbels made extensive reference to the disabilities under which Negroes suffered in the United States. Through films, articles, lectures, Nazi propagandists censured Americans for their hypocrisy. Nor did they neglect stressing the slums and other seamy sides of American life, going so far as to revive pictures of Hoovertowns from the days of the depression. Nonetheless Nazi propaganda utterly failed. Despite the admitted injustices and inequalities of American life, intelligent people the world over, particularly in Europe, recognized that political means for the amelioration of these conditions existed, and that in many respects they were rapidly improving. On the other hand, Nazi cultural terror was almost total and no political freedom existed to check or reverse it.

With some modifications the same propaganda line is now being employed by the Soviet Union, and circulated with a brazenness and virulence never matched by the Nazis—but this time with impressive effects on large sectors of non-Communist opinion in Western Europe and England. The intellectual classes, scientists, men of letters, teachers, publicists, who play a greater role in influencing public opinion abroad than their opposite numbers in this country, have been especially responsive to the Communist campaign of defamation. Many of them are under no illusion about the state of Soviet culture and its repressions. But they have become convinced that the processes of American freedom no longer function as in the past, that the critical safeguards and mechanisms by which American democracy has remedied abuses and evils in its body politic have been undermined, if not destroyed, by an hysterical anti-Communist fever. Even many Americans who are non-Communist have been repeating this line.

As we have seen, a prime responsibility for this state of affairs can without doubt be attributed to what has actually been happening in the United States. Zealous individuals and groups, expressing themselves with anger and unrestraint on the shortcomings of national policy and leadership, have been guilty of "cultural vigilantism." In addition, exaggerated reports and unfounded accusations that make sensational newspaper headlines set up multiple echoes abroad. As a result of this scandalous indifference to the truth, Senator McCarthy's charges have had the boomerang effect of convincing many people abroad and at home that it is enough to be accused by him of being a "red agent" to earn the accolade of a devoted and loyal public servant. If anything, all this testifies to an unregimented culture, particularly when directed against the state. Unfortunately, most Europeans are badly informed about the federal structure of the American republic and the division of federal powers. Any silly demand by some superintendent of education in a distant state or an arbitrary pronouncement by a local police chief which he has no authority to enforce, or an asinine speech on the floor of a state legislative chamber, or in Congress, is often blazoned forth abroad as an expression of national policy. The demand of a local citizens group, exercising their political right to form voluntary associations and their natural right to make fools of themselves, that the local library withdraw a Communist book or periodical, is equated with the *official* policy of Communist regimes in continuously censoring the publication and distribution of books in every field. Nor must we overlook the effects of the denial of visas to some distinguished non-Communists and the occasional hardships of the security and loyalty program, which raise large and difficult issues that have still not been adequately met, even after gross injustices have been remedied.

But just as responsible for the misleading impression of the current state of affairs in America are the exaggerations of critics reporting the American scene. No less a person than Bertrand Russell in a communication in the *Manchester Guardian* last year wrote: "In Germany under Hitler, and in Russia under Stalin, nobody ventured to pass a political remark without first looking behind the door to make sure no one was listening. This used to be considered a mark of a Police State. It is no longer, for when I last visited America, I found the same state of things there." And more recently in the *New York Sunday Times* he added: "In America, almost as much as in Russia, you must think what your neighbor thinks or rather what your neighbor thinks it pays to think." Since writing the above Mr. Russell has explained in a letter to the *Manchester Guardian* that he does not believe that conditions here are as bad as in the Soviet Union but this has not prevented him from asserting that "a reign of terror" exists in the United States. The effect of this phrase is precisely to reintroduce into the minds of his readers the cultural equation he disavows. An injustice, of course, is an injustice whether it happens occasionally to one person or to millions systematically, but except when writing about the United States, Mr. Russell would not dream of designating with the expression "a reign of terror" the scattered events of injustice, foolishness and hardship which provoked his outburst and which, when they cannot be countered by courage, are remediable by due process of law or by due constitutional process neither of which has been abridged.

Professing a friendship for America and a vital concern in preserving its freedom, Mr. Russell expresses this friendship and concern by writing:

> Professors of economics who are told that it is their duty to indoctrinate the young against communism are considered subversive if they know what the doctrines of communism are; only those who have not read Marx are considered competent to combat his doctrines by the policemen who have professors at their mercy.

Americans who are unaware of these facts, says Mr. Russell, are like the Germans who were ignorant of what went on in Nazi concentration camps. Those who deny that these are the facts are worse than ignorant; they wish to destroy American freedom. The only fact Mr. Russell cites is one case of apparent injustice under the loyalty program described in an American magazine of large circulation. On the strength of this, and presumably a few other cases widely discussed in the American press, Mr. Russell asserts there are "many thousands" of such cases not known to Americans but known to Europeans. "The shocking things that are done in America are known in every country of the Eastern hemisphere although most Americans remain unaware of them." One wonders who informs Europeans about what happens in the United States, and if they learn these things from reading the American press, how most Americans can remain unaware of them.

Barely a few months after Mr. Russell proclaimed to the entire world, and to the delight of neutralists and Communists, that the United States was being swept by a "reign of terror," the American Civil Liberties Union as well as the American Jewish Committee made public reports on the state of civil rights in America in connection with the celebration of the 161st anniversary of Bill of Rights Day. Neither organization is inclined to easy optimism and they have consistently and properly played the role of Cassandra in discussing threats to freedom. Although it is admitted that the record is far from shining, both organizations express some satisfaction with the rate of progress, and a moderate optimism for the future progress of civil rights in various fields of American life. Indeed, the report of the American Jewish Committee states that especially in the field of racial relations unprecedented progress in maintaining and extending civil rights has been achieved in the five-year period from 1948 to 1953—a period which roughly covers the cold war. (*New York Times,* Dec. 15, 1952.) Neither report, it is almost gratuitous to add, received any notice abroad.

I believe a case can be made out for the view, on Mr. Russell's own criteria, that the state of freedom when he was last domiciled in this country was not too unlike that of today. He was the victim of an outrage, first at C.C.N.Y.* and then at the Barnes Institute. In 1940 over forty teachers were dismissed for membership in the Communist Party or refusing to testify concerning

* *Cf. The Bertrand Russell Case,* edited by John Dewey and H. M. Kallen, N. Y., 1941.

Freedom in American Culture

their membership. The Sedition Trials against members of domestic Fascist groups were begun, and the eighteen members of the Trotskyist group were convicted under the Smith Act. But Mr. Russell never even dreamed of characterizing this complex of events as a "reign of terror."

Mr. Russell as a visitor may not have experienced a representative side of American life. But what shall we say of the following remark of Mr. Robert M. Hutchins: "Everywhere in the U.S. university professors, whether or not they have tenure, are silenced by the general atmosphere of repression that now prevails."* And this at a time when professors have actually been more outspoken than ever in the past against arbitrary actions by university and state authorities as was clearly evidenced in the Universities of Ohio, Chicago and California. Aside from a few members of the Communist Party, whose case is discussed below, the facts are that no professor who was in the habit of speaking up five years ago has been silenced, many who were silent five years ago are speaking up, while those who were silent five, ten, fifteen years ago and are still silent cannot be regarded as victims of a reign of terror. It is not necessary to picture the situation as ideal—or to deny the episodic outbreaks of intolerance towards professors with unpopular views (when was the U.S. free of them?) to recognize Mr. Hutchins' statement as a fantastic exaggeration, and no more accurate in its description of the situation than a characterization of the state of academic freedom at the University of Chicago under Mr. Hutchins would be if it were based only on Mr. Hutchins' outrageous dismissal of Mr. Couch. Why, it was not so many years ago that college professors were regarded by visitors from abroad as "the third sex" in American life. Today as a group they are as intellectually bold as any profession in the nation. The number of attempts to impose tests for loyalty has undoubtedly risen but whereas in the past such tests would have been accepted supinely

---

* *Ethics,* Vol. XLVI, No. 2, January 1951.

either with equanimity or without protest, today there is more vigorous opposition on the part of teachers to arbitrary action by legislatures and boards of trustees than ever before in the history of American education.

Now and again other individuals, some even in official posts, take up Mr. Hutchins' cry and assert that American college teachers are petrified with fear, unwilling to discuss controversial issues or to protest measures of which they disapprove. Many different things are here confused. It is true that the number of criticisms and attacks on the schools has increased, and here and there some fantastic things have occurred like the dismissal from a rural college in the West of a temporary teacher on a one year appointment because he signed a petition to the President asking for amnesty for the defendants convicted under the Smith Act. But it is just as true that college teachers have never fought back so unitedly, spiritedly, and so successfully as today. They won on the key point in the University of California case; they helped put to rout the House Committee on Un-American Activities when it sought to check on textbooks; they are slowly turning the tide against loyalty oaths; they have condemned investigations by Congressional committees often and vigorously.

To circulate the myth that "everywhere in the U. S. university professors" have been cowed or silenced by Senators McCarthy and McCarran or whoever else is identified with the spirit of repression is not only to circulate an untruth but may, if given credence, actually contribute to bringing about such a state of affairs. It is to discourage teachers from continuing their role as active defenders of academic freedom. My own impression is that teachers today are more aroused and more active in behalf of academic freedom than they have ever been in my thirty-five years of experience as college student and teacher.

The amount of actual repression in colleges cannot be assessed by subjective impressions and even statistical data are not conclusive because they do not register certain imponderables. But without some reference to statistical data subjective impressions

Freedom in American Culture

are often extremely misleading. The best and most recent tables of cases involving academic freedom and tenure are those published by the Committee on Academic Freedom and Tenure of the American Association of University Professors:

Statistical Tables of Cases for the Seven Calendar Years 1945-1951

CASES *

	1945	1946	1947	1948	1949	1950	1951
Pending January 1	74	71	36	47	56	61	68
Revived from former years	5	4	6	4	2	2	2
Opened since January 1	43	32	39	35	38	40	50
Total dealt with during year ..	122	107	81	86	96	103	120
Closed	51	71	34	30	35	35	45
Pending at end of year	71	36	47	56	61	68	75

DISPOSITION OF CASES *

	1945	1946	1947	1948	1949	1950	1951
Withdrawn by complainant after preliminary investigation	10	12	10	7	7	7	5
Rejected after preliminary investigation	8	12	10	15	14	12	12
Statement published or planned without visits	4	3	4	1	1	1	3
Visit of inquiry made or planned	33	20	8	5	2	5	5
Adjustment made or being sought	48	44	32	36	34	38	36
Procedure not yet determined .	19	16	17	22	38	40	59
Total	122	107	81	86	96	103	120

* Each "case" refers to a single controversy. Committee A also deals with a number of situations not classified as "cases"; such situations are not included in these tabulations.

Bulletin of the AAUP, Spring 1952, p. 109.

The tables are significant because they throw light on the *comparative* situations before and after the period of the cold war.

In presenting these tables the chairman of Committee attributes the small increase in the number of cases in the last year not to ideological or political factors but to the usual endemic professional causes. He writes:

> While the members of the staff in the Washington office have dealt during the past year with a somewhat larger than normal number of cases, as the accompanying tables indicate, these have arisen largely from the usual types of disagreement between professors and their colleagues and from the natural dislocations involved in the transition from the years of overload caused by the influx of veterans and the diminished enrollments arising from the draft and from the calling of reservists to duty.
>
> *loc. cit.*

Despite Mr. Hutchins this is not a picture of a terrorized profession.

Even a normally level-headed man like the drama critic of the *New York Times* seems to have sucked on the mandrake root and narcotized his sense of humor and proportion. Commenting on a poor drama season in New York, Mr. Brooks Atkinson attributes it to Senator McCarthy and to the public denunciations of a few actors as stalking horses for the Communist Party—as if New York never had a poor drama season before. He concludes with the charge that the American drama is being just as much terrorized by toughs and ruffians as the drama in Moscow!

Recently a professional liberal figure appeared on a television program on the state of civil liberties in America. At a moment when the cameras brought him so close that one could almost look down his throat, he was shouting: "It's getting so that a man can't open his mouth in this country." Whether the thousands of people who got a glimpse of his tonsils appreciated the irony of the situation is doubtful. What is not doubtful is that millions here, and still more millions abroad, are being sold a bill of goods which reads that the demagogues, crackpots and cranks who make the newspaper headlines in virtue of our queer sense of news value have destroyed the structure of American freedom, and that we are now living under a cultural terror almost as bad as that prevailing in the Soviet Union.

The notion that there is hardly any difference between American democratic culture and Soviet totalitarian culture, if it becomes more widely accepted in Western Europe, may very well be disastrous to current efforts—even military efforts—to unify Western defense against Communist aggression. To understand the psychological attitude which such belief generates it may be instructive to consider an historical parallel of fateful significance.

From 1929 to 1933 the Kremlin laid down as a canonic and mandatory directive for all national satellite Communist parties its notorious theory of "social fascism." According to this theory social democracy, in all its variants, and fascism were, in the words of Stalin, "not opposites but twins." Among its other consequences this doctrine largely contributed to the triumph of Hitler over the Weimar Republic. The millions, whose orthodox political faith led them to accept Stalin's dictum, saw no reason to support German social democracy in its struggles against Hitler. Since the doctrine proclaimed that the Socialists were no better than Fascists, their choice was pictured to them as narrowed between Tweedledum and Tweedledee. This split the German working class, whose united strength might have prevented the access of Hitler to power and the advent of the second world war. On the other hand, despite their opposition to democratic and social-democratic regimes, the six million Communist voters found these regimes endurable, for these regimes permitted criticism, social reforms, free trade unions. By accepting Stalin's doctrine of social fascism they lost their fear of Hitler, since Hitler, as a twin of social democracy, could be no worse than his socially identical twin. They blithely looked forward to continuing under Hitler the exercise of the democratic freedoms they enjoyed under the Weimar Republic. They expected to follow Hitler into power in the same way as Hitler, exploiting the privileges of agitation granted by the Weimar Republic, succeeded his predecessors. *Nach Hitler kommen Wir!* was a favorite slogan. The rude awakening and the understanding of the differences between social democracy and fascism came to many of them only on the execution block and in the concentration camps.

Although conditions in present day Europe are far different from those that existed before Hitler, the psychological and political consequences of belief in the monstrously false equation between American democracy and all its imperfections and the Soviet police state may be just as disastrous in the current struggle for the survival of a free world. The continued existence of freedom in Western Europe depends upon these states making common cause with American democracy. American economic and military aid on the whole has had no political strings attached. It does not even remotely imperil European independence. But if it is believed that the world is equally threatened by two different police states, then even those Europeans who dislike the Soviet Union have no reason, in the event of an extension of hostilities, to make common cause with an America which, if we are to believe Messrs. Russell, Hutchins, and others, is barely distinguishable from Stalin's Russia. And contrariwise, why worry too much about Stalin's victory, if in the end what Soviet communism represents is not too different from American culture today in which, oddly enough, even its critics, foreign as well as domestic, can earn comfortable incomes crying stinking fish! to large audiences.

Mr. Russell assures us that he personally recognizes that the impositions making for conformity are greater in the Soviet Union than in the United States, and that in the event of a showdown his hopes will be on the United States. But I have verified again and again that his exaggerations serve to reinforce neutralist sentiment abroad all the more strongly because Mr. Russell is so distinguished an anti-Communist. Only an extraordinary sense of humor or extraordinary powers of observation could have led Mr. Russell to write: "Senator McCarthy's emissaries and his allies in the F.B.I. are perpetually snooping, and if by some misfortune you were to quote with approval some remark by Jefferson you would probably lose your job and find yourself behind bars." But Europeans reading this utterly ridiculous charge and giving it credence are not likely to bother about further nuances in the degrees of cultural terror recognized by Mr. Russell. For them, this is fascism! At best their reaction is "a plague on both of your charnel houses of culture" —an attitude which the Communist Party declares, for obvious reasons, to be an honorable one for those who cannot give unconditional support to communism.

The American public is not yet aware of the strength and stubbornness of this neutralist sentiment in Europe whose manifestations, except in official quarters, take on a more anti-American form almost every month. When they do become aware of it, there may be a violent resurgence of isolationist sentiment. European liberalism itself will come under fire as in effect neutralist, and even the profession of anti-communism by American liberalism will be suspect in the light of the fact that the exaggerated, unmeasured, and hysterical cries of "hysteria" by some liberal groups and organizations have been cleverly exploited by Communists for wonderful propaganda abroad.

"The American people," Mr. Hutchins tells us, "now find themselves blocking the revolutionary aspirations of oppressed peoples abroad and declining at home to permit the kind of criticism that has been our glory, and I think our salvation, in the past." (*Loc. cit.*)

To which revolutionary aspirations of which oppressed people is Mr. Hutchins referring? North Korea? South Korea? Is he implying that the American people refused to permit their government to help by the Marshall Plan and other measures the British Socialist regime carry on? Is he perchance charging us with blocking the revolutionary aspirations of Yugoslavia? He surely cannot mean Israel, which in many ways has done more revolutionary things than most countries of the world, or India, whom we continue to help on a generous scale despite her neutralism. Does he mean the oppressed people of Mao's China now writhing under a terror that makes Chang Kai-shek's rule as tame as a tea party? Does Mr. Hutchins want us to help the Chinese masses overthrow their present despots? Or does he mean that, by refusing to recognize these despots and reward them for defying the U.N., we are blocking *their* revolutionary aspirations?

Subsequent to the time he penned this indictment, the United States wrongly joined England and France in refusing to give the Tunisian *nationalists* a hearing before the U.N. and then under a barrage of criticism from the American people reversed itself. But it is a far cry from *nationalism* to social revolution, for in some countries the most powerful feudal elements exploit nationalistic feeling to prevent fundamental social reforms. Any attempt on the part of the U.S. government to ally itself with some local national groups over the heads of a legitimate government is almost certain to bring vehement charges of dollar imperialism. Under some circumstances this risk should be taken, but the decision has to be made from case to case with an eye on the larger strategy of defending and extending global freedom. Mr. Hutchins' blithe formula makes no more sense than its exact opposite.

And precisely what kind of domestic criticisms are we failing to permit today which we permitted in the past and which saved us in the past? Is it the criticism of our foreign policy which Mr. Taft makes, and which Mr. Taft and Mr. Hutchins both used to make in the days of the America First Committee? But Mr. Taft's book, strongly critical of American foreign policy, was on the best-seller list when it appeared a few years ago. Is it criticism from the opposite quarter? But Justice Douglas' book, which expresses such a criticism, was also on the best-seller list! Whose voice are we stifling? Certainly not Mr. Hutchins'.

Here we are—pilloried before the entire world as unrelievedly reactionary both in our domestic and foreign policy because on some point or other these critics are displeased with it as is the author, probably the reader, and numerous others. But instead of specifying in a concrete way what should be done and agitating for it, Hr. Hutchins uses a brush as broad as a comet's tail to smear America.

Why should there be so much misconception about the state of freedom in the United States? The answer is only partly due to the wild, undiscriminating, unscrupulous harangues of Senator McCarthy. For even the attitudes and actions of the government, the chief target of McCarthy's campaigns, have come under fire as evidencing the eclipse of freedom in the United States. Although some of the government's actions are indeed blameworthy they do not warrant this wholesale, irresponsible denunciation.

In the main—if we disregard the motives of malice and exhibitionism—the misconceptions may be traced to a failure to recognize some important distinctions, and an ignorance about the Communist movement so carefully nurtured as to be almost perverse. I shall briefly explain these distinctions and show their bearing on some troubled areas of American life.

There is first the distinction, already discussed, between heresy and conspiracy. As we have seen, in a democracy there can be no justification for any kind of conspiracy, for any movement which by secret, underground organization plays outside the rules of the game and seeks to subvert the institutions or processes that are part of the democratic system. Anyone acquainted with the official instructions under which members of the Communist Party operate will recognize that they are a conspiratorial group. Intelligent democrats are therefore justified in barring them from any position in which, were conspiratorial intent carried out—an intent clearly evidenced by their voluntary act of continued membership in the Communist Party—undesirable results would ensue. Heresies, on the other hand, honestly affirmed and publicly defended, are essential to the healthy functioning of the democratic process. Most of the foolishness encountered in recent years is a consequence of the identification of heresy and conspiracy from opposite quarters. The foolish reactionary regards heretics as conspirators. The equally foolish, ritualistic "liberal" regards conspirators as if they were merely heretics. *Our moral obligation in political life is to the toleration of dissent, no matter how heretical, not the toleration of conspiracy, no matter what its disguise.* The only qualification here flows from the fact that since no right is absolute or unlimited, since every right must be evaluated in terms of its consequences on other rights, certain situations of emergency or crisis may lead to temporary restrictions upon freedom of expression. This leads us to a second distinction.

The second distinction is between the exercise of rights, like rights of speech, press and assembly, in times of peace or situations of normal life, and in times of crisis or war. There is general agreement that the punishment of overt criminal acts is justified at any time. But what about an incitement to a criminal act or its advocacy which does not go beyond the realm of utterance? No right is absolute, because its exercise may have social consequences which in the interests of other rights require its abridgment. Every child knows that the right to life and safety in a crowded theater makes it wrong for anyone to exercise his right of speech falsely to cry "fire" and cause panic and stampede. "Since," as Justice Holmes once put it, "the character of every act depends upon the circumstances in which it is done," an act of speech that would be trivial in times of peace might become malicious or criminal in times of emergency, crisis or war. There are many situations in which the necessity of saving the country is the overriding consideration. One does have to go as far as Thomas Jefferson (whom I risk quoting, *vide* Mr. Russell) who once wrote in answer to a correspondent, J. B. Colvin: "A strict observance of the written laws is doubtless *one* of the high duties of a good citizen but it is not the *highest*. The laws of necessity, of self-preservation, of saving our country when in danger, are of higher obligation. To lose our country by a scrupulous adherence to written law, would be to lose the law itself, with life, liberty, property and all those who are enjoying them with us; thus absurdly sacrificing the end to the means."

The difficulty here is to determine when such a situation is present, how to assess the existence and degree of the dangers, and *who* is to assess them. But it seems to me incontestable that such situations *may* arise and that whatever agency or government declares the state of emergency to exist, such declaration should be limited in duration, and *renewable* only by vote of Congress. Without holding the right to the expression of heresy at any time and place to be absolute—for even the right to non-heretical speech cannot be absolute—it still seems wise to tolerate the expression even of Communist, fascist and other heresies, lest in outlawing them we include other kinds of heresies, and deprive ourselves of the opportunity to acquire possibly sounder ideas than our own.

It is interesting to observe that in discussing fascism liberals were aware of the theoretical difficulty in justifying the abridgment of free expression on the part of a free culture. But on the whole they were satisfied that in relation to fascism there was no betrayal of principle in putting obstacles in the way of those who used freedom of speech to advocate its suppression, particularly when Hitler was at the height of his power. In relation to communism, however, there has been nowhere near so much agreement among them, partly because the illusions of the Popular Front period exist about communism, at home and abroad. Bertrand Russell writing in 1939 about the internal dangers of fascism, said:

> Does the principle of free speech require us to put no obstacle in the way of those who advocate its suppression? Does the principle of tolerance require us to tolerate those who advocate intolerance?
> There is, of course, one obvious limitation upon the principle of free speech: if an act is illegal, it is logical to make it illegal to advocate it. . . . To prohibit the advocacy of illegalities is therefore not enough; some further limitation

upon the principle of free speech is necessary if incitement to violence is to be effectively prevented . . . the ordinary citizen, if he is on the whole content with his form of government, has a right to prohibit any organized attempt to overthrow it by force and *any propaganda obviously likely to promote such an attempt.* . . . When, as in the case of the fascist, the aims of the rebels are fundamentally opposed to a governmental theory accepted by the majority, and when, further, it is obvious that *violence is intended to be used at a suitable moment,* there is every justification for preventing the growth of organized power in the hands of a rebellious minority. For if this is not done, internal peace is jeopardized, and the kind of community that most men desire can no longer be preserved. . . . Liberal principles will not survive of themselves; like all other principles, they require vigorous assertion when they are challenged.

> *Freedom: Its Meaning,* 1940, N. Y. pp. 254-255; ed. by Anshen. My italics. (Quoted with permission of the publisher Harcourt, Brace & Co.)

The third distinction is between responsible, policy-making and sensitive posts in government and civil affairs, and occupations that cannot be so classified. The precise line of division is hard to draw. Even a position as clerk in the Department of Justice such as Judith Coplon filled may be extremely strategic, while the post of foreman of a road building crew may not be. But an actor's job reciting from another's script is certainly not strategic.

Some reasonable principles can be formulated as a guide to four types of situation. First, there are situations, e.g., in plants where restricted work is being done, in which the risk is so great that Communist conspirators may defeat the purposes of the work being done, that membership in the Communist Party should be *ipso facto* sufficient grounds for dismissal. There are other situations, such as government service and schools, in which, although this risk may be lessened by supervision, the introduction of these processes of supervision would be demoralizing. Here, too, membership should be a *prima facie* bar. There are still other situations in which the processes of supervision can easily be introduced without demoralizing consequences or great expense. Here membership should not be a bar, but specific performance should be the only test. Finally, there are situations in which there is little or no risk, e.g. performers on radio and film. Here, too, specific performance is alone relevant. In this last case, it goes without saying that the right of individuals to publish the truth about the political affiliations of such performers or to picket peacefully in protest cannot be proscribed without violating the Bill of Rights. The moral responsibility to withstand public pressures of this kind rests with the employer and the public itself. If we disapprove of unwise or unfair picketing, we should either picket in turn or make some other kind of protest instead of calling for police measures.

The really difficult cases are those in which we are considering applicants for posts where a man's ideas, particularly if he holds them with a tenacity that can be called fanatical, may have a bearing on his eligibility. There is a great danger that this may be misunderstood and I therefore wish to put this matter as carefully as possible. I wish to repeat that what I am now discussing is not freedom of expression *per se* but certain types of expression insofar as they bear upon professional fitness for specific responsible posts *before* assignment has been made to such posts.

Some thinkers have denied that ideas are ever relevant to action, that fanatics, no matter what ideas they are fanatical about, are entitled to the same opportunities, other things being equal, as anyone else. This seems to rest on a confusion between two propositions: (1) Belief in an idea is *logically* irrelevant to the performance of action where the term "logical" is understood as strict entailment. The fact that a man believes that Jews should be boycotted in business does not mean that he *necessarily* will boycott them. (2) Belief in an idea is *psychologically* irrelevant to the performance of actions. The first is true, the second is false. *Ideas are plans of action.* Whether this is affirmed as a logical or as merely a psychological truth depends on one's school of thought. But there is common agreement that whatever else ideas are, when believed, they are *at least* plans of action. In respect, therefore, to evaluating the probabilities that an individual will act on an idea when an opportunity presents itself, we must recognize that there is an important difference between entertaining an idea and *firmly believing it.* That is why *fanaticism* may be very dangerous in some situations and cannot be contained merely by counterposing a liberal attitude to it. In the quest for *truth,* there is no answer to fanaticism, as Bertrand Russell correctly says, except a liberalism which holds that everything is open to question. Here he is eternally right. His words remind one of Justice Holmes' famous observation that to have questioned one's own first principles is the mark of a civilized mind. *But with respect to the requirements of action or the implementing of policy,* sanctioned after free discussion in a democratic community, a fanatically held idea, even by a man who is not a conspirator, may be considered relevant in addition to his professional qualifications in appraising his fitness for a post. If, however, he has successfully held a post, and is not a member of an underground conspiratorial group, then the expression of any ideas, no matter how extreme or crackpot, should not be considered evidence of unfitness independently of its effects on his actual conduct or professional work.

Let me illustrate what I mean. Suppose a physician fanatically believed that hopelessly ill people should not have their lives prolonged. So long as the community did not approve of the practice of euthanasia, it would not be wise to permit such a man to run a hospital for the aged and infirm. He might, however, be acceptable for some other position. Suppose a man was a fanatical anti-Semite convinced of the authenticity of the *Protocol of Zion* and the legend of blood-ritual murders. We would be foolish to entrust him with the education of our children, even if he were an excellent geographer. It is conceivable that he might be useful elsewhere. Or finally suppose that a man fanatically believed that the Marshall Plan was an instrument of Wall Street to despoliate Western Europe. Even if he were not a member of the Communist Party, it would hardly be wise to consider him for the post of supervisor of the plan. In all these situations, ideas are relevant to professional qualification but not to employment in general.

As a rule of action, however, this principle cannot be *generally* applied because of the difficulty in establishing the degree of tenacity with which an idea is held, and because of the necessity of examining other aspects of the situation. But enough has been said, I hope, to refute the notion that the ideas a man holds and the *way* he holds them are *never* relevant in considering his fitness for positions of responsibility and trust. No one questioned Senator Borah's right to know whether Mr. Thurman Arnold believed that the anti-trust laws should be enforced before approving his appointment to a post whose responsibility included prosecution of violators of those laws.

If we bear these distinctions in mind, I believe we can use them as guide lines for intelligent policy in many fields. We need not fall victim to pressure groups which under the banner of anti-communism seek to further their narrow economic or sectarian interests in housing, price controls, government regulation or public education. Nor need we permit ourselves to be morally intimidated by other groups which under the traditional war cries of liberalism unwittingly pressure us into allowing a free field for subversion, infiltration and espionage.

I wish to examine in detail some of the consequences of the failure to make some of these distinctions. I take as an illustration a widely distributed pamphlet by the Public Affairs Committee, *Loyalty in a Democracy* edited by Maxwell Stewart.*

* It is a report of a round table on the problem of loyalty held under the chairmanship of Professor Robert E. Cushman of Cornell. The participants in the round table are listed as follows: "Alan Barth, Eleanor Bontecou, Alexander Brooks, Lawrence Chamberlain, Vern Countryman, Robert Cushman, Thomas Emerson, Denna F. Fleming, Roma Gans, Howard Henderson, Erling Hunt, Richard Kennan, Alfred McLung Lee, Patrick Malan, Carey McWilliams, Maxwell Stewart, H. W. Han and others." The chairman refers to the pamphlet as

Heresy, Yes — Conspiracy, No

This pamphlet is an all-out attack on the government's security and loyalty program which not only misstates central facts but proceeds on the assumption that the attempt to bar conspirators and other security risks from government posts flows from the premise that some citizens are not entitled to the rights and privileges of the Bill of Rights. It not only fails to distinguish between heresy and conspiracy but fails to distinguish between the rights to a fair trial, which the Bill of Rights gives even to conspirators, with the rights to a job. Because I believe that no man whether a member of the Republican, Democratic, Socialist or Communist Party should be deprived of freedom of speech and assembly, denied bail when charged with a crime, etc., I must believe, according to this position, that I cannot deny to a conspirator, a member of the Communist Party, the privilege of holding a federal job. I must dismiss him, as I would anybody else, only *after* he has committed his acts of sabotage or espionage.

Criticizing not merely the procedures of some legislative committees but of the federal loyalty program itself, the report states:

> But the challenge to our democratic institutions is not primarily in these procedures; it is in the assumption upon which they rest. Once you concede that there are certain citizens of the United States—adults, sane, and law-abiding—who are not entitled to the rights and privileges guaranteed to all Americans by the Bill of Rights, you have given away a large part of your case.

To assert that this premise is the basis of the loyalty program is a monstrously false allegation. There have always been special qualifications for government employment which all Americans entitled to the full privileges of the Bill of Rights have had to

an "outgrowth of the discussion" and "a joint product of many minds." It is not without significance in this connection that Messrs. Maxwell Stewart and Carey McWilliams have been staunch defenders of the procedures and verdict of the notorious Moscow Trials.

76

meet. The loyalty and security program adds certain additional qualifications in these difficult times. Some of its procedures undoubtedly are in need of improvement but the report of the Public Affairs Committee instead of making specific recommendations to improve the program in effect calls for its abandonment. This is the position taken in Alan Barth's *The Loyalty of Free Men*—one so extreme that even the rather doctrinaire Dr. Chafee gags on it. The Public Affairs Committee follows Mr. Barth in suggesting that: "Possibly it would be better if we would honestly admit that we cannot without grave injustice determine in advance *with exactness* who is likely to commit acts of espionage and sabotage, and leave the problem, *as we have in the past,* to be dealt with by legislation prescribing punishment for acts of disloyalty *after they had been committed.*" (My italics, p. 28.)

The word "possibly" is used to soften the shock of this passage: it should read "actually," for a glance at the three recommendations the Committee makes in effect involves the abandonment, as advocated by Mr. Barth, of the entire security and loyalty program. To leave matters *"as we have in the past"* is to betray a complete indifference to what happened in the past. The revelations of the Hiss case, to mention only the activities of one Communist ring in government, seem completely lost upon the Committee. Because we cannot say *"with exactness"* who is likely to commit acts of espionage and sabotage in all cases, it does not follow that we cannot say with great probability who is likely to commit acts of such a character in some cases. In how many life situations can we say with exactness what will happen? Do we therefore do nothing on the basis of good evidence to forestall dire eventualities? Not everybody exposed to a deadly plague will come down with it or transmit it but there is a sufficient likelihood to justify isolating him. There are some people, it is true, who come down with the plague who have never been suspected of being exposed to it. Were anyone to argue that therefore we should not isolate those who unquestionably have been exposed to it, he would convict himself of absurdity. Yet apparently this is the way Mr. Barth and the Public Affairs Committee think. Because some who commit sabotage are not known to be Communists or members of the Communist Party, it is not sensible, according to them, to assume it is likely that those who we know *are* members of the Communist Party will be disloyal. To punish acts of disloyalty *after they have been committed,* instead of trying to prevent disloyalty, among those who have clearly expressed their intent by membership in the Communist Party, is like saying that instead of trying to prevent a man with the *intent* of committting arson from carrying out his plans, we wait until he has burned the house down and then punish him.

For all that Mr. Barth and the Public Affairs Committee panel say about the Communist movement, they do not really believe that it is a conspiracy. They want to protect us from spies, saboteurs and foreign agents but they would do it—and here are their practical proposals—by (a) an educational campaign to develop "true loyalty" in all citizens, (b) strengthening and enforcing present laws and (c) using "modern methods of personnel selection" including psychiatry to hire people rather than judging them by their "associations or conventional behavior." It is not clear whether known membership in the Communist Party would bar a person from being hired but, it is made clear that once hired he would be judged *only* by his performance, even if it subsequently became known that he was a member of the Communist Party. Such membership in the eyes of the panel has less predictive weight concerning a man's *political* reliability than psychiatric findings.

The only comment we need make here on the psychiatric angle is to inquire which would be a more reliable index of a man's *political* loyalty to the United States, a report by psychiatrist Dr. Carl Binger, and psychologist H. Murray, the experts in the Hiss trials, or the fact that an individual was a member of the Communist Party which purges its ranks of all members who do not give primary allegiance to the Kremlin? And what in the world has psychiatry, whose uses in many contexts I do not con-

Freedom in American Culture

test, to do with political loyalty to democracy? Are there no psychiatrists who are Fascists or Communists?

Much more important is the plain implication that even if the membership of Hiss, Perlo, Coe and their friends had been established *after* their probationary period in government service had been completed, they would *not* have been dismissed unless caught, charged, and convicted of committing a crime. Membership *as such* in an espionage group would not be sufficient ground for dismissal, and certainly not the refusal to answer a question about such membership if the answers were self-incriminating.

The significance of this panel report of the Public Affairs Committee can be gauged not only from its boldness in maintaining that procedural safeguards against conspirators constitute an attack on the civil liberties of heretics but from its misstatements of fact, false alternatives, and substitution of irrelevant issues.

"Not a single foreign agent or saboteur has been uncovered by the loyalty investigation," (p.9) it writes. If members of the Communist Party are not foreign agents, then perhaps so. But the function of the loyalty program is not to detect saboteurs but only to keep out those for whom some evidence exists that they will become such. If the panel does not know that the factual discovery of active spies is the function of the F.B.I. it has no business discussing the question. But it does know, since in one place it maintains that we do not need a loyalty program since the F.B.I. does its work so well. Why then the repeated emphasis on the fact that saboteurs have not been discovered by the Loyalty Board?

Joining in the hysterical outcry that professors are being intimidated into silence, the panel report states: "Undoubtedly the Lattimore case, involving weeks of newspaper headlines and testimony under the Klieg lights of television, frightened thousands of university professors. They shuddered at the thought that the same fate could overtake them. They and thousands of other prominent people were reluctant to risk attack by criticizing the loyalty program." This compounds misleading innuendo with in-

79

vention. It implies that Lattimore was questioned because he attacked the loyalty program. This is false. (Nor was he questioned under Klieg lights.) Lattimore was charged with being the architect of American policy in Asia and serving as a ranking Soviet agent. He was never even questioned about the loyalty program. To assert that thousands of university professors were frightened into not criticizing the government loyalty program makes one wonder who counted them. Almost half the panel of the Public Affairs Committee consists of professors. What makes them believe that their colleagues are less courageous than they are? Surely, a refusal to endorse a program which would abolish all loyalty and security provisions instead of improving them, thus making it easier to commit treason and sabotage, is not conclusive evidence of fear on the part of college professors. Professors as a group have not been less critical of one or another aspects of the loyalty program than other groups. In fact, with respect to loyalty oaths they have been the *leaders* of a national opposition.

One final illustration of the intellectual disingenuousness of this report of the Public Affairs Committee must be considered in virtue of the gravity of the theme. Like many other groups, it is critical of the Smith Act, which is its right. But instead of expressing its opposition in a forthright way it resorts to "cagey" language and charges that the Act confers on the Attorney General powers which tend to obscure the "obvious and vital distinction between discussing [*sic!*] violent revolution and preparing to achieve it." But the Smith Act, justifiably or not, proscribes *not* the discussion of violent revolution but its advocacy. The Supreme Court itself *discussed* violent revolution; to suggest that the Act which it upheld overlooked "the obvious and vital" distinction between *discussing* violent revolution and *preparation* for it is absurd. If the report had read "There is an obvious and vital distinction between *teaching and advocating* violent revolution and preparing to achieve it," every reader would have seen that the distinction is neither obvious nor vital, and that the whole case for the Smith Act, even if we finally reject it, rests upon the contention, so ably argued by Justice Learned Hand, whose position was affirmed, that there are situations in history when advocating violent revolution and preparing for it are continuous parts of one dangerous process.

I know of nothing better calculated to produce a dozen Senator McCarthys than the implementation of the position defended in this report of the Public Affairs Committee. Undoubtedly everyone concerned in this issue, including Senator McCarthy, is sincere and patriotic. But in their own ways both positions are fatal to the preservation of democratic institutions.

Outside government employment one cannot formulate rules of action that will hold generally, for circumstances are too diverse. As far as professional activity is concerned, the basic requirement is that certain forms of professional conduct and integrity be recognized, administered by the professional groups themselves in the same way as committees on ethical practices function in the medical and legal fields. Within the framework of these principles of ethical conduct, the widest latitude should be permitted to heresies. An unceasing defense must be conducted against the ever present tendency of special interests, fearful of the results of free inquiry and doubt, to limit freedom of experiment and dissent. At the same time any groups, and not only Communist groups, which organize secretly to pervert the ends of a profession should be exposed, not so much on political grounds as on professional grounds, and measures adopted to prevent them from victimizing the unsuspecting.

In these unparalleled times of perplexity, anxiety and danger, it is not too Utopian to hope that with the willing use of our intelligence we may be able to withstand the totalitarian war against our free culture—and indeed carry the war for cultural freedom by proper *psychological* means into the enemy's territory—without losing our own traditions of freedom, variety, dissent and democratic fellowship.

The truth of the matter is that many American men and

women of good will, and large sections of American liberalism, particularly in the universities, are much less concerned with the outrages of Communist totalitarianism against their victims, and the threats to their own freedom in the extension of the Kremlin's power, than they were with the outrages of Fascist totalitarianism and the threats of a victory by Hitler. Who does not remember the ferment and stir on American campuses from 1933 to 1939 even before the worst iniquities of Hitlerism were known? The committees, the meetings, the mass demonstrations and picketings, the pamphlets and leaflets against Fascism were almost an everyday occurrence. Anyone who suggested that we should try to understand the Germans despite their distasteful foreign policy, that we should send ambassadors of good will, build cultural bridges, would have been shouted down. Had he said that all the excitement about Nazism and Fascism was a form of hysteria because, after all, Hitler had so few followers *in this country,* and those mostly cranks and comic opera figures, he would have been considered a Nazi apologist.

If we match Hitler's first six years with the six years that have elapsed since the cessation of hostilities, we find that Stalin has absorbed more countries, killed more people, extirpated more democratic institutions more thoroughly, than even the psychotic barbarian, Hitler. Where is the excitement, the moral indignation, the impassioned protest? In 1935 I could rouse the academic community to Hitler's latest decree or to the attempt of some Polish Universities to make Jewish students sit on "yellow benches." In 1948 when I sought to organize a protest against the cold-blooded execution of Czech students after the Communist coup d'état, I could hardly raise a corporal's guard in addition to members of the old Committee for Cultural Freedom and their friends. The stalwarts who shouted against Hitler, against Dollfuss, against Mussolini, Franco, Chang Kai-shek, Pilsudski, Metaxes, were silent before the bloody events in Latvia, Estonia, Lithuania, Poland, Romania, Bulgaria, Czechoslovakia, Greece, Eastern Germany, which not only destroyed every vestige of academic freedom but took the lives of thousands of democratic students and professors. I could rouse them with a resolution or a meeting of protest against Argentina. But although these individuals are not Communists, they are apathetic or cynical to the global Communist threat. They are convinced that our liberties are in greater danger from American fascism than from any other source.

So long as this remains true and American liberals do not take the leadership in the struggle against communism, they create the conditions in which demagogues thrive who oppose communism and liberalism both. It is only under such liberal leadership that peace may be won without appeasement; and, if it comes to a struggle, it is under liberal leadership that democratic institutions and the rights of heresy have the best chances of being preserved.

In the course of our discussion we have found one phrase cropping up again and again which constitutes a stone of stumbling on the path to an intelligent position. This phrase is "guilt by association." Although we have touched upon it in passing, it might be rewarding to examine more closely this expression and the use made of it in current thought.

Chapter 4

WHAT IS "GUILT BY ASSOCIATION"?

From time to time certain phrases catch the public fancy. They get fixed in popular consciousness and enjoy a vogue both in the academy and the market place. Repetition gives them a patina of familiarity so that their use soothes the understanding instead of challenging it. Gradually these phrases begin to be employed in all sorts of contexts until they function not as summaries of thought, but as substitutes, like flags run up to show the color of our emotions.

Such a phrase is "guilt by association." In view of presidential directives to the Civil Service Commission to review and unify the discordant procedures in existing loyalty and security programs, its analysis is no mere theoretical exercise. Men's liberties, reputation, and livelihood may depend upon the proper interpretation of this expression.

The origin of the phrase is obscure but its current use almost universal. It appears even in Supreme Court decisions, with a minority charging in a vigorous dissent that a certain piece of legislation (the Feinberg Law) commits our society to a belief in the pernicious doctrine of "guilt by association," whereas the majority holds that there is nothing pernicious in the principle

84

behind the practices so vehemently denounced by their fellow-justices.

Even long before the phrase "guilt by association" appeared in a dissenting opinion of the Supreme Court, it had been used in many quarters to hamper exposure and criticism of Communist Party activities. It has been argued that nothing can be legitimately inferred about an individual's qualifications for any post from the fact that he is a member of the Communist Party. To make any such inference, we still hear, is to lapse into the horrible sin of attributing "guilt by association" and to betray the heritage of American freedom. The very same person who recognizes that under certain circumstances membership in the Society of Friends, Ethical Culture, and similar groups may be relevant in favorably assessing individual worth or qualifications for a position, will passionately deny that membership in a conspiratorial party, whose control commission rigorously excludes inactive people or dissenters, is ever relevant in making an unfavorable assessment! In effect such a person, while believing in "innocence by association" or "fitness by association," disbelieves in "guilt by association" or "unfitness by association." Yet these expressions are on all fours in their ambiguity.

In the whole discussion of the tangled questions of national security, professional integrity, and personal freedom, now raging throughout the country, "guilt by association" is the most overworked phrase in circulation. Even an organization with such a long and honorable history as the American Association of University Professors has invoked the phrase, as a protective mantle, around the right of members of the Communist Party to teach in our colleges and universities on the same terms as any other individuals. The Academic Freedom Committee of the American Civil Liberties Union has similarly denounced those who would exclude members of the Communist Party from colleges on grounds of professional unfitness as having fallen victim to the diseased thinking that guilt can be evidenced by association. The Public Affairs Committee in its pamphlet, *Loyalty in a*

Heresy, Yes — Conspiracy, No

Democracy, has an entire section devoted to "guilt by association," and throughout the discussion the most horrendous consequences are attributed to judgments based on it.

Many groups and individuals who are vociferous in their condemnation of "guilt by association" show not the slightest reluctance in imputing guilt by association when criticizing their political opponents. The most extraordinary amalgams of "guilt by association" on the most tenuous of grounds have been created to discredit political opponents who are at the same time themselves accused of resorting to this mode of thinking.

Nowhere, however, has an extended analysis of the expression, "guilt by association," been made in order to determine its different meanings and to distinguish between its legitimate and illegitimate uses and applications. Until this is done not only may our practices be unjust and illiberal to the individuals affected by our policies, but our counsels are likely to be confused in devising intelligent safeguards against Communist penetration.

The meaning of the phrase "guilt by association" is ambiguous because of the ambiguity of the key terms "guilt" and "association." There is *criminal* guilt which makes a man subject to penal sanctions—fines, loss of his liberty, and, in extreme cases, even of his life. There is *moral* guilt which is not legally punishable but which may incur, in addition to a judgment of blame and disapproval, certain social sanctions from the community. Except to those who regard the particular laws that are being violated as unjust, criminal guilt usually carries with it the stigma of moral guilt. Anglo-Saxon jurisprudence does not recognize criminal guilt by association except in certain cases of conspiracy in which the association takes a specific form.

The kind of situation in which the phrase "guilt by association" is most frequently applied is one in which moral guilt is involved. The question arises over the degree and justification of the sanctions the community adopts towards those who are presumably guilty. Some cases present no difficulties. A candidate for a judi-

What Is "Guilt By Association"?

cial post is shown to be an intimate associate of racketeers and gangsters. No one asserts his criminal guilt. But certainly those responsible for his election or selection would feel justified in denying him office. And judging by his efforts to exonerate himself from the charge, where corruption is not rife, the candidate acts as if he, too, believes that his associations with others are relevant in considering his qualifications.

Common sense and common practice, reflected in such expressions as "a man is judged by the company he keeps," "birds of a feather," etc., recognize the wisdom of appraising certain kinds of association in considering the fitness of an individual to fill positions requiring public confidence. A crony of notorious gamblers is not likely to be considered for the post of bank teller even if it is demonstrable that all he does is to hold their money belt or bank their money. He would be eligible to drive a dump truck but hardly an armored money truck.

Suppose, however, a judge already holding office associates with disreputable elements in the community. What action of reprisal, if any, would the community be justified in taking, even if there were no evidence of *criminal* guilt? This question underscores the ambiguity of the term "association." For the answer is indeterminate until we know what kind of association exists between him and them, and for what purposes. "Association" is an equivocal word for the most diverse kinds of relationships among men,* ranging from active co-operation through membership in an organization, to chance meetings and other innocuous contacts, to continuous encounters for purposes of debate and refutation. For example, a man joins the Communist Party, and by virtue of his membership actively co-operates in subverting the purposes of the institution in which the Communist Party is secretly functioning. A second man joins a co-operative or a trade union which Communists subsequently join or capture. A third man, perhaps a minister seeking to save lost souls, frequents Communist meet-

* Cf., Lovejoy, *Journal of Philosophy*, February 14, 1952, p. 88.

ings in order to argue with and against Communists. All three relationships are forms of associations, but moral guilt is present only in the first case. In the other two cases the association is perfectly innocent and sometimes commendable. Most of the tearful effects produced by the charge that a conspirator is being made a victim of the doctrine of "guilt by association" consists in transferring the connotations that the phrase has in the second and third contexts to the first.

With these preliminary distinctions in mind, some light may be thrown on the question whether inferences based on an individual's continued membership in the Communist Party constitutes unreasonable imputation of criminal or moral "guilt by association." The American legal tradition holds that all guilt is personal. That this is not violated by the provisions of the Smith Act, which forbids the advocacy of the overthrow of government by force or violence, must be recognized even by those who have their doubts about its wisdom, or who would have preferred to see the leaders of the Communist Party charged with failure to register as foreign agents. For one thing, an *act* of membership is personal. But more important, no member of the Communist Party has so far been legally punished, or held criminally guilty, on grounds of his membership alone. In each case the government has sought to prove that by some specific act or deed, involved in an advocacy which is part of the process of preparation, the defendant in question has been guilty of teaching the necessity of the violent overthrow of democratic government or of conspiring to do so.

Much more controversial is the question whether in barring members of the Communist Party from public employment, federal or local, we are invoking the principle of "guilt by association" in an objectionable way. It is at this point that many confuse "criminal guilt" with "moral guilt." If a member of the Communist Party is kept out of an atomic weapons plant or any other strategic or policy-making post, he is not being charged with "criminal guilt by association" because some other members of the Communist Party have been guilty of espionage. His guilt is *moral*, and it is personal. Nor is he being charged with mere association of the innocuous variety previously mentioned, but with an *act* of membership in an organization whose structure, discipline, and controls make it impossible for any person to remain in it without actively co-operating in the achievement of its purposes. Since these purposes are conspiratorial, there is every justification to consider his act of membership as directly relevant to his professional qualifications.

Whatever may have been the case in the past, a man does not today somnambulistically stumble into the Communist Party. If he remains a member, this is *prima facie* evidence that he is a hardened conspirator and that he accepts its orders and directives. If ever an individual were found who had joined and remained a member of the Communist Party under the impression that it was merely a branch, say, of a Temperance Union or a Benevolent Association for Diffusing Joy Among the Sexes, he would be ineligible on grounds of lack of intelligence for any responsible job.

The situation is quite different, however, with membership in "front" organizations or those listed as "subversive" by the Attorney General, other than the Communist Party and similar conspiratorial political groups of fascist hue. We are assuming for purposes of this analysis that such groups have been correctly identified and the procedures by which this has been done are both public and subject to judicial review. That this has not yet been done is a serious weakness in the Federal loyalty program, but one which is not irremediable.

Since the actual purposes of some of these organizations have been carefully disguised, many well-meaning people have at one time or another been taken in. To infer from the act of membership in *such* organizations, the moral guilt of co-operation in achieving the ulterior ends of the Communist Party "fraction" operating behind the scenes, may be a sad mistake. It is here that some grave injustices have been done to individuals by denying them access to responsible posts because unscrupulous groups capitalized on their idealism or naïveté. As a rule it is in situations of this type that the phrase about avoiding "guilt by association" may be legitimately used in warning or pleading against lumping together the sheep and the goats.

No single formula can be a guide to intelligent decision in such situations, but only tested knowledge acquired in long and close study of front organizations, Communist ideology, and the turns and zigzags in the strategy and tactics of the Kremlin's war against the West. A blameless life as an investment broker or as a minister of the gospel, even a brilliant career as a corporation lawyer or in the military services, does not of itself qualify a man as an expert in this field. Since literally hundreds of thousands have unwittingly or wittingly passed through Communist fronts, and since the number of sensitive positions in government and industry increases daily, great care must be exercised lest in the interests of security, we are needlessly committing individual injustices.

It cannot be too much emphasized that the problem is not to determine the presence or degree of criminal guilt involved by membership in "subversive groups," but the presence and degree of risk involved in employing in strategic posts those who hold, or who have held, such membership. The technical task of detecting actual espionage agents or saboteurs must be left to special agencies.

In judging the significance of an individual's membership in a subversive organization, the following are some of the more important considerations:

(1) The number of such organizations he is a member of. A man may be fooled once, twice, or even three times. But beyond a certain point we are justified in concluding that he is a willing fool, not criminally guilty of anything, but morally obtuse in

What Is "Guilt By Association"?

lending his name, prestige and sometimes substantial means for exploitation by the enemies of freedom.

(2) The degree and character of activity in such organizations. Was he merely a name on a letterhead or a member of the executive committee where the Communist Party fraction usually shows its hand?

(3) The time and place of such activity. Most Communist "fronts" have been fathered by the party. Others have been captured or kidnapped from original organizers who were anything but Communists. Some individuals who have struggled to prevent capture remain to continue the struggle until excluded. It is ironical that even some anti-Communists have been considered poor loyalty and security risks because of membership in an organization, originally non-Communist, but subsequently captured. In some places a local group, free of Communist Party taint, will affiliate with a national organization with high-sounding aims and name, without realizing that it is a front.

(4) Most important of all is the extent of the open co-operation between the front organization and the Communist Party. Any member of the International Labor Defense, the former legal defense arm of the Communist Party, which used to attack in unbridled fashion the American Civil Liberties Union for its defense of the civil liberties of all political groups, could hardly have failed to be aware of its character. On the other hand, in the late thirties a member of the American League Against War and Fascism might very well have been ignorant of the fact that it was a Communist Party front organization even though it was organized, according to well-authenticated public testimony, by Urevitch, a Comintern agent, in the swank apartment of A. A. Heller, sugar daddy of many Communist Party fronts. Since the usefulness of a front organization to the Communist Party depends upon its not being publicly identified as a front, whenever such organizations are exposed they are often killed and new ones set up in their place. This has been especially true among Communist youth front organizations which are the most important

91

single source from which the Communist Party recruits its most devoted cadres.

These various factors cannot be weighed mechanically. Each individual case must be considered in the light of general principles and its specific aspects. Allowance must also be made for the climate of opinion in the years when the struggle against Hitler seemed the all-absorbing task. These were the days when generous hopes ran high—a tribute to the trustfulness and good will of so many Americans—that the Kremlin would cultivate its own garden instead of embarking upon a program of world conquest.

Despite reports to the contrary abroad, the United States is still a country in which public opinion is largely molded by voluntary associations of private citizens. These associations also perform invaluable public services on a national, and especially local levels. Whether in the cause of peace or social welfare or education, civil liberties, and national defense, the overwhelming majority of these organizations have never found it necessary to join forces with totalitarians of any stripe, with bigots, and cultural vigilantes. No program to safeguard American democracy can be anything but self-defeating which discourages the existence and multiplication of such voluntary associations. We must not permit the existence of disingenuous front organizations to interfere with the continuous fight for good causes—whether popular or unpopular. Unless we fight for them, not only when the popular current is with us but when the going is rough and hard, good causes become lost causes. Communism on a global scale is the main danger, but there are plenty of evils on our own doorstep whose solution will make it easier to face and conquer the greatest threat to free institutions since the days of Salamis and Marathon.

As we have seen, the recurrent problem faced by liberals is the degree of tolerance to be extended to those who are dedicated to the destruction of liberal society. The administrative answer to the problem has been the loyalty and security program. The political answer to the problem has been the Smith Act and the opinions upholding it. Very few decisions in the history of the Supreme Court have created such doubt and confusion among liberals as the decision affirming the conviction of the leaders of the Communist Party under the Smith Act. It therefore invites careful study.

Chapter 5

REFLECTIONS ON THE SMITH ACT

I

The Smith Act makes it unlawful for any person to advocate the overthrow of the government by force and violence (Section Two) or for any person to attempt to commit or to conspire to commit such advocacy (Section Three).

This Act and the various judicial opinions on its constitutionality are among the most discussed, and the most unread, of modern official documents. In any such discussion, several sorts of issues must be distinguished. One is the constitutionality of the Act. A second is its wisdom. A third is the justice of its application to the Communist Party. Another way of putting this may focalize the moot points better. Is the law behind the indictment of the leaders of the Communist Party constitutional? Constitutional or not, is it wise to have brought the charge? Were the defendants, i.e., the leaders of the Communist Party, guilty of the charge—do they actually advocate the use of "force and violence"? [1]

[1] Not enough study has been given to the various opinions which entered into the decision on the Smith Act. Of particular significance is the opinion of Judge Learned Hand of the United States Court of Appeals, affirming the con-

Reflections on the Smith Act

The constitutionality of the Smith Act, it may be argued, is a matter of history since in fact the Supreme Court has decided the question. However, no adjudication of any Congressional legislation as constitutional can be regarded as final; the Supreme Court can always reverse itself by adopting the fiction that a new case before it, apparently involving the very same issues on which it has taken a stand, is in some respects relevantly different, and therefore provides the ground for a new decision. Both cases then become precedents to be cited by the Court on subsequent occasions for whichever decision it sees fit to make.

But most discussion about whether a piece of legislation is constitutional or not actually is a discussion about whether it is wise or not, "democratic" or not, enlightened or not. Anyone who reflects upon the number and variety of laws declared constitutional in the past, some of which supported the institution of slavery, will admit at once that an act may be constitutional and unwise, and, like the Federal Income Tax when it was first adopted, wise and unconstitutional. I shall therefore be more concerned with the wisdom of this act than with its constitutionality.

There is one preliminary question which must be cleared up concerning "the right to revolution," since it has been asserted that the Smith Act abrogates this right. Reference is made to this right, not in the Constitution, but in the Declaration of Independence, where it does not appear as an absolute right * but as one justified under certain conditions. Only when life, liberty and

---

viction of the defendants. His finding was the basis of Chief Justice Vinson's opinion which, although derived from the earlier decision, treats the main themes in a pedestrian way. Much more distinguished are the concurrent opinions of Justice Jackson and Frankfurter who treat profoundly the deeper issues of the case at bar.

* It may not be supererogatory to remind the reader of the exact words: ". . . Prudence, indeed, will dictate that governments long established should not be changed for light and transient causes. . . . But, when a long train of abuse and usurpations, pursuing invariably the same object, evinces a design to reduce [mankind] under absolute despotism, it is their right, it is their duty, to throw off such government, and to provide new guards for their future security."

Heresy, Yes—Conspiracy, No

the pursuit of happiness are threatened with destruction do "the people" have a right to overthrow their rulers. The Declaration distinguishes between revolutions of this character and "insurrections" of minorities which the English king is accused of fomenting among the American colonists.

Some writers have inferred that because there is a justification for revolution in situations in which democratic processes are absent, a similar justification therefore exists in situations in which these processes are the rule. This overlooks the various connotations of the term "right." The term "right" may be used in the legal sense and the moral sense. Legally, a right is any claim to goods or services or privileges, made by one or more individuals, and which society stands ready to enforce. Legally, therefore, it is utter nonsense to speak of the right to revolution. Justice Hand disposes effectively of the claim that there is a *legal* right to advocate violence when he says, in his opinion for the Court of Appeals which found the Smith Act constitutional:

> The advocacy of violence may, or may not, fail: but in neither case can there be any 'right' to use it. Revolutions are often 'right'; but a 'right of revolution' is a contradiction in terms, for a society which acknowledged it, could not stop at tolerating conspiracies to overthrow it, but must include their execution.

However, in all historical situations, whether democratic or not, individuals have a moral right to revolution in the sense that, if they are rationally convinced that their fundamental values can be preserved only by the overthrow of the existing regime, they are morally justified in making the attempt. Believing what they do, it may even be their duty to make the attempt. But by the same token, individuals who are rationally convinced that any attempt to overthrow the existing regime by force and violence will destroy their fundamental values, will have a moral right to suppress the revolutionists.

This does not mean that in any particular historical situation

96

Reflections on the Smith Act

both sides are equally justified in their analysis of the values involved and of the needs and interests in which values are rooted. One or another side may be hasty, partial, or mistaken. So long as the processes of reflective inquiry are kept open, what appear to be ultimate and inarbitrable conflicts of interest may prove to be negotiable. When such conflicts are not negotiable, what is shown is not that moral values have no objective reality but that they are not universal.*

There is nothing self-contradictory in asserting that, in *any* society, human beings have a moral right or rational claim to revolution. What *is* self-contradictory is the belief, by someone who regards himself as a principled democrat, in the right to revolution in a democratic society. Societies whose democratic processes operate unabridged and whose decisions truly rest upon the freely given consent of a majority, may act in such a way as to cause moral men to use revolutionary means to overthrow them. But when men act in this manner, they cannot sincerely or consistently call themselves democrats, even when they consider themselves God's angry men. Democratic government and good government are not identical in meaning. That democratic government is more likely to produce good government than non-democratic government is only an empirical hypothesis, warranted by most of the historical evidence but not by all of it.

These considerations may appear to be abstract, but failure to think them through almost invariably leads to confusion. To one who accepts the principles and institutional practices that define a democracy, there is neither a moral nor a legal right to use force and violence to overthrow a democracy which satisfies the definition, merely because its fruits are personally unsatisfactory. On the other hand, while he may not have a legal right to overthrow a dictatorship, because it writes the rules of law, he cer-

* For further elaboration of this point see my article in COMMENTARY, March 1948, "Why Democracy Is Better," and my "The Desirable and Emotive in Dewey's Ethics" in *John Dewey: Philosopher of Science and Freedom*. (New York, 1950).

tainly has a moral right to do so, because by his action he is passing judgment on the existing rules of law.

On the assumption that they are sincerely convinced of the badness of democracy, we may grant to the Hitlers and Stalins, and to other totalitarians of the more reasonable Platonic brood, the "moral" right to revolt against a democracy, provided we understand that as democrats we have the "moral" right—nay, duty—to crush them, when and if they make the attempt, or prepare for that attempt. Any criticism of the Smith Act as undemocratic by totalitarians, especially of the Communist and Fascist stripe, we can dismiss as a piece of indecent hypocrisy.

My concern is with the Smith Act from the point of view of a believer in democracy. All such believers would admit that legislation which punishes the overt act of revolt or insurrection should be enacted and enforced. But the Smith Act makes punishable, not the overt actions, which are covered by other legislation, but the advocacy of, or incitement to, the use of force or violence. Further, it makes punishable a conspiracy to teach any doctrine containing such advocacy or incitement.

What is a "conspiracy"? Some clarification is necessary at this point. In many contexts, the word "conspiracy" refers to nonverbal overt behavior. As usually employed outside of legal contexts, it designates active planning with others and involves something more than the use of words. The verb "to conspire," however, has a much more comprehensive meaning. It denotes, not merely the overt act of conspiracy, but the process of conspiring. On occasions, the use of speech, oral and written, between two or more persons may be considered as part of the process of conspiring—depending on the place, the circumstances, and the nature of the words used.

Many people who are critical of the Smith Act concentrate their fire against section three which makes it illegal "to conspire" to advocate the use of force and violence. Since there was no evidence indicated of "conspiracy," in the usual sense of overt non-verbal behavior—say accumulation of arms—they conclude

Reflections on the Smith Act

that it is absurd to have charged the Communist defendants with having attempted "to conspire." This criticism is based on the assumption that the use of words by themselves can never be evidence of an attempt "to conspire."

It is the great merit of Justice Jackson's opinion to call attention to the legal fact that in our system of law conspiracies are adjudged to exist on the basis of the same *kind* of evidence that was introduced in the case of the Communist Party leaders. The legal rule concerning conspiracy in interstate commerce, for example, and the admissibility of evidence chiefly of a verbal kind in establishing the existence of such conspiracy, has never been challenged by the opponents of the Smith Act.

"Conspiracies of labor-unions, trade associations, and news agencies," writes Justice Jackson in his concurring opinion on the Smith Act, "have been condemned although accomplished, evidenced, and carried out, like the conspiracy here, chiefly by letter-writing, meetings, speeches, and organizations." He goes on to cite from an opinion of Justice Holmes involving the Sherman Anti-Trust Act: "Coming next to the objection that no overt act is laid, the answer is that the Sherman Act punishes the conspiracies at which it is aimed on the common law footing,—that is to say, it does not make the doing of any act other than the act of conspiring, a condition of liability." To which Justice Jackson adds the dry observation: "It is not to be supposed that the power of Congress to protect the nation's existence is more limited than its power to protect interstate commerce."

Consequently, there is a legal warrant to accept as evidence of conspiracy to do something unlawful, speech, writing and organizational activity. The main question, then, is not Section Three of the Smith Act, which forbids conspiracy to do what is proscribed in Section Two, but Section Two itself, which forbids the advocacy of the overthrow of government by force or violence. If it is wrong to advocate the use of force and violence, it is wrong to conspire to do so. But is it wrong to advocate the use of force and violence?

Heresy, Yes—Conspiracy, No

Since the First Amendment enjoins Congress from passing any laws abridging freedom of speech, some opponents of the Smith Act regard it as unconstitutional on this ground. But, if the first amendment were construed literally, this would make even laws against criminal libel unconstitutional. Whoever reads the First Amendment as if it made the right to speech absolute and unconditioned would find himself committed to the same kind of absurdities as anyone who took the statement in the Declaration of Independence about all men being created free and equal as a proposition in theology or biology instead of political ethics.

Outside of legal circles, this appeal to the right of free speech as an absolute is so common and is buttressed so often by invoking mistakenly the position of Justices Holmes and Brandeis, that it is pertinent here to quote from an opinion of Justice Holmes speaking for a unanimous court:

> The First Amendment while prohibiting legislation against free speech as such cannot have been, and obviously was not, intended to give immunity for every possible use of language. . . . We venture to believe that neither Hamilton nor Madison, nor any other competent person then or later, ever supposed that to make criminal the counselling of a murder within the jurisdiction of Congress would be an unconstitutional interference with free speech.*

If a democracy does not accept the belief in absolute rights, how does it morally distinguish itself from a dictatorship? I shall consider this question later; but for the moment I wish to point out that the defendants tried under the Smith Act did not fall back upon any assertion of the absolute right of freedom of advocacy. Their main contention was that, even if the charge were true, such advocacy did not constitute a "clear and present" danger of the violent overthrow of the government.

This in principle recognizes what common sense has always acknowledged, viz., that if an act is criminal or immoral, it is

---

* Frohwerk v. United States, 249 U. S. 204, 395 Ct. 249, 250, 63 L.Ed. 501, cited in Justice Jackson's concurring opinion.

wrong to advocate or counsel its commission even if the liability for such advocacy is not enforced. I cannot resist quoting from an earlier opinion of Justice Hand a generation ago which expresses with felicity the logic, the ethics, and the psychology of the matter:

> One may not counsel or advise others to violate the law as it stands. Words are not only the keys of persuasion, but the triggers of action, and those which have no purport but to counsel the violation of law cannot by any latitude of interpretation be a part of that public opinion which is the final source of government in a democratic state.

II

The general principle which limits the right to free speech is not expressed in the Constitution but in a famous decision written by Justice Holmes, in which he stated that "the question in every case is whether the words are used in such circumstances and are of such a nature as to create a clear and present danger that will bring about the substantive evils that Congress has a right to prevent."

Like the phrase "due process of law," the phrase "clear and present" danger seems to have a fluid meaning. How clear must the danger be? To whom must the danger be clear? How present —today, this year, or the current century? And how great the danger? The Justices of the present court are at loggerheads with each other as to the exact meaning to give the phrase. Most discussions are frankly concerned more with what the words *should* mean, i.e., how they should be interpreted in specific cases, than with what they *did* mean to Holmes and Brandeis. What is true of constitutional interpretation generally is true of interpretations of dicta like "clear and present danger"—what seems reasonable to the Court at any given time is read back into the original intent of Holmes' words.

If we examine the context in which Holmes first used the

phrase, we may be able to get a better notion of what he had in mind, independently of whether we desire to accept or reject his proposed criterion. In the Schenk case the defendant was charged with obstructing, recruiting, and causing military insubordination by denouncing conscription. The most inciting sentence of the handbill, only a few of which were circulated, was, according to Justice Vincent, the following: "You must do your share to maintain, support and uphold the rights of the people of this country."

It was this action—the distribution of a handbill with such a mild incitement—which Holmes, speaking for a unanimous court, held a "clear and present danger" of imperiling the conscription program and causing military insubordination. It follows at once that Holmes could not have meant by his criterion an action that threatened to be successful. No one in his most fantastic dream could imagine that the circulation of a few leaflets by a lone individual would successfully undermine the American program of conscription. Nonetheless, Justice Douglas in his minority opinion on the Smith Act denies that "a clear and present danger" of revolutionary overthrow exists on the ground that the Communist petitioners have not "the slightest chance of achieving their aims."

Now it so happens, although Justice Douglas is unaware of it, that the Kremlin often instructs its fifth columns to make a bid for the conquest of political power by force and violence even when the probability of success is extremely small, and even when the direst predictions of failure have been made by those ordered to seize power. The reasons for this need not now concern us: they flow from strategic considerations in the Kremlin's plans for world domination. In the 1920's such futile insurrections took place in Thuringia, Hamburg, and Canton. Even a wildly improbable effort at overthrow, one foredoomed to failure, may have very grave consequences for the community. Whatever the "clear and present danger" formula may mean, to any reasonable person it cannot mean that speech advocating a crime

Reflections on the Smith Act

should be curbed only when it is extremely probable that the crime will be successful.

What is relevant in determining whether or not to invoke the clear and present danger formula, is the probability of *an attempt being made*, not the probability of the attempt succeeding. The probability that an attempt will actually be made to carry out what is advocated, is a function of two things: the readiness of those advocating revolutionary overthrow to act when they believe the situation is ripe—something which the jury is called on to decide—and, second, the political state of the world, the temper of the times, the objective threats to the existence of democratic institutions—which the court pronounces on (for no good reason that I can see, since this is not a matter of law but of fact).

The majority opinion interprets the phrase in the same way as Judge Learned Hand does: "In each case (courts) must ask whether the gravity of the 'evil,' discounted by its improbability, justifies such invasion of free speech as is necessary to avoid the danger." The term "evil" refers to the substantive evils Congress has a right to prevent, and the term "improbability" is used synonymously here with "remoteness." How remote is the danger of the Communist conspiracy making some attempt to carry out what it advocates?

All of the opinions in the Smith Act, except for the dissents of Justices Black and Douglas, recognize that the phrase "clear and present danger" is no shibboleth, and that in every case its intelligent use requires an analysis of the particular situation. Some consistency there must be, however, if these words are not to become entirely arbitrary. What seems extremely puzzling to me is how anyone can approve of the determination that a clear and present danger existed in the Schenk case—when Justice Holmes first formulated his principle—and contest the finding that a clear and present danger exists in the case of Dennis *et al.*, who are an integral part of a highly organized international conspiracy. For my own part, it seems to me that the Supreme Court was clearly unjustified in its decision in the Schenk case. The whole incident was trivial, and there was not the remotest chance that Schenk could have had any influence on the American conscription program. I do not believe it can fairly be construed even as an attempt to obstruct that program.

To approve of the decision in the Schenk case and disapprove of it in the Dennis case, as so many liberals have done, makes no sense at all. This is all the truer because instead of referring the Schenk case back for retrial so that the *jury* could determine the *facts* about the clear and present danger, the Court made such determination itself. Justices Black and Douglas who believe that the jury should have passed on this point in the case of Dennis *et al.* do not criticize either the decision or procedure in the Schenk case. So far as I know Norman Thomas was the only outstanding liberal figure who, although approving of "the clear and present danger" interpretation, emphatically criticized the Court in the Schenk case both for taking jurisdiction to determine the facts and for its decision on the facts.

As the Smith Act has now been interpreted by the courts, it applies only to cases in which a "clear and present" danger exists that an attempt at revolutionary overthrow will be made. Now the question arises: who is to be the judge of whether or not a clear and present danger exists? Two different things have been confused in the court opinions on this question. The first question is whether or not the gravity and dangers of the times justifies, in the interest of national security, restrictions on the freedom of speech to advocate revolutionary overthrow. The second question is whether or not the specific case at bar, in which the defendants have been charged with conspiracy to advocate revolutionary overthrow, is one in which a clear and present danger flows from *this particular advocacy*. The opinion of the majority of the judges is that both of these questions are questions for the Court to decide. My own view is that the first question is one for Congress to decide since it involves a conflict of social interests—the interest in national security and the interest in free speech. The second question is one for the jury to decide. I shall discuss these two questions separately.

The first question, as Justice Frankfurter points out in his remarkable concurring opinion, is one which obviously falls within the legislative power. It is a matter of policy. And responsibility for policy rests with the elected representatives who may be refused our confidence at election time, and not with judges who are beyond reach. As far as policy goes, a judge's vote counts for one and no more than one, and is cast like every other citizen's vote. Justice Frankfurter's words in this connection ought to be inscribed in letters of gold on the portals of the Supreme Court. "Our duty to abstain from confounding policy with constitutionality demands perceptive humility as well as self-restraint in not declaring unconstitutional what in a judge's private judgment is unwise and even dangerous."

Leaving aside now the question of constitutionality, was Congress justified in assuming that there exists a clear and present danger of sufficient gravity to warrant restriction on advocacy of revolutionary overthrow? That a danger to our national survival exists which is clear, present, flourishing, and extremely powerful, seems to me to be undeniable to any sober view. This danger flows from the unremitting crusade of the Kremlin, now using open violence, now subversion and espionage, against the United States. These dangers may be *distinguished* in their internal and external aspects, but they cannot be *separated*. It is communism as an international movement whose capital is Moscow which is the enemy of American democracy; and the American Communist Party, no matter what its size or influence (which is not entirely inconsiderable), is an integral part of that movement. Whoever overlooks this has overlooked the main point. For without this organic tie to the Soviet state apparatus with all its engines of war, espionage and terror, the American Communist Party would have only nuisance value, its members would be ineffectual, candidates for the political psychopathic ward now inhabited by various other Communist splinter groups like the

Trotskyites. It is not the speech of members of the Communist Party which makes them dangerous but their organizational ties, for this in effect makes them a para-military fifth column of a powerful state, ready to strike whenever their foreign masters give the word.

The aim of the Smith Act was certainly justified in the light of the available facts. But the method of achieving this aim— making powerless the Soviet fifth column—was inept. The proscription should have been placed, not on speech to achieve revolutionary overthrow, but on organization to achieve it, and not merely any organization but an organization set up and controlled by a foreign power.

I know a gentle, rather weak-headed old man, formerly a member of the I.W.W., who vehemently makes speeches advocating insurrection by the working classes outside the parliamentary process, and the destruction not only of the state, in which he professes not to believe, but of capitalists as a class. He sounds bloodthirsty, but anyone who hears him knows that it is all rheum and wind. Technically, however, according to the Smith Act, Section Two, Paragraph A, Subhead 1, this feeble, harmless old man would be liable to prosecution and punishment. Now, surely Congress did not intend this.

In 1940 the leaders of the Trotskyist Socialist Workers Party were found guilty of violating the Smith Act. I have always been mystified as to why the Supreme Court refused to pass on the constitutionality of the Smith Act in this case. Although like other Communists they denied it, this Trotskyist faction does believe in, and firmly advocates, the revolutionary overthrow of the American government by force and violence. It accepts the thesis and Resolutions of the first four Congresses of the Communist International, and if anything, is theoretically more intransigent than official Communists whom it has regarded, first as "centrists," and then as "thermidorians." It has all the venom of the Stalinists but not the fangs. Although professing loyalty to the Soviet Union as a "worker's state"—one which would

Reflections on the Smith Act

shoot them out of hand if it could reach them!—this group's advocacies and activities never constituted the slightest threat to the security or survival of the United States. The reason is that, although organized, they are completely independent of any foreign power, do not take orders from the Kremlin, and do not collaborate in the espionage activities of the Communist Party. Their prosecution was, not merely foolish, but scandalous, and was ordered by President Roosevelt in payment of a political debt to Daniel Tobin whose control of the Teamster's Union was being threatened by a Minneapolis local, controlled by Trotskyists. Certainly, Congress did not have such groups in mind when it passed the Smith Act. Yet they were liable under Section Two, Paragraph A, Subhead 3, which outlaws any organization which advocates revolutionary overthrow.

Judge Hand admits that the wording of the Act, literally construed, would "make criminal the fulminations of a half-crazy zealot on a soap-box, calling for an immediate march on Washington." As the Supreme Court has interpreted the Act, however, it has remedied the deficiency by in effect introducing "the clear and present danger" clause. Although Judge Hand is apparently dubious about the wisdom of revising the language of the Smith Act, it seems to me that it would be a marked step in clarification, as well as an obstacle to arbitrary misinterpretation by a future court, were Congress to amend the Smith Act in order to insert the italicized words in the relevant sections as follows:

(A) It shall be unlawful for any person—

(1) To knowingly or willfully advocate, abet, advise, or teach, *in the case that it constitutes a clear and present danger,* the duty, necessity, desirability or propriety of overthrowing or destroying any government in the United States by force or violence. . . .

(3) To organize or help to organize, *in the case that it constitutes a clear and present danger,* any society, group, or assembly of persons who teach, advocate, or encourage the overthrow or destruction of any government in the United States by force and violence. . . .

Heresy, Yes — Conspiracy, No

A certain area of ambiguity will always remain, since what constitutes "a clear and present danger" will have to be determined in each case. But the explicit presence of such a phrase in the law itself would go a long way towards discouraging indiscriminate use of the Smith Act against private individuals sounding off on their own, and societies of crackpots and amateur conspirators who are greater threats to the peace of mind of their parents and wives than to the security of the nation. I believe this amendment desirable despite the fact that the widely heralded predictions, made with such hysterical fervor, that the Smith Act would be used against liberals, democrats, and socialists in an attempt to suppress thought have not materialized.

This brings me to the second question, referred to above, namely whether any particular advocacy of the use of revolutionary violence constitutes a clear and present danger. In the case of the Communist Party defendants, the jury was called upon to determine only whether they violated the statute but not whether such violation constituted a clear and present danger. That determination was made by Judge Medina as a matter of law, affirmed by Judge Hand, and upheld by Justice Vinson who wrote the majority opinion of the Supreme Court. Judge Medina in his instructions to the jury advised them as follows:

> If you are satisfied that the evidence establishes beyond a reasonable doubt that the defendants, or any of them, are guilty of a violation of the statute, as I have interpreted it to you, I find it as a matter of law that there is a sufficient danger of a substantive evil that the Congress has a right to prevent, to justify the application of the statute under the first amendment of the Constitution.
>
> This is a matter of law with which you have no concern. It is a finding on a matter of law which I deem essential to support my ruling that the case should be submitted to you to pass on the guilt or innocence of the defendants.

I agree with the finding but I cannot see in what way this is a matter of law. It seems to me that sufficient evidence was introduced, or could easily have been introduced, to convince any but Communists, their sympathizers, and doctrinaire pacifists who believe Stalin has a loving heart, that the international Communist movement, of which these defendants were trusted members, constitutes a clear and present threat to the preservation of free American institutions and our national independence. The only valid point Justice Douglas' dissent makes is that this question should have been considered by the jury since it is a question of fact. But whether Court or jury should pass on this question, Justice Douglas himself denies in the most emphatic way that the existence of the Communist movement creates any clear and present danger to the nation.

If this is a question of fact it is best answered by those who have some familiarity with the relevant fact—and on the question of the Communist movement Justice Douglas has given no evidence of special familiarity.

The late Justice Brandeis was supposed to have introduced a revolution in the approach of the Supreme Court by trying to dig out the empirical data bearing on the effects of social legislation like minimum wage laws, instead of trying to deduce wise policies from ambiguous legal expressions. Although the Justices of the Supreme Court in some recent cases have shown increasing awareness of some of the grosser historical facts about the Communist movement in modern times, on the whole they have been seriously remiss in acquainting themselves with the verifiable facts about Communist theory, practice, and organization. I do not know what judicial qualifications Justice Frank Murphy had for his elevation to the Supreme Court, but his decision in the Schneiderman case, in which he found that the Communist Party did not believe in what it expressly said it believed, betrays a sublime indifference to the easily verifiable truth. Although of late, and especially in considering the Smith Act, the Supreme Court Justices have shown a commendable spirit in repairing the gaps in their knowledge, even Justice Frankfurter, who has read belatedly, alas, the Canadian *Report of the Royal Commission to*

Heresy, Yes — Conspiracy, No

Investigate Communication of Secret and Confidential Information to Agents of a Foreign Power, adds in a footnote to an opinion which otherwise ranks with the best of Holmes and Brandeis: "There appears to be little reliable evidence demonstrating directly that the Communist Party in this country has recruited persons willing to engage in espionage or other unlawful activity on behalf of the Soviet Union." Not only does sworn testimony and corroborative evidence exist, supplied by former secretaries of the Communist Party and by former active underground agents that the American Communist Party did recruit its members for espionage work and other unlawful activity; it is also part of the public record which individuals of the Central Committee were liaison officers with the three Soviet espionage organizations in this country, and were entrusted with the selection of personnel.

Justice Vinson offers a mild characterization of the nature of the Communist Party and of the historical situation in justification of the Court's finding of a clear and present danger. He says:

> The formation by petitioners of such a highly organized conspiracy, with rigidly disciplined members subject to call when the leaders, these petitioners, felt that the time had come for action, coupled with the inflammable nature of world conditions, similar uprisings in other countries, and the touch-and-go nature of our relations with countries to whom petitioners were in the very least ideologically attuned, convince us that their convictions were justified on this score.

To this Justice Douglas acidly retorts: "That ruling is in my view not responsive to the issue in the case. We might as well say that the speech of petitioners is outlawed because Soviet Russia and her Red Army are a threat to peace." And why not? Under certain circumstances this might very well be the case. The elementary duty of the court, including Justice Douglas, is to study the techniques of infiltration, penetration, and open warfare waged by the Soviet Union and its agencies against the United

Reflections on the Smith Act

States in Korea, Berlin, Western Europe, South and Central America, and Asia, and to assess the cumulative effects of its campaign of subversion and defamation. The members of the Communist Party are literally the fifth column of the Red Army, and the success and strategic position of that Army are certainly relevant in considering the danger, not merely of Communist advocacy, but of Communist organization in this country.

Justice Douglas does admit "that the nature of communism as a force on the world scene would, of course, be relevant to the issue of clear and present danger of petitioners' advocacy within the United States." But he makes no attempt to consider that nature. Instead he regards the political strength and position of the Communist Party in *this* country, ignoring its ties with the international Communist movement, as of "primary consideration," and scoffs at the notion that by their efforts, including their capacities for sabotage and espionage, they have even "the slightest chance of *achieving* their aims" (my italics). Of course, considered in isolation, the Communist Party has not the slightest chance of succeeding in its aims. But the point which Justice Douglas so elaborately misses is that they do *not* work in isolation but in a co-ordinated strategy which has behind it the power of a regime which controls the human and natural resources of a quarter of the world. Nor, as we have already seen, is the likelihood of the success of the conspiratorial action the decisive matter. An unsuccessful attempt can be productive of great misery. One plant needlessly struck, one atomic installation sabotaged, some key state secrets betrayed, in conjunction with the general strategy of the Soviet assault, may have effects out of all proportion to their apparent proximate causes. It is true that there are other laws besides the Smith Act which cover sabotage and espionage, but Justice Frankfurter is surely justified in calling attention to the fact that, according to the *Report* of the Royal Canadian Commission investigating the Communist espionage network, "conspiratorial characteristics of the Party similar to those shown in the evidence now before us were instrumental in developing the necessary motivation to cooperate in the espionage."

At the time Justice Douglas wrote his dissent, virtual war between one section of the Communist International and the United States as part of the U.N. was raging in Korea, the Communist war of nerves against the West was being thrown into high gear, neutralism was registering gains in Europe, and the shocking record of Communist espionage lay revealed, if only in part, before the world. To deny under these circumstances that an organization of some tens of thousands conspirators, with a reliable periphery of some hundreds of thousands, constitutes a clear and present danger to the security of the nation is to manifest a stubborn will to believe that Providence or luck will protect those who are too blind to protect themselves.

III

That the Communist Party, despite its denials, actually advocates the use of force and violence is apparent from all its basic documents. The contention that the use of force and violence is reserved only to meet insurrectionary threats from non-Communists *after* Communists have peacefully and democratically come to power is disingenuous. A similar characterization must be made of the dodge adopted by John Strachey, when he was a Communist, in resisting the threat of deportation, needless at the time, by a nervous Attorney General. Communists, he said, do not advocate the use of violence; they merely predict it. But this runs counter to the entire Communist conception of the nature of a belief as a guide to action. Communists are safe in predicting the use of force and violence because in reality they advocate that use. Their very theory of knowledge instructs them that, in social affairs at least, all concepts are not merely predictive but directive.

The subterfuge that the use of force and violence is only a defensive measure, taken in advance against an anticipated reaction, is a contribution of Stalin to the ideological strategy of Bolshevism. Lenin and Trotsky were much more forthright on this score. In fact in the post-Leninist struggle for succession, Trotsky accused Stalin of lack of revolutionary integrity for not advocating insurrection as an offensive tactic in the conquering of state power. To which Stalin replied:

> An original peculiarity of the revolutionary tactics of this period must be pointed out. This peculiarity consists therein that the revolution attempted to carry out every, or almost every step of its attack under the appearance of defense. There is no doubt that the refusal to permit the transfer of troops was a serious aggressive act of the revolution; nevertheless this attack was undertaken under the slogan of the defense of Petrograd against a possible attack of the external enemy. There is no doubt that the formation of the revolutionary committee was a still more serious attack against the Provisional Government; *nevertheless it was carried out under the slogan of the defense of the Petrograd Soviets against possible attacks of the counter-revolution.*
>
> In *Errors of Trotskyism,* London, 1925, Eng. trans., pp. 225-226.

Communist Parties throughout the world have learned this lesson well. But they were not always so careful in the past as the following citation from William Z. Foster's, *Towards Soviet America,* shows:

> Even before the seizure of power, the workers will organize the Red Guard. . . . The leader of the revolution in all its stages is the Communist Party. . . . Under the dictatorship all the Capitalist parties—Republican, Democratic, Progressive, [La Follette type] Socialist, etc.,—will be liquidated, the Communist Party alone functioning as the Party of the toiling masses. Likewise, will be dissolved all other organizations that are political props of all bourgeois rule, including chambers of commerce, employer's associations, rotary clubs, American Legion, Y.M.C.A., and such fraternal orders as the Masons, Odd Fellows, Elks, Knights of Columbus, etc. (p. 275).

Heresy, Yes—Conspiracy, No

This is the real meaning behind "Communism as the twentieth century version of Jeffersonian democracy."

IV

Some words must be said about the implication in Justice Douglas' opinion that the law upheld by the majority decision hardly differs from the law of the Soviet state, as expressed by Vishinsky when he said: "In our state, naturally there can be no place for freedom of speech, press, and so on for the foes of socialism."

It would be difficult to find in the annals of the Supreme Court an observation so unjustifiable and injudicious. Hardly anything could be more explicit in Judge Medina's instructions to the jury, in Judge Hand's opinion, and in Justice Vinson's majority decision than the continually reiterated assertion: "It is perfectly lawful and proper for the defendants or anyone else to advocate reforms and changes in the laws, which seem to them to be salutary and necessary. No one has suggested that the defendants transgressed any laws by advocating such reforms and changes. No syllable of the indictment refers to any such matters."

The charge was not conspiracy to advocate the abolition of capitalism or the establishment of socialism. The charge bore on the advocacy of, and conspiracy to advocate the use of, force and violence to overthrow the state irrespective of the economic program of the defendants. Justice Douglas must surely be able to see the difference between denying a man certain freedoms to propose economic change and denying him the freedom to advocate that these reforms be carried out by force and violence.

To be sure, every state must evaluate the rights of the individual by its consequences upon society or upon the rights of other individuals. That is why, in the interest of social welfare or national security, which expresses the rights of other individuals, any particular right might be abridged. No right can be unconditionally affirmed independently of how it affects the community. This is true both in a democracy and in a totalitarian dictatorship. What then is the difference?

The differences are many and fundamental. In a democracy the social welfare or national security in whose name a right may be abridged is determined by the community or its responsible representatives—responsible, in the sense that they can be removed. Freely given consent of the majority enters in a way completely absent in a dictatorship. Secondly, the processes by which the decision is made are open, so that the opposition can be heard. Third, the decision is limited, renewable, and abolishable. The mandate is not made in perpetuity. Fourth, a democracy, as Professor A. E. Ewing has well pointed out, regards the freedoms of the individual as possessing an intrinsic worth, essential to the integrity of the individual personality, itself the object of supreme worth, and therefore moves slowly and reluctantly towards the abridgment of individual rights. It waits for periods of genuine crisis, of genuine, clear and present danger to the security and safety of the community. A totalitarian dictatorship has no regard for the intrinsic worth of human freedom and personality and moves immediately, brutally, and arbitrarily towards suppression of all opposition which threatens not the security of the community but the monopoly of physical power and intellectual authority of the dictatorship.

We have previously pointed out that *from the point of view of a democrat* one has a moral right to advocate the use of force and violence in a dictatorship where the processes do not exist which make possible the removal of evils and injustices. Again from the point of view of a democrat, one has no moral right to advocate the use of force and violence against the democratic community if, as a consequence of open and honest processes of inquiry, discussion, and decision, it is possible to remove evils and injustices.

In short we must reject Justice Douglas' comparison of Vishinsky's dictum with the law as expressed by his colleagues on the Supreme Court Bench as a gratuitous piece of demagogic rhetoric no less injudicious and irresponsible because it is made by a member of the highest judiciary body in the land.

V

The Smith Act is imperfectly phrased. Were it to be interpreted literally it could easily lend itself to abuse. The main, if not avowed, purposes of the Act—to prevent the organization of the Communist conspiracy from growing to a point where it could become dangerous, to make known to the people of the United States the nature of the Communist movement so that individuals who joined it would know what they were getting themselves into—could have been achieved by invoking other legislation, particularly the provision calling for the registration of agents of a foreign government. An overwhelming case could have been made out in court for the indictment of the Communist Party of the U.S.A. as an agency of the Soviet regime, and of every member who continued in it, as an agent of a foreign power. Although the listing of such agents would carry no *legal* sanctions, it is not likely that any but the hardened core of conspirators would be prepared to flaunt publicly the fact of their primary allegiance to an enemy power of their native country. The Communist Party would, of course, seek to mask itself behind other organizations, but it would do that less successfully than it does today. The Progressive Party and the American Labor Party in New York are today notorious Communist Party fronts but they cannot be molested under the Smith Act because they are careful to avoid teaching or advocating the desirability of revolutionary overthrow. Nor would they—(or should they)— be molested under the Foreign Agents Registration Act. But if the mechanism by which they were set up were ever publicly exposed, those individuals who moved behind the scenes might be required to be listed under the Foreign Agents Registration Act.

Nonetheless the Supreme Court has so interpreted the Smith

Act as to really amend it. Advocacy of violent overthrow is illegal only when such advocacy constitutes a clear and present danger to the security of our democracy. The general principle behind that interpretation is unassailable except in the eyes of those ritualistic liberals who have forsaken the primary tenet in the faith of a liberal, *viz., the use of intelligence* to determine which of the conflicting claims behind the conflict of rights is to receive priority. A way should be found to leave the determination of the fact that a clear and present danger exists to the jury or to Congress, instead of making this subject to legal determination by the bench at any level.

Although the wisdom of enacting the Smith Law was doubtful, the wisdom of now repealing it is even more doubtful. For if the Smith Act were repealed it would give a new lease of life to an illusion whose widespread and pernicious character was to a not inconsiderable degree responsible for the original enactment of the law. This illusion is that the Communist Party is a political party like any other on the American scene, and therefore entitled to the same political rights and privileges as all other American political parties. It is amazing how pervasive this attitude has been among certain circles, especially in the colleges and universities. Here is a man who applies for a commission in the Army, a research post in a key plant, an important professorship in which he has an opportunity to influence thousands. If he has the technical qualifications, he is entitled to the position no matter whether he is a member of the Republican or Democratic or Socialist Party. Given knowledge of what these parties are, there can be no doubt about this. But, then, nine times out of ten one hears—or used to hear—"and since the Communist Party is a legal party, just like any other, a member of the Communist Party is also entitled to the post for which he has technical qualifications, just like anyone else."

That the Communist Party, although legal, was an organized conspiratorial movement to destroy the structure of freedom in every aspect of political and cultural life, was either not known or ignored. As a result of the court trials held under the Smith Act, the facts about the Communist Party have become widely known. These facts enjoy the authority of having proven themselves in the sharp debate and prolonged inquiry of the legal process. To repeal the Smith Act instead of continuing the process of reasonable amendment would probably lead many to assume, either that the Communist Party had changed its character, or that it did not really advocate the overthrow of democratic institutions by force and violence. Both assumptions would be false.

So long as the cold war rages between the Soviet Union and the democratic West, the Smith Act, now the law of the land, can by amendment and intelligent enforcement serve a therapeutic function without endangering the tradition of American rights and liberties.

In the long run, however, neither laws nor security agencies, as necessary as they are, can constitute a lasting defence of democratic institutions, if the will to freedom is not strong in a people. On several occasions the world has observed the consequences of the absence of a firm commitment to freedom on the part of governments and peoples. The Weimar Republic and Czechoslovakia are both illustrations of what happens when citizens idly watch conspirators paralyze the defensive powers of a democracy, avoid the fatiguing task of exposing and struggling against the conspirators in their multifarious guises and activities in the shop, on the street, in the schools, and rely mainly on the protective arm of the state itself infected with the germs of conspiracy.

Even when the democratic state itself is vigorous and free of infiltration, the legitimate desire to extirpate conspiracy, especially where it is allied with an external enemy, may lead it into adopting hasty administrative and legislative measures. These may have consequences prejudicial to the functioning of free institutions unless the rank and file citizens themselves preserve a democratic atmosphere in public and social life which encourages criticism and correction of governmental errors or excesses, and which at the same time limits the receptiveness to conspiracy. This requires participation of individuals and voluntary association on every level of political and social life. There is no short cut to, or guarantee of, intelligent participation—or enlightened public opinion. It is best furthered by an enlightened public education.

This is particularly true of the United States. The public schools on every level, including the private college, have played the most powerful role in the symbiotic process which has knit the United States into a unified culture. A unified culture, as distinct from a uniform one, recognizes that diversity of religion, cosmic outlook, local customs and personal belief are compatible with a common acceptance of the basic political patterns of democratic behavior.

Today our educational institutions have, if anything, an even more important role. If faith in freedom, and reliance on intelligence in settling problems, are to be strengthened during the long years of anxiety and danger ahead, it is to the schools we must look to develop the values, habits and attitudes which constitute the free man's second nature.

Part Two

ACADEMIC FREEDOM

The New School knows that no man can teach well, nor should he be permitted to teach at all, unless he is prepared "to follow the truth of scholarship wherever it may lead." No inquiry is ever made as to whether a lecturer's private views are conservative, liberal, or radical; orthodox or agnostic; views of the aristocrat or commoner. Jealously safeguarding this precious principle, the New School stoutly affirms that a member of any political party or group which asserts the right to dictate in matters of science or scientific opinion is not free to teach the truth and thereby is disqualified as a teacher.

Equally the New School holds that discrimination on grounds of race, religion or country of origin either among teachers or students runs counter to every profession of freedom and has no place in American education.

—from New School Bulletin
Vol. 10, No. 19 January 5, 1953, p. 2.

Chapter 6

THE DANGER OF AUTHORITARIAN
ATTITUDES IN EDUCATION

I

To both Thomas Jefferson and John Dewey, the cohesion of a free society rests neither on supernatural nor natural sanctions but on community of interest. But only in a perfect or angelic society are all interests, to the extent that we can speak of interests, always shared or common. Because every individual, no matter what his social origins and relations, is a unique center of experience, because in a finite world not all desires can be gratified by all individuals at the same time, some rational principle or process of decision, which settles conflicts of interests, must be given priority over any special interest.

War, myth, custom, use and wont also serve as principles or processes of decision. But by themselves no one can regard them as rational in character. For a rational principle is one which permits every interest to find a voice and to receive a hearing, to persuade and be open to persuasion, to offer evidence for itself and to examine evidence against itself. A rational principle leads to an *informed* decision, not one determined by caprice or violence. Even if the informed decision is blocked or stopped by the brute weight of another principle of decision, that does not make it less informed.

The survival of a free society, especially in a world where its destruction is the aim of a powerful totalitarian society, makes it essential not only that the decisions of its leaders be informed, but that the support or criticism such decisions receive also be informed. That is why freedom requires a principle of rational authority, recognized as primary in all its educational enterprises and embodied in active habits of inquiry.

Such authority not only differs from the spirit of authoritarianism but is opposed to it. The term "authority" and the term "authoritarian" have the same root but are widely different in meaning. "Authority" is on the whole an emotively neutral word. "Authoritarian" markedly suggests something objectionable. Every authoritarian rule is an authority but not all authority is authoritarian. And happily so, for the social life of man would be impossible without some authority.

In criticizing authoritarian attitudes, then, we shall not be criticizing authority but rather inquiring into the kind and expression of authority most necessary for the enrichment of life. Without some authority there would be perpetual conflict and disorder, but this in no way justifies the equation of authority with any kind of peace and order. The authority of freedom is obviously different from the authority of tyranny. A similar relation holds between "tradition" and "traditionalism."

In order to understand the meaning of authoritarianism in education, we must briefly indicate what the purposes and ideals of democratic education are to which authoritarianism is hostile. Among these purposes and ideals may be listed: (1) the development of intellectual and emotional maturity, (2) the readiness to meet the challenge of new experiences on the basis of relevant knowledge, (3) the acquisition of techniques and values that are themselves tested in present experience, (4) the deepening of moral awareness and responsibility, and (5) finally, the cultivation of intelligent loyalty to the underlying values of the democratic community as distinct from any particular political expression of these values. These are large terms which have to be interpreted a little differently on different educational levels. Roughly speaking, however, we may say that the pervasive ideal of democratic education—or liberal education today—is to achieve a community of persons who, on the basis of reliable knowledge about themselves and the world in which they live, can develop freely in a free society. We shall therefore call those tendencies in education authoritarian which, by blocking the roads of inquiry, prevent freedom of intelligent choice; which, by discouraging critical participation in the processes of learning, obstruct individual growth; which, by imposing dogmas of doctrine or program, blind students to relevant alternatives and encourage conformity rather than diversity; which, in short, fail to recognize that the supreme and ultimate authority, the final validating source of all other authorities in human experience is the self-critical authority of critical method—or intelligence.

II

The danger of authoritarian attitudes in teaching comes from so many quarters that one is embarrassed to decide where to begin the enumeration. For purposes of exposition I shall divide them into two classes: those that come from outside the school, and those that come from within the school.

Threats that come from outside the school may all be characterized as attempts to invade the *relative autonomy* of the school as an educational agency and to limit the freedom of the teacher as a professionally qualified educator. Such threats come from special groups which, perhaps for the most worthy and sometimes less worthy reasons, seek to pressure schools and teachers into emphasizing particular studies or into emphasizing them in a particular way to reach predetermined conclusions. Note that I used the phrase *"relative autonomy"* when I spoke of the relation of the school, teacher, and society. For it is neither possible nor desirable for the school and teacher to isolate them-selves, especially in a democracy, from the great social events, movements, and problems of their community. But the main point here is this: professionally qualified educators, as individuals and as a group, are the only ones that can be entrusted with the de-cisions which determine what is relevant *educationally* to the needs of their charges, and what emphasis it is to receive. Other-wise the whole concept of teaching as a profession has no validity. The mere fact that the individual is a parent no more qualifies him to determine what the best *educational* regimen is for his child than what the best medical regimen is. As a parent, he is free, of course, to select the type of education he desires for his child—secular or parochial. As a citizen he is, of course, vitally concerned in the physical and psychological conditions under which his child is receiving instructions. His cooperation in help-ing to solve problems in these areas is most welcome. But all this is still a far cry from the assumption of educational authority or expertness.

If this is true for the parent, then *a fortiori* it is true of the businessman, the military man, the churchman, or any other man afire with zeal as to how best to save the nation and the world by reforming or revising the curriculum. To *propose* materials for instruction is one thing; to high-pressure, to denounce, or to intimidate is another. It is clear that no course of study imposed on teachers, against their better educational judgment, will be properly taught. Everyone can recall lessons endured, or taught half-heartedly, by teachers who did not see their educational sig-nificance but who had received instructions from their superiors who in turn were bowing to what they thought was the voice of the public coming from the mouths of an irate self-appointed committee, or out of the editorial pages or special feature col-umns of newspapers. Apparently the only thing that newspaper columnists today seem to be agreed upon is their claim to educa-tional omniscience.

In ordinary times the relative autonomy of the educational

process is commonly recognized. In extraordinary times, especially times of trouble like our own, the tendency to breach this autonomy becomes very strong—almost irresistible.

It is a commonplace that the struggle between the Communist and democratic ideologies in the next historic period will be decisive for the future of world culture. Nothing is more natural than the request by those alarmed at the prospects of Communist victory that the schools should enroll themselves in the struggle. But it is a dangerous request, if it means more than a request that the school, at the appropriate levels and courses, should critically evaluate the history, theory, and practice of communism—something that every live school system will already have been doing. And it is a dangerous request when nationalistic and ultra-patriotic organizations on the crest of a wave of justifiably angry public opinion seek to impose their own ideas on teachers as to how communism should be taught as the preconditional commitment for studying it, sometimes even for *not* studying it.

Each field has its own virtues, and the classroom in a democracy is not a field of battle. If communism, as I believe, is the greatest menace to human freedom in the world today, I believe it can be shown in the same way we show that certain growths are cancerous and not benign. If this is the truth, then we do not need more than the critical methods of inquiring into the truth to establish it. And if it is not the truth, then, since we are committed to the value of making intelligent decisions, we should be eager to discover it. Sentiment, no matter how exalted, is not a substitute for analysis. If the truth may make us free, we are not free to deny or ignore the truth wherever we find it. Not all expressions of anti-communism are prodemocratic—something we learned from Franco and Hitler—just as not all expressions of anti-fascism are prodemocratic something we have learned from Stalin and his lieutenants everywhere. When it comes to understanding, patriotism is not enough. The only way to win the argument against communism in the minds of men—where ultimately it must be won if democracy is to survive—is by showing that it is condemned not merely by authority of past tradition but by the outcome of present inquiry.

This means that teachers today must make an intensive study of the ideas of communism as of fascism and other forms of totalitarianism and not permit themselves to be bullied or frightened into failing to examine these doctrines lest the study itself be misinterpreted as advocacy. No matter how ardent one may be as an adherent of democracy, if he does not, *wherever it is relevant,* consider in a scientific spirit the arguments of its opponents from any quarter, he is giving way to an authoritarian attitude. Those who come knocking at the school door with ultimatistic demands or taboos concerning what teachers *should* teach and *how* they must teach, and with ready-made formulas about the meaning of democracy and its alternatives, must be asked to show their professional qualifications as educators before they are taken seriously.

III

A second source of danger to the relative autonomy of the educational process emanates from some propaganda agencies among certain businessmen and professional groups. This has come to a head in a campaign so to influence the educational curriculum of our schools as to identify, on the one hand, the free-enterprise system with democracy, and, on the other hand, the welfare state with a creeping socialism which inevitably develops into the paralysis and paresis of communism. The whole subject, of course, broken down into problems of manageable proportion on the proper levels, should be an integral part of the social-science curriculum. As a *proposal* for study it is probably carrying coals to Newcastle. But as a demand that the views and sentiments described above be a *conclusion* which the study *must* reach, it is a piece of intellectual impertinence. If a free economy in the classic sense were identical with democracy, we would have less democracy in the United States than we actually do have, for the free economy of the past is certainly quite different from the economy, regulated in a thousand ways both by big government and by big industry, under which we now live. If growth in social security spells slavery, we would have less freedom, less criticism today than we ever have had in the past, which is notoriously not true. And certainly Great Britain is not behind the United States in civil freedoms even though it is far ahead of it in social-welfare legislation and socialization.

The very terms "capitalism" and "socialism" are today incurably ambiguous, more often epithets of abuse than of description. It should be one of the tasks of our social-science teachers to show how these words are often used as substitutes for clear ideas, noisy rhetorical blanks that distract us from the complex problems that resist total solutions.

There is a third source of danger to the relative autonomy of the schools which comes from very sincere individuals who are dedicated to the democratic way of life. I refer to those who maintain that this way of life is *logically* dependent upon certain religious truths which, if denied, leave democratic values hanging in the air. Consequently, in order to avoid inconsistency, they believe that the curriculum of a democracy, particularly in its higher institutions, must at some point give instruction in religion—since a non-religious school is an irreligious school and an irreligious school a necessarily non-democratic one. The argument has many variations and the proposals to implement it take many forms.

I think it is demonstrable that neither the meaning nor the validity of moral ideas rests on supernatural foundations. But suppose for a moment they did. Introduced into the curriculum in any form—how would the study of these supernatural foundations be conducted? Like assertions made in secular disciplines for which evidence is asked and critically assessed? But a *critical* evaluation of dogmas is the last thing which many of those who believe religion has a place in schools want. It is not hard to imagine what the reaction would be of those who accept one religious dogma or another, to a critical negative judgment on that dogma. No, religious dogmas can be imparted only by those who have faith to others of the same faith. Whatever place they have in human experience, they have no place in the public schools.

Sometimes the argument made for the introduction of religious instruction into public schools is that it alone can provide the unifying and "living faith" which individuals need to sustain themselves in an uncertain and often tragic world. (*See* Canon Bell, *Life,* October 16, 1950.) It is claimed that the need and necessity of such faith is recognized even by totalitarian cultures, where it is met by fraudulent and monstrously false glorifications of men and doctrines which nonetheless are quite effective psychologically as morale builders and sustainers. It is then urged that religion in a democracy should play an analogous function.

But it is precisely in a democracy that ideas, secular or religious, cannot function like ideas in a totalitarian culture. For their hypnotic character in the latter depends upon the complete absence of critical dissent, the mobilization of all psychological techniques to insure conformity, which are foreign to the spirit of a democratic society. It is simply false to assume that faith in a functioning democracy can be of the same psychological character as faith in a totalitarian culture. We did not have to believe in democracy in the same way as fanatical Nazis believed in Nazism in order to survive Hitler's attack. Nor do we today have to indoctrinate belief in democracy in the brutalitarian way in which the Communists regiment the minds and hearts of their youth, in order to survive the Kremlin's crusade against freedom.*

The tendency of religious, economic and nationalist groups to

* "A democrat cannot be fanatical in the same way as a Nazi or a Stalinist, for whom an unanalyzed end justifies the use of any means. But it does not follow that because he is humane and intelligent a democrat cannot be passionate and active in his faith, that he must be a political Hamlet, irresolute before the combination of toughness and chicanery with which the enemies of democracy confront him." *Cf.* my "The Autonomy of Democratic Faith," in *Living, Reading and Thinking,* edited by Chamberlain, Pressey, and Waters, p. 654, New York, 1948.

scan the curriculum and the materials of instruction in order to see whether the appropriate position is taken on some special topic creates a major obstacle to critical teaching. Professionally qualified teachers are the best judges of what texts are suitable for educational purposes and not *ad hoc* committees that regard no education as sound which challenges their private prejudices masquerading as common first principles. The best educational experience shows that, if many conflicting sources are made available to students rather than specially restricted material, they more readily acquire the intellectual sophistication which gives them an immunity to the tricks and semantic corruptions of totalitarian demagogy. For example, instead of barring the *Daily Worker* from the classroom, the good teacher can sometimes make as effective use of it as he can of the *New York Times*. If we are interested in exposing the logic of the total lie, I know of no better specimen material today than official Communist literature. And yet we occasionally read of committees of strong-willed, well-intentioned, but intellectually undiscriminating citizens who ransack the libraries of their schools and triumphantly flourish books and materials that may actually be helpful to the teacher in exposing communism, as evidence of subversion.

But is not the development of loyalty to our country a legitimate objective of our schools? Certainly, but nothing follows from that unless we are aware of what it is in our country and our culture which evokes our loyalties. The Loyalists of 1776 are considered differently from the Loyalists of 1861 in our history. Josiah Royce somewhere says that "true loyalty includes some element of free choice," and without making this a definition, I believe that a loyalty which depends merely on habituation, or conditioned reflexes, on the fact that there is nothing else imaginably conceivable to be loyal to, is universally regarded in the Western tradition as less worthy than a loyalty which is freely given and freely informed about alternative objects of loyalty. It is the existence of freedom and of free institutions which is the primary justification of loyalty to America. Free men cannot be loyal to slave states. That universities under nazism and communism made loyalty to their regimes a prime goal of instruction is one of the reasons we condemn them.

That American schools develop loyalties to the community of which they are a part is an indisputable fact—as indisputable as that the schools in societies less free than ours develop loyalties to their communities. What we should be concerned with then is that the loyalties American schools develop reflect the distinctively libertarian aspects of our traditions and not the chauvinism which perverts the natural piety for the sources of our being.

Let us then recognize that loyalty to America and to democracy does not mean loyalty to American*ism* or to the Democratic Party or any other party. It does not mean loyalty to any one group or class or sectional interest or to a program for free enterprise or controlled economy. It does not mean conformity; those who are not critical of the failings of democracy are less loyal than those who are.

If we interpret loyalty in this way, it is something that cannot be commanded. It cannot be sworn to. It cannot be tested by oaths. It grows slowly as the student's mind and body mature, gathers force as he understands, and tries to live up to his understanding of the democratic process, and when freedom is challenged or threatened, wells up spontaneously, fed by all the hidden springs of emotion.

Our deepest loyalties are seldom avowed. They are expressed best not in words but in actions. When the loyalty of a generation comes into question or has to be proved, there is already an acknowledgment that education and other social institutions have been remiss in their functions. The man who must be urged to say, "I love you," because his actions leave doubts, is a doubtful lover whose words mean less the more frantically they are solicited of him. If the only evidence we have of a person's loyalty is his use of a certain form of words on request, we are lost. Loyalty to American democratic traditions, processes, and values is a virtue beyond price; but if our schools do well in achieving their task of developing free and informed minds, this virtue shall be added unto them.

IV

So far I have been discussing the more overt authoritarian threats to the relative autonomy of the educational process. I wish now to consider the more subtle dangers which come from authoritarian attitudes within the school itself and which threaten not the relative autonomy of education but its quality and critical integrity. These are harder to guard against because habituation in certain traditional ways has given us a sense that they are natural and unalterable.

The first and most obvious expression of authoritarian attitude reflects the undemocratic organizational structure of many schools in various sections of the country, and even in a few metropolitan centers. Through a hierarchy of command, instructions and directives are transmitted to the classroom teacher from above without opportunity on his part to participate in their justification—if any. Where the teacher is a passive agent in executing orders, he is likely to regard the student as a passive agent in the classroom, as a living subject who must absorb nonliving subjects, conditioned to accept certain conclusions by virtue of the teacher's authority rather than the authority of evidence and method. Evidence, however, has little persuasive authority unless it is preceded by intelligent questioning and doubt. But one of the most common manifestations of totalitarian attitudes towards students is impatience with doubt, opposition, and the half-articulate bewilderments, which as often betray genuine difficulties in the subject matter being taught, as they do the personal difficulties of the learner.

Many teachers love to be asked questions but only those they can answer. There are, I fear, too few who can gracefully acknowledge that they do not know or that they were mistaken. It is a myth that the young in *intellectual* matters are naturally rebellious and it is the easiest thing in the world to silence them by ridicule, cold indifference, or the show of outraged dignity. There is a deeper courtesy than the conventionalities of outwardly polite behavior. This consists in recognizing the educational significance of the process by which the student reaches an uncoerced conclusion—or rather a conclusion coerced only by the materials he is dealing with. "It is not I who tell this," the teacher's attitude should say, "but the facts in the case"—if there are facts. There is, of course, "ancestral wisdom," but when it is invoked it must be invoked because of its wisdom, not because of its ancestry. And wisdom, whether ancestral or present, needs no external authority.

Whatever one may think of progressive education—and it must not be judged by its detractors or by the effusions of some of its mindless advocates—it places respect for the personality of any child on the same moral level as respect for the personality of our own children. Such respect emphatically does not mean that the teacher is "to let pupils do what they want to, when and how they want to do it," as progressive education is cheaply caricatured; it does mean that we have a moral obligation to let students see the *sense* behind what we ask them to do, and the when and how of it.

Authoritarianism on the part of teachers may take other forms. The teacher may follow a psychologically inoffensive course but a methodologically vicious one by indoctrinating for some special point of view which is imposed on the student because of the instructor's predetermined commitment to some faith—religious, political, economic. I do not want to discuss the general question of indoctrination here or the occasions on which indoctrination may be justified, as for example, when we induce children to take certain moral attitudes by nonrational means because they are not yet sufficiently mature to understand the rational grounds for them. I am referring specifically to indoctrination by irrational means in behalf of some controversial conclusion.

Indoctrination of this sort by the teacher is not merely authoritarian; it is dishonestly authoritarian. Instead of openly proclaiming a bias which the student can do something to nullify if he is aware of it, it conceals its bias. It abuses a position of trust and by insidious means may predispose and color the mind of a student so that he can no longer see or objectively appraise any other side than the one in which he has been indoctrinated.

If we bear in mind that we are defining authoritarian attitudes in terms of their effect on the continuous search for new modes of significant experience, new truths, and more reliable methods of inquiry, we find that just as not all who shout peace believe in peace, so not all who are professional scientists exhibit at crucial times a scientific temper. In all fields of the arts and sciences there are reigning orthodoxies. These orthodoxies are usually established on the basis of the warranted conclusions of the best available methods. But there is always an emotional wrench when some customary doctrine or theory is challenged. More often than not, the challenge is absurd or irresponsible. When this takes place there are some scientists who, not content with exposing absurdity, wish to prevent it from being uttered. In their excess of zeal for the truth they act like absolutists who forget that at best we can only reach probabilities in inquiry, that no theory can make scientific headway in a free culture unless it gets itself progressively confirmed, and that the best protection against *theoretical* error is exposure, not suppression.

Not so long ago we were confronted by the sad spectacle of scientific men evincing little faith in the logic and ethics of their own professional activity. Upon the publication of Dr. Velikovsky's book, *Worlds in Collision,* which confuses legend, myth, and warranted assertions, a campaign was undertaken by scientific men not merely to refute it, which was easy enough, but to prevent its publication, which was intellectually reprehensible. Nor is this the only instance of self-defeating and utterly unnecessary scientific orthodoxy. Here and there some administrator, happily no scientist, will vehemently oppose the presentation of the political-biology of Lysenko, overlooking the fact that the exposure of charlatanism is much more deadly to it than its proscription. I do not mean to suggest that scientists are under any necessity of examining seriously every crackpot theory that demands a hearing. They would have little time left for their own research, if they did. But I do mean to suggest that, unless they scrupulously avoid any attempt to prevent others from hearing what they may justifiably ignore, they are giving evidence of an incipient authoritarianism which, if unchecked, may become virulent. The best scientists, it should be pointed out, have a saving grace as well as a sense of humor about their most fundamental commitments.

V

I come finally to the consideration of a type of educational philosophy which would make it easier, despite its own professions of democratic allegiance, for authoritarian attitudes to develop. This is a position which is marked by basic theoretical confusion—and to be confused in these matters is much worse than being clear-headedly wrong. For a clear head can set itself right. It is held in inchoate form by different types of teachers of different social persuasions but on occasion it receives theoretical formulation. According to this school of thought an adequate philosophy of education must at the same time be a philosophy of *politics* whose task is to hatch political programs in alliance with the state. Public education becomes the ally of certain forward-looking groups in the community—and what group does not regard itself as forward-looking?—and commits itself to an advocacy of one or another social or political goal that recommends itself to the majority of educators after they have freely discussed what the goals should be.

Those who would make the schools either instruments of political conservatism or revolutionary transformation usually profess impatience with the ideals which John Dewey has made central to his educational philosophy—individual growth, participation, and the supremacy of critical intelligence. For them this is insufficient. In an amazing mixture of pedagese and poppycock, they contend that emphasis on critical method *prevents* human beings from solving problems and achieving goals. As if the methods of scientific inquiry did not recommend themselves *precisely* because they were better ways of reaching reliable solutions than other alternatives.

There is nothing new in the proposal that "education in its most comprehensive sense should become the copartner of politics . . ." (Brameld, *School and Society,* November 13, 1948). We know which partner is sure to dominate which. The proposal is in fact the hallmark of illiberalism in education—and this remains true irrespective of whether an educator wants to use public education to teach the necessity of "a thoroughly reconstituted domestic economy" or the necessity of a thoroughly stabilized *status quo* capitalist economy, whether he takes as his grand design "international world government" or rampant American chauvinism, whether it is the "old deal" or the "new deal." The schools cannot harness themselves to any political program, no matter how self-righteous or apparently benevolent, without handing over the reins, as has been the case only too often in the past, to drivers who have other goals than the development of emotional and intellectual maturity. It is not for the schools to dedicate themselves to any grand political designs. Their task is to develop the powers to recognize the grand designs which events are shaping for us, to show that they are not fated, but rather that there may be alternatives to them which our own ideas and actions may help to realize, and above all to train the faculties of critical assessment and evaluation. All this is involved in the educational effort to bring alive in students and *to keep* alive the readiness and willingness to inquire—and to act intelligently.

It is one thing to say that the schools cannot be impartial about their own commitment to the quest for truth, beauty, and integrity; it is quite another to say that they cannot be impartial in considering specific *programs* encountered in their quest.

But it is sometimes objected that it is inconsistent to oppose commitment to a specific doctrine and yet urge commitment to a method or to the ideal of the inquiring mind. This objection is completely without force with respect to the problems of education and rests on a failure to see what commitment to critical method means. Critical method is self-corrective. It is self-aware in that it can formulate alternatives to itself in the way in which Charles Peirce distinguishes four methods of fixing belief. To be committed to this method does not exclude the consideration of other methods. But to be committed to a doctrine or program, if it means anything at all different from critical analysis of hypotheses, is in practice to exclude other doctrines as species of error known in advance. For if these errors are not held to be errors in advance but only *after* inquiry, there is no more commitment involved than there is in any genuine discovery of truth. In that case we are not committed to programs but only to the *process* of finding out.

Some partisans of grand designs who urge that education commit itself to a political program are dimly aware of the dangerous alley into which it leads. For after all, if a school is committed to a political program, what shall we do with a teacher who is opposed to the program? And what will happen to the school in a community which opposes the commitment? Unless it is to impose a conformity of belief, the school must leave the processes of inquiry open. And some planners of the grand design assure us that, of course, this is what they propose to do. They do *not* advocate indoctrination but at most a kind of harmless propaganda. Well, then, if all programs are subject to critical evaluation, with the possibility of individual rejection left open, then what point is there in committing a system of education to a program *in advance* of specific inquiries? If anything is worth believing, honest pursuit of the proper method will lead to it. To beat the air with demands that the school commit itself to one program rather than another, and then blandly to deny that any indoctrination is intended, simply does not add up. Such a position, if it is not a form of spoofing or does not testify to a lack of ingenuousness, is muddled from beginning to end. *Religious* sal-

138

vationists at least make no bones of the fact that they believe in indoctrination; *political* salvationists, alas, lack the courage of their confusions.

VI

I have described many varieties and sources of authoritarian attitudes in teaching. It would be absurd to assume that the danger to free teaching in a free society is equal from all of them at any one time. Wisdom here consists in keeping a sense of proportion in relation to transitory nuisances, even when acute, and the underlying massive threats which may change the whole cultural landscape. At the present time, the greatest danger to free teaching lies in the failure to distinguish carefully between the rights to heretical belief, which every freely and honestly inquiring mind has, and the practice of conspiracy, a right no one has in a democracy unless it is the moral right of an undemocratic rebel who is prepared to risk the consequences of his rebellion.

The teachers of this country do not need lessons in patriotism from anybody. Over the years I have found that the best way to meet authoritarianism, wherever it raises its head, is not to yield to it but to fight it openly. A lost battle is not a lost war. More than one dour prediction about the future of American education has been falsified in less than the lifetime of the prophet.

Today we are involved in a desperate international civil war to preserve the political freedom which is the *sine qua non* of all other freedoms. If those who teach do not show wisdom and courage in their professional activity, if they permit educational leadership and initiative to pass from their hands into those that are untrained and unqualified, then educational freedom may be an unintended casualty of political victory. Here as elsewhere— the readiness is all.

This raises the question of the nature of academic freedom. But something must first be said of the role of the teacher in a democratic society before we ask why he should enjoy the freedom to exercise that role and what such freedom means.

Chapter 7

THE VOCATION OF THE TEACHER

Next to the child's parents his teachers play the greatest role in his life. If we think of the teacher as a composite person of all who have ministered to the child's educational needs from kindergarten to college days, it is safe to say that the child spends almost as much time in the presence of his teacher as of his parents—or at least one of them, his father.

Some parents are convinced that their children's teachers exercise more influence than they do themselves on their children's lives, on their daily choices and long-range decisions. As a rule this is an exaggeration; the environment of the street, of companions and friends is just as important, if not more so. But its very exaggeration testifies to the strength of the view that the teacher has a profound effect upon the developing personality of his students.

As adults when we look back on our educational past, we remember teachers, not methods or techniques or even the special content of their instruction. Their influence on our lives, our ideals of conduct, standards of judgment, secret ambitions and hopes, even our choice of life careers is often unknown to them. Unconsciously we learn from everyone but we have a tendency

The Vocation of the Teacher

to resist those whose explicit business is not to teach us. Only to the teacher do we willingly open ourselves to influence without feeling belittled or resentful or ashamed of our ignorance. In some ways the relation of teacher and student is as intimate as that of the physician and patient. There is still a kernel of truth in the ancient notion that the teacher, especially in his concern for wisdom, is the physician of the soul. He occupies a privileged position of trust not always reflected in the emoluments or social esteem accorded him by the community.

In some cultures learning goes on without professional teachers. But in our own urban culture, much of the knowledge, many of the skills, and most of the values which the young used to acquire in the past through direct participation in the daily life processes of an earlier, predominantly agricultural economy, are now made the subject of focal instruction through formal schooling. The result is that when a crisis develops in urban societies, what the teacher is doing, or failing to do, becomes a question of public concern.

Particularly is this true in a democratic society which relies upon the educational process to impart the knowledge and strengthen the values that sustain faith in freedom and promote wise decisions on matters of affecting the public welfare. The teacher has a key role in a democratic society because he is expected to be not the servant of some partisan interest but of the spirit of disinterested inquiry which serves the common interest. He thereby must keep always open the channels of communication to doubt and fresh discovery. It is expected that his first devotion will be not to a technique or school of thought or a subject but to the final source of all democratic institutions, the unique persons of the young men and women, growing up in a troubled and dangerous world. It is no wonder then that when tensions mount in a community, the schools and teachers become the object of suddenly awakened interest.

Our own days of alarm and turmoil have provided many occasions for such interest. From all sides the teacher is buffeted by pressure groups which criticize him for doing this or not doing that, for truckling to the student's needs or imposing tasks upon them foreign to the world they live in. In the eyes of some he must prove his loyalty before that of any other group. Real estate boards lecture him on how American history is to be taught and business men, who would resent anyone telling *them* how to run their factory or market their product, lay down the law to him on how to teach everything from the three R's to the secrets of politics and the mysteries of faith. The textbooks he uses are often perused with suspicious eyes by representatives of religious, national or racial minorities as well as self-appointed guardians of the national heritage. And as if this were not enough, he is prematurely wept over by the bleeding hearts of ritualistic liberalism as a victim of hysteria, terrorized into fearful silence, even as he manages to fend off reactionary groups and get on with his work. It sometimes seems as if the teacher were the only one who remains calm in the excited hubbub swirling around him.

The fundamental freedom the teacher wants is the freedom to do his job. What that job is, is a question always in order but rarely more opportune to ask and answer than today. Unless the community understands it, the teacher will suffer from constant harassments and the community, before long, from poor and mean-spirited teaching.

The first answer to the question: What should the function of the teacher be? may sound like a paradox. The function of the teacher is ultimately to make himself dispensable in the process of education. For the best education is one which develops within the individual the power, skill and resources necessary to self-education. Life to the very end may be considered a school but it is not a classroom. He who cannot learn from his own experiences and from the experiences of others without the benefit of teachers never outgrows the estate of the child.

To develop the capacity for self-education in his students, the teacher must aim to achieve a number of interrelated ends. Of these the most important are emotional and intellectual maturity.

The Vocation of the Teacher

What is emotional maturity? Although hard to define its most adequate indication is the *habit of reasonable expectation*. The immature are those who, ignorant of the world they live in, its dangers and challenges, are blind optimists, trusting to chance or some surrogate for father to put things right. Or they are hysterics, defeated by their fears, refusing to recognize that the grave problems which beset us can yield only to thoughtful action. Sometimes they alternate in a panicky cycle between these two moods.

There can be no emotional maturity, of course, without knowledge but knowledge of the ways of *things* is not sufficient to achieve it. Ability to handle formulas or to predict the interacting behaviors of material substances, as many teachers know, can go hand in hand with an opacity to human relationships and the complexity of social interactions. Emotional maturity seems to depend more upon knowledge of self and others, upon proper historical perspective, an awareness of how often the best of men fall short of their own ideals. It avoids the assumption that because men are not angels, they are beasts, and conversely. The emotionally mature do not lose their sense of wonder and awe at the spectacle of human existence against the infinite backdrop of the cosmos but neither are they continually being surprised by events. They do not confuse innocence with virtue or deplore human finitude as natural depravity. They are skeptical of large claims without being cynical, and their faith, even when deep, is not fanatical.

Emotional maturity is a slow growth. It cannot be forced or acquired like mathematical skill at a very early age. And like most virtues it is more likely to be achieved by indirection as a consequence of the pursuit of other ends than by directly striving for it.

Intellectual maturity is manifested in the capacity for reasonable assessment of evidence. A man who can handle figures perfectly may be a perfect fool about politics and a person whose political judgments are shrewd may commit blunder upon blunder in thinking about budgets or tariffs or the control of atomic energy. Intellectual maturity not only is insight into what constitutes evidence but into the kinds and degrees of evidence appropriate to different fields. There is no necessary carryover from one discipline to another which explains why a learned man so often sounds like a dunce when he ventures, without sufficient preparation, outside of his own specialty.

The function of the teacher is not merely to teach the student how to think—as if this were an abstract skill, apart from subject matters thought about—but to get him thinking *in* and *about* the major fields of human interest. A student who thinks in history as he does in mathematics, about people as about electrons, about a work of art as about a court decision, is a poor thinker. The laws of valid inference are the same for all fields but the truth of an assertion depends upon more than logic although any assertion which violates the laws of logic must be false if not meaningless. Thinking is effective only when it reveals command of subject matter.

It follows from this that the teacher who wishes to develop emotional and intellectual maturity in his students will nurture in them a respect for—but not worship of—fact. To be intellectually responsible means an insistence that ideas about the world be tested by the facts already known, even if unpleasant, and by other facts to be sought for, and that in the absence of sufficient evidence, judgment be suspended. To suspend judgment is never easy particularly about matters which are urgent and require action. But it is well to remember that we do not need to be certain in order to act; and that our doubts may be settled through the intelligent quest for the evidence by which we seek to appease them.

Respect for fact is not enough, there must be respect for authority—not the authority of a person, an institution, dogma, or doctrine—but the authority of rational method. The teacher cannot substitute his own person as an authority even when he asks the student of tender years to take some things on faith. The

The Vocation of the Teacher

child cannot grasp the mathematical proof that twice two is four or the evidence that the earth is round at the time when he is first asked to believe these truths. But at the same time that he acquires these beliefs, he must be encouraged to think out for himself whatever he can, his powers of thought developed, so that when he reaches higher levels of instruction, what he has accepted on faith he can test by rational analysis.

Indoctrination is the deliberate use of non-rational means, or the dishonest use of irrational means, to induce beliefs. The second kind of indoctrination is never justified, and the first only in the early years before the powers of intelligence have been awakened. Any kind of indoctrination on the high school or college level is a violation of the integrity of the student's person, of his right to his own personal growth. John Dewey maintained that psychic indoctrination of the student in behalf of predetermined conclusions was morally as indefensible as physical assault by the stronger against the weaker. No teacher worthy of teaching in a free society, he believed, would indoctrinate or accept instructions to indoctrinate from any organization whatsoever.

The teacher must often resist the request of students who wish to rest in the comfortable securities of approved ideas, "to be told" the answers to problems which may not even have known solutions. A recent study shows that many scientists probably found their life interest as a result of a teacher giving them a problem to work out for themselves. The teacher cannot begin too soon to encourage independence. "Men's minds," says Santayana, "are more gregarious than their bodies." The rarest of the virtues of the mind, today as always, is intellectual courage, the strength to stand alone if necessary against the fashion of the moment. But, as distinct from caprice, it must be rooted in the love of truth and disciplined by an awareness of fact.

The good teacher develops a sense for fact in his students but not, we said, a worship of facts. Facts are significant only insofar as they bear on ideas, theories, principles, confirming or disconfirming them. That things are so is not as interesting as why they are so. Particularly in history and social science when students believe they understand why things are so, the teacher should provoke them into asking, wherever it is relevant, whether things had to be so, whether they should have been so, whether they could have been different. The historical disciplines can be fruitfully studied not only as a record of what actually happened or developed and why; but a record of what might have been. In this and other ways the teacher seeks to stretch the *imagination* of his students, their feeling for alternatives and possibilities, in order to liberate them from the tyranny of the established. Despite rumors to the contrary, the intellectually young are more likely to be traditionalists and conformists than rebels, and to accept what has happened as a source both of historical legitimacy and moral validity. But it is not difficult to make them understand that the facts alone—important as they are—do not always determine great historical events and policies; that human ideals, cold and desperate courage, willingness to risk something in action, and sometimes even chance, play their part, too. The belief that they can make a difference in a world that is still developing has a liberating, and sometimes a stirring effect, on the young who feel helpless because of their numbers and dwarfed by the magnitude of the problems which beset our times.

A good teacher is something of an actor, and the less self-conscious he is the better he is. And like an actor he must communicate by contagion a certain excitement about ideas, their dramatic conflicts, their relation to material interests, and their fascinating careers and transformations in the world. But having motivated his students, the teacher must discreetly retire and let them carry on under judicious guidance. For although they rarely believe it, they profit only from what *they* do, not from what they hear him say or see him do.

No taboo can be laid down on what subject matter or ideas the teacher is to consider if he is to teach well. Those who would bar controversial subjects, dangerous ideas, the study of fascism or

The Vocation of the Teacher

communism, and other political ideas from the classroom, when the din of these clashing doctrines can be heard in every market-place, indeed in every home, are really preventing intelligent discussion of the issues whose resolution determines the future.

The teacher must, of course, recognize certain criteria of relevance—he should not wander aimlessly all over the universe—but it is he and only he, who is the best judge of what the educational needs of his students require.

The good teacher knows how to use all sorts of materials, even those turned out by the enemies of democracy. Sometimes in order to bring home a sense of the latent strength of positions which the student will encounter in the world, the teacher must play devil's advocate. For a while, he leaves the student wriggling on the hook of doubt and uncertainty until the latter feels sufficiently moved to meet the challenge to his fundamental convictions by reaching out for further facts and arguments and wrestling free to more stable beliefs.

What of moral and spiritual values? Is it any part of the teacher's calling to develop the character of his students, to influence the constellation of values in which the quality of personality finds expression? The answer must be tentatively affirmative—tentative because experience shows that didactic efforts to "improve" students by preaching or scolding or disciplining are futile. Spiritual growth and the quickening of moral perception seems to me to be the natural by-product of emotional and intellectual maturity and not the result of explicit lessons in virtue.

The responsibility of the teacher in this respect is discharged by exercising his vocation to make every occasion of learning one for both thought and feeling—aesthetic, moral or practical. The student who does not see anything "neat" about a geometrical demonstration, who has not grasped the significant form in a play or poem or painting, who misses the way in which ideas are related to episodes in a thinker's biography or a culture's history has had something less than a complete experience. Every teacher inspires as well as instructs in virtue of the ideals of excellence or the vision of greatness he holds up to his students and in his judgments on men and affairs and movements of the past and present.

More important still, whether he knows it or not, the teacher by his manner and practice serves as a living example to his students. His values and judgments have immense authority for them. Discourtesy, indifference, courting popularity, flippancy, superficiality, bullying and dogmatism are the seven deadly sins of teaching and the students are very keen in sensing them, and reacting in kind to each other. The profoundest moral impression the teacher can make on his students is by his humility before the truth, and the objective methods of seeking it. That is why he cannot wear the collar of any cult or party which presumes to dictate to him what he should believe or teach, and at the same time fulfill his obligations to the community, to his colleagues, or to his students.

It is necessary for the teacher to guard against the effect of teaching immature minds in a relatively isolated academic environment, and of constant exposure to the young in need of guidance. The older some teachers grow the more they resemble their students intellectually—and the more likely they are to treat all other human beings as students. That is why in addition to his own intellectual interests, pursued on the highest level of scholarship, it is wise for the teacher to have some experience with the world of affairs in some non-professional contexts. Those who scoff at professors because "they never had to meet a payroll" would find themselves just as much at a loss if *they* had to meet a well-prepared, intellectually alert and searching class. But there are other avenues of fruitful approach to the world outside the classroom which do not involve finance. (Besides, teachers think they know enough about finance when they puzzle about how to make ends meet.) Exploring fields which bring them into active association with adults and adult minds enriches their experience of the world and people and improves their

The Vocation of the Teacher

qualities as teachers. Communities which place restrictions upon the activities of teachers as citizens, of teachers as normal men and women, in the end defeat the best educational interest of their children.

The teacher, like anyone else, desires a certain material security for himself and his family. But no man in his senses chooses teaching as a road to fortune. Except for the few who alas! take up teaching because they have failed in everything else, the teacher is, or should be, an individual who finds a personal fulfillment in his work. His deepest satisfactions come from seeing his students develop as thinking persons, agreeing or disagreeing with him as independent minds, and knowing that the characters of the men and women of tomorrow owe more to the daily efforts of himself and his colleagues than to that of any other group. It is the teachers, more than the poets, who are the unacknowledged legislators of the free world.

The community entrusts the teacher with its most precious possessions. He is aware that he holds a position of high responsibility no matter what subject he teaches, and not only because he stands *in loco parentis*. But it is difficult to carry out one's trust in an atmosphere of suspicion, or even of excessive and fussy supervision. No one who is watched can perform the vocation of teacher properly; no one who needs to be watched should be permitted to follow the vocation of teacher. Once he is certified as professionally competent, the community must have implicit faith in him. After all, no one who is not in his classroom practically all the time, can tell whether a teacher is failing to fulfill his unspoken commitments to his vocation or betraying his trust. Even if such supervision were practicable, it would not be desirable. No trust can or should be placed in those who receive instructions to betray their trust, like members of the Ku Klux Klan and the Communist Party. Educators themselves can eliminate from their ranks the few unfaithful ones without the help of the state power. But these questions I shall discuss in greater detail in subsequent chapters.

Heresy, Yes—Conspiracy, No

The selection of teachers should be the occasion for the most careful thought, particularly on the college level where only too often it is assumed that anyone who knows anything is therefore qualified to teach it. But technical knowledge and intelligence are necessary but not sufficient criteria of the good teacher. The good teacher should have a feeling for the vocation, literally the calling, of teaching and should enjoy its exercise. Instead of being apologetic about his work, he should take pride in it, and dignity. He should have a warm sympathy for students, their difficulties and problems, and must get to know them not as names or numbers to be graded, but as individual persons. He should have a vital concern for the traditions of intellectual freedom and seek to arouse in those he teaches a passion for freedom.

The classroom relation between the teacher and student on any level, the give and take between them as the student gropes his way from one position to another, should be considered privileged almost in the same way as the relation between physician and patient, and, in one particular, like the relation between the priest and communicant.

The classroom is a laboratory in which students experiment with ideas, trying to reach some clarity or firm ground of belief. In that quest they should be encouraged to hold, defend and test any view which seems valid in the light of evidence. They will probably abandon many more ideas than they accept in the course of their intellectual development.

That is why it seems to me impermissible for a teacher to answer questions about a student's beliefs or positions on any subject which has been discussed in the classroom or to reveal any information, religious or political, about a student's expression of opinion in the classroom to any group or agency, except at the request of the student himself.

There is nothing that a teacher says that he should not be able to say in public, if he pleases. There is nothing a student says in the classroom for which he should be held accountable outside the classroom. The recognition of this seems to me to be part of the credo of a good teacher.

If we recruit enough good teachers, we need not fear for the future of free society in an age of anxiety. If it can withstand assaults from without, then despite the calamity howlers it will never fall from within.

If we recognize this as the vocation of the teacher, we can better appreciate the case for academic freedom.

Chapter 8

THE CASE FOR ACADEMIC FREEDOM

There are many things human beings believe with an intensity much stronger than is warranted by the arguments they can muster for them. Some individuals have therefore been inclined to conclude that all such beliefs are emotional rather than cognitive. Those who do not mince matters call these beliefs prejudices, and frankly proclaim that such prejudices, no matter how limited, parochial, or personal, are both inescapable and legitimate. No one, they say, can prove his ultimate preferences, and one preference is as valid as another.

It is true that the belief in the desirability of academic freedom is often held with an intensity which is stronger than the arguments usually advanced in its behalf. But it is not true that this is an infallible sign that the belief is an ultimate prejudice or preference. For very often the belief can be buttressed by additional arguments, and by evidence that alternative positions have still less to be said for them. Considered in their totality, these arguments and evidence increase the weight of the grounds for one's convictions. But they take time to develop, time that is not always available in the thick of discussion. More important is the recognition that rational argument and evidence are *rele-*

The Case for Academic Freedom

vant to certain beliefs even if the intensity of belief is not an exact and continuous function of the strength of the former. It is enough to recognize that a belief (or preference) can grow more reasonable in consequence of argument and evidence.

Belief in the desirability of academic freedom is a belief which is held, especially in certain academic quarters, with an intensity hardly warranted by the arguments usually advanced for it. There is something intellectually strange about the looseness of the thinking and writing about the subject of academic freedom. It is more often a theme for rhetorical fervor than of logical analysis. As a doctrine it is approached in academic circles as sacred folk lore. In consequence when the belief in academic freedom is openly criticized, when the shock of surprise has worn off the criticism is hysterically denounced instead of being rationally refuted. A striking illustration of this recently occurred. An incompletely educated young man with a flair for dialectic and debate wrote a brilliantly wrong-headed book, *God and Man at Yale,* attacking what he called "the superstitions" of academic freedom. He based his attack on what he considered were democratic premises, and reached the conclusion that academic freedom, if it could be defended at all, could only mean the freedom of the community or of private associations of men and women "to supervise the educational activities and aims" of the public and private schools they respectively supported.

So far as I am aware not a single attempt was made to meet Mr. Buckley's arguments on rational grounds. He was roundly abused, denounced as a Fascist of sorts, and cited as part of a deplorable trend to conformity in the American cultural pattern. Later on I shall examine Mr. Buckley's chief arguments and attempt to show that his conclusions rest either upon dubious assumptions or upon invalid inferences from assumptions that are not dubious. But here I wish to point out that if his book is evidence of a deplorable trend, the reception it has received is evidence of a trend no less deplorable.

Heresy, Yes—Conspiracy, No

I

What is academic freedom? Academic freedom is a specific kind of freedom. It is the freedom of professionally qualified persons to inquire, discover, publish and teach the truth as they see it in the field of their competence, without any control or authority except the control or authority of the rational methods by which truth is established. Insofar as it acknowledges intellectual discipline or restraint from a community, it is only from the community of qualified scholars which accepts the authority of rational inquiry.

Like every other freedom, academic freedom, although it has an intrinsic value, is not absolute. It must be judged by its consequences on a whole cluster of other freedoms (values). The *justification* of academic freedom must therefore lie in its fruits.

Before going on to treat of its justifications, a word or two must be said of the relationship between academic freedom and other civil freedoms. A large measure of academic freedom may exist even in the absence of widely distributed civil freedoms. The slaves who were sometimes used as pedagogues in ancient Greece and Rome may have been given freedom to teach some disciplines as they thought best. Within the framework of certain key assumptions of Christian doctrine, a considerable degree of academic freedom was enjoyed by the medieval university at a time when civil freedoms for the citizens of the community was hardly an embryonic concept. In the German Empire although the traditions of *Lern und Lehr Freiheit* were somewhat circumscribed by the royal will, university professors enjoyed a greater academic freedom than that possessed at the time by professors in more democratic countries like England and the United States.

On the other hand, where academic freedom does not exist in secular institutions or is severely limited in institutions of higher learning, civil liberties are not likely to flourish. This is a matter of degree and historic context depending upon the grounds for the restriction. In the United States, the two main causes, until

The Case for Academic Freedom

quite recently, for restriction upon academic freedom were religious unorthodoxy or disbelief and unconventional personal or moral behavior. In the latter case it was not what the professor believed or taught which was found objectionable but something about his personal life. Conditions varied from section to section, and sometimes from one university to another. In Southern universities doctrines and practices would not be tolerated which were matters of course in the North. In the past, metropolitan universities have, on the whole, extended the largest measure of freedom to teachers, partly because their presidents were men of sufficient distinction to prevent boards of trustees from interfering with the details of the educational process; partly because life in a large city allowed an anonymity impossible in the small town; partly because the large university was more conscious of public relations and tolerated many things in order to avoid scandal; and partly because administrators accepted the ideals of academic freedom.

In virtue of the remission of taxes and other privileges extended to it, every university is a semi-public institution subsisting to some extent upon public largesse. It receives complete or partial support from the community. No college or university of quality can flourish on an income derived *solely* from student fees. In many situations it seems reasonable to expect that those who carry the burden of support of an institution should be entitled to lay down or control its policies. But academic situations are not among them. The presupposition of academic freedom is that whatever administrative control may legitimately be exercised by any board of trustees, governors or regents on university policy, it cannot be extended to limit the right of the faculty, as individuals and groups, to pursue, publish and teach the truth as it sees fit. From this it follows at once that the conditions and enforcement of the rules of tenure must ultimately lie in the hand of the faculty.

Why should the community recognize the validity of this claim to academic freedom? The main reason is that in this way new truth and new knowledge is won more easily than if any specific doctrine or dogma is laid down as an inviolable guide. The history of thought is to a large extent the history of intellectual mutation and heresy. The discipline of reflective inquiry, of experiment, and critical discussion is a severe test on claims to truth. To add to these tests external, and therefore irrelevant, criteria is to establish needless obstacles to the growth of human knowledge.

Second, insofar as wisdom lies in the intelligent choice of alternatives, academic freedom by enabling alternative policies to be stated, and by permitting inquiry into facts which are relevant to decision of policy, contributes to the development of human wisdom. The very independence the university extends to the scholar offers us a better assurance that his judgment will be objective than if he held his post on condition that he accepted certain dogmas whose truth he could not question. His independence and training fit him especially for objective judgment on those controversial issues which arouse and sometimes divide the community.

Third, although there is no guarantee that freedom to inquire and teach insures the solution of technical problems in medicine, engineering, economics and other applied disciplines, it provides a climate more hospitable to fresh vision and invention in these fields than would be found in its absence. The universities supply society with its great specialists.

Fourth, academic freedom, permitting challenge, question and debate, subject to no authority but intelligence, develops a critical temper among students without which they cannot achieve intellectual maturity. In an era where propaganda and advertising are highly developed techniques of eliciting non-rational consent to propositions of dubious character, the desirability of intellectual sophisticaton can hardly be overestimated.

Finally, limitations today upon academic freedom *tend* to weaken the vitality of intellectual and cultural freedom in the community at large. Where safety and conformity are the rule

The Case for Academic Freedom

in institutions of higher learning, apathy and indifference will often be found in the public market place of ideas, too. This was not always the case in the past, as the history of ideas in England shows.

All of these justifications, and no complete list has been intended, have one thing in common. They point to the fact that academic freedom exists not merely for the sake of the professor but for the sake of the community also, and that its ultimate fruits are to be found not in the private, professional delight of the connoisseur of ideas, although this has merit, too, but in the public good which includes, let us hope, the multiplied private delights of others besides professors.

That academic freedom is something which concerns others besides the academic community is the source of a two-fold responsibility—of the general community to the academic community, and of the academic community to the general community. This two-fold responsibility is not always recognized.

This two-fold responsibility would not exist, or it would take a radically different form, if the college and university functioned as a business or profit-making institution without any public subsidy whatsoever or any remission of taxation. In such a situation, subject only to the laws against fraud, the institution would function as a business. Those who were dissatisfied with it would cease to patronize it. On the other hand, members of the faculty would have no claim upon the community for any help or support.

But no liberal educational institution of any worth functions as a business or factory. The academic freedom and tenure of its faculty (for without security of tenure academic freedom is a myth) cannot depend upon the "gate receipts." In the last analysis only the general community can underwrite them. The plain fact is that no educational system can be completely autonomous of the community which directly or indirectly supports it.

The nature of the community to which the university owes responsibility is not easy to define. Obviously it is not to a political party. Nor is it to the administration of the nation or state or city. It is not to the majority of the voters at any time in any region in which the institution may be located. The university serves a community always "in the making," so to speak, and in which natural piety to the values and achievements of previous generations is joined to intelligent anticipation of the needs of generations to come—without in any way neglecting the legitimate concerns of the present. At a certain moment the opinions and beliefs accepted in a university may be quite different from those entertained by a majority of the community. But this very majority must stand prepared to defend the right of the university to disagree with it, its right to be loyal to the community "in the making," provided such disagreement flows from its vocation of inquiry. The more democratic a given community is, the more it seeks to participate and cooperate through its voluntary associations in the educational experience provided by the university, the more aware it must be of the limits of its justifiable powers.

But if the public community cannot claim absolute right to control of the educational process neither can the academic community claim the absolute right to carry on its activities independently of its effects on the community. There are two generic conditions under which the community can legitimately limit the academic freedom of an educational institution: (a) if it could be established that it was unable to achieve its proper educational goals—the advancement of learning, the encouragement of insight and creativity, and the transmission of the knowledge, skills and values which constitute the minimum indispensables of a liberal and professional education, and (b) if despite the achievement of these goals, it violated other moral values which on reflection appear more weighty or fundamental.

It is hard to imagine a situation in which the exercise of academic freedom, as we have defined it, by professionally qualified men and women would result in the intellectual failure presupposed by the first condition. If such a situation of academic breakdown and intellectual bankruptcy existed, presumably it would be discovered by representatives of other academic institutions before the community became aware of it.

The situation presupposed by the second condition although improbable is not so difficult to imagine.

The logic of the situation may appear clearer if we consider briefly an analogy between academic freedom and medical freedom. Medical freedom is freedom to inquire, to experiment and to apply the findings of research to human beings in quest of health. The community supports medical research and practice by qualified practitioners because it believes that the health of the community is thereby furthered by it. Were this in fact not the case, or were it the case, and physicians carried their inquiry to a point where they cruelly experimented, out of sheer love of knowledge, on human beings—thus violating our sense of the indefeasible dignity of man—the community would have a moral justification in abridging medical freedom. But since neither of these dread possibilities is actually true, there can be no warrant for the community to interfere with the autonomy of the medical profession in holding whatever medical theory or adopting any medical practice which qualified physicians believe required by the ends of their profession. Were the community sincerely convinced that a basic moral norm were threatened by the effects of teaching a specific medical theory or adopting a method of research it would be justified at most in refusing to subsidize the teaching of the subject in which this allegedly pernicious theory or practice was found. It would not be justified in dictating that any practitioner state conclusions which ran counter to his findings. The community may not want the medical truth established because it may consider the price in suffering paid for that truth too high. But it cannot make obligatory the teaching of a medical untruth. For example, it is conceivable that under the sway of some religious or sentimental moral doctrine the community might be strongly opposed to the vivisection of animals in medical research and forbade the practice. One could not justifiably oppose such a restriction on the grounds of medical freedom although one could find other adequate grounds for opposing the restriction. It would constitute a violation of medical freedom if the community insisted that medical schools teach the untruth that vivisection on animals has never led to discoveries beneficial to man. It is not a violation of medical freedom to prevent the dissemination of the facts about birth control—as ill judged as such a taboo may be. It would be a violation of medical freedom to prescribe the dissemination of untruths about birth control.

Mutatis mutandis, these distinctions hold for academic freedom. The democratic community can legitimately determine whether or not to support the formal educational process of schooling. If the results of the schooling are unacceptable to it, if it has evidence that the education supplied is failing to achieve the ends for which it was introduced, the community is within its rights in withdrawing its support. If the results of the schooling are technically satisfactory but at the same time violate basic *reflective* moral norms, it is also justified in withholding its support. But where this is not the case, it has no valid ground for interfering with the autonomy of the teaching profession by abridging the freedom of teachers to hold any doctrine whatsoever on any subject of inquiry, or their freedom to adopt any pedagogical device or method in imparting the results of inquiry. The legislature of a state may not regard the study of geometry as necessary in the curriculum. If it dropped the subject from the course of study, its action may be rightfully challenged on many grounds. But it cannot be indicted for violating anyone's academic freedom. However, were the legislature to decree, as one Western state is supposed to have done, that hereafter the value of π should be taught as exactly three, such an action would not only be foolish but would constitute a violation of academic freedom. Similarly, it would be foolish but not a violation of academic freedom for a legislature to proscribe the teaching of biology or economics; but it would be both foolish *and* a violation of academic freedom to *prescribe* that any particular theory—say,

The Case for Academic Freedom

the germ-theory of disease, the hypothesis of organic evolution, the theory of marginal utility—be taught as truth or exposed as error. If any subject is to be taught, then the principles of academic freedom require that those who have been professionally certified as competent, and only those, teach it.

If this conclusion is valid and binding even upon the duly constituted authorities of the democratic community, *viz.*, those who are responsible to the electorate, it should be all the more valid and binding on the self-constituted pressure groups of any kind who seek to tell teachers what they should teach and how.

Despite current detractors of American higher education, there is no valid empirical evidence that American colleges and universities are failing to achieve the ends of the democratic educational process. Whatever shortcomings and limitations exist can be remedied by the autonomous activities of the educational profession itself. Indeed, during the last two decades the most impressive curricular changes have been introduced throughout the country. Never in the history of American education have teachers been so intent on defining, implementing and testing the objectives of liberal education in a democratic society. Common and individual needs of students have been met by a reasonable variety in curricular programs. Those unable to profit educationally from a conventional regimen of studies are able to find courses of study appropriate to their interests and capacities no less, and sometimes more, instructive. On the score of educational preparation and achievement there is certainly no justification for limitation of academic freedom or intervention by the state.

Nor has the functioning of our academic institutions in any way violated ethical values central to the democratic way of life —leaving aside the altogether different problem posed by the practice of segregation in some states. As an institution, the college or university in America, at the very least, has contributed as much to an understanding of, and intelligent loyalty to, democratic ideals as any other American institution whether it be the press, the church, labor or business.

Heresy, Yes—Conspiracy, No

The question of the relationship between academic freedom and democratic loyalty we shall discuss in greater detail after we clarify some misconceptions about the nature of academic freedom.

II

We often hear it said that academic freedom is the freedom to teach the truth. There is no freedom to teach error. There are truths about the world; there are truths about man and society; there are truths about human values. And only those in the possession of these truths, and who possess the necessary skills of imparting them, are entitled to academic freedom.

Something like this view must have been held by the president of a West Coast University who is reported as saying in justification of his recommendation that a scientist be dismissed for supporting the views of Lysenko: "Any scientist who has such poor power of discrimination to choose to support Lysenko's genetics against all the weight of evidence is not much of a scientist or has lost the freedom that an instructor should possess." (*New York Times,* February 24, 1949)

These are two entirely different things. A failure to discriminate between them would help Communists destroy academic freedom. If the scientist in question has lost his freedom to inquire into the truth by virtue of Communist Party membership, that is one thing. But if he has pitted his own independent judgment against the weight of scientific evidence, then, even if he is a thousand times wrong, he must be protected against dismissal. The very nature of scientific method permits anyone to challenge any of its conclusions. Its self-corrective procedures are the only assurance we need that the truth will be found.

After all, the important point about Lysenko is not whether his theory is right or wrong, or whether, as some Soviet apologists have been saying, "there may be something in it," but rather that the weapons of political terror and the dread authority of the Politburo were used to settle a scientific dispute. It is this use

The Case for Academic Freedom

of the police to decide questions of science which marks the cultural barbarism of the Soviet regime.

We must lean over backward to avoid the very shadow of suspicion that a man is not free to challenge even universally accepted truth.

This view that academic freedom is freedom to teach the truth is usually held by those who believe they have the absolute truth about the world, man and society—absolute truth which extends to man's supernatural ends as well as his natural ends. One need only ask for the absolute truths, belief in which qualifies the individual for the enjoyment of academic freedom, to see how dubious they are. Certainly no one has the right to teach error— so long as it is recognized as such. "Error has no rights," says Monsignor Ryan. Of course. Neither has truth in the abstract. Only human beings have rights. A scholar has no right to lie. But he has a right to err in his quest for the truth.

Anyone who at the outset of his academic career believed that the circle could be squared, that the world was flat, that Kemmerer's experiments proved the inheritance of acquired characteristics, would probably not be certified by his peers as competent to teach mathematics, geography or biology. But if he were once certified, he would have the academic right to be wrong. If there were any infallible criterion of absolute truth, one might infer from the proposition that no one had a right to teach error, that no one was free to teach anything but the truth. Most of the time, however, we are quite confident that some belief about a phenomenon is erroneous without having the corresponding degree of certainty as to which belief is the correct one. We are quite confident that cancer is not caused by lack of piety or excessive consumption of buttermilk. But, alas, we are not anywhere near so confident as to what actually causes it. The number of wrong answers that can be given to a problem is usually indefinite; the number of correct answers is usually one. The fact that yesterday's heresy has often turned out to be today's orthodoxy, and that today's orthodoxy may be regarded as tomorrow's absurdity should make us hesitate about insisting that only what is known to be absolutely true should be taught.

That is why we must amend the proposed conception of academic freedom as freedom to teach the truth with the phrase "as one sees it." Even this is not sufficient. "As one sees it" may be an expression of what is arbitrary and fantastic. We have a right to demand of the inquirer into truth, and of those who aim to teach the truth or aid in its search, that their assertion be *warranted*. What makes a conclusion warranted is how it is derived from evidential grounds. The scholar and teacher has a right to teach the truth as he sees it in the light of reflective inquiry and in relation to all the evidence available to him. When a man receives his credentials as a scholar and teacher from his peers it is presupposed that he has demonstrated his capacity and inclination to reach conclusions according to the best methods of rational inquiry current in his particular field. It is not necessary that he agree with any specific conclusions or subscribe to any specific doctrine. It is the *way* in which he reaches his conclusions which makes him a member of the community of scholars. Correspondingly, an individual entrusted with a teaching post is not judged by whether he teaches the truth but by *how* he teaches, by the techniques and methods with which he motivates interest, elicits intellectual activity and intelligent perception on the part of his students. He can teach the truths about a subject—whether it be French grammar or analytic geometry, a thousand times over. He is a poor teacher unless he teaches in a certain way, unless his students have an understanding grasp of the truths or warranted conclusions about the subject matter. Once an individual, after a probationary period in which his teaching has been tested, has been certified as a competent teacher, then unless evidence crops up which points to betrayal of professional trust or to membership in an educationally conspiratorial organization, his academic freedom must be defended to the limit.

This means that the academic community must defend not any

particular heresy which the teacher reaches but his right to profess that heresy no matter how abominable it may seem both to
the academic and general community. Whoever touches one
teacher because his doctrine is troublesome or pernicious touches
all. Does this mean that the teacher or scholar is to be privileged
and to seek immunity from criticism behind a rhetorical smoke
screen about academic freedom? Not at all. The civil rights of the
ordinary citizen guarantees him the freedom to criticize anyone
he pleases, scholar or not, to listen to anyone according to his needs,
and to talk sense or nonsense according to his capacities. But
beyond this, and much more important, the general community,
which upholds the rights of academic freedom, expects the academic community to apply the same solvent of criticism to the
conclusions of the heretical and orthodox, the traditionalist and
the trail blazer, the bringer of glad tidings and the prophets of
doom. Continuous, forthright criticism; vigorous, informed, and
incisive discussion; that is the circumambient atmosphere in which
ideas must make their way in the academic community. Extremism, crackpottism, fellow traveling, whether Fascist or Communist, have a hard time surviving when faced by a succession of
gusty challenges. The pity of it is that this criticism and discussion have been wanting in recent years, particularly with reference
to the intellectual excesses of totalitarian fellow travelers. And
what members of the academic community have failed to do
through the appropriate techniques of mutual criticism, members
of the general community and their representatives have sought
to do by the utterly inappropriate methods of suppression.

III

We must now consider a plausible argument which would grant
academic freedom to scholars and teachers only in matters of
fact, which can be established by scientific method, or in disciplines like mathematics and logic, in which conclusions can be
demonstrated. In fields which involve "values" or "policies" or

Heresy, Yes—Conspiracy, No

"judgments of good or bad," it is argued that since conclusions cannot be verified by experiment or established by analysis, the democratic community is justified in seeing to it that *its* "values" are taught to students and not that of its opponents. That is to say, if "values" are merely prejudices, so that it cannot be established that one value is better than another, then the "prejudices" of the democratic community, which bears the financial burden of education, must be favored rather than the "prejudices" of any particular teacher or set of teachers. This position claims to rest on the democratic assumption that there are no experts in wisdom, that every individual citizen is as much a consumer in respect to values as any other, and that therefore the majority of the consumers (whether as citizens or as parents) are justified in imposing a "value orthodoxy" on schools and colleges which the individual teacher may explicate, criticize within certain limits, but not deny or undermine. If the value-orthodoxy of a democratic community is the belief in freedom, then no teacher may invoke the shibboleth of academic freedom to attack or subvert the value of freedom or advocate totalitarianism. So runs the argument.

Freed of irrelevant accretions, this is the position of Mr. Buckley, and I suspect of some tough-minded positivists whose value prejudices, however, are quite different from those of Mr. Buckley. The presupposition of the argument is that a sharp dichotomy exists between facts on the one hand, and values or policies on the other. But there is hardly any field which concerns itself only with matters of pure fact or only with matters of pure policy. The empirical disciplines especially represent an intermixture of both. Even those who profess to keep facts and values or policies in separate compartments cannot in practice sustain the division.

The best illustration is provided by Mr. Buckley himself. Although he himself is convinced that a free enterprise economy is desirable for many reasons—indeed he believes that the survival of democracy depends upon the preservation of a free economy—he acknowledges that it is possible that a majority of Americans, the citizens, the consumers, the ultimate taxpayers, may want, not a free market economy, but one which would make for a greater re-distribution of wealth. But he then goes on to chide authors of textbooks in economics who assume that the American people desire a greater redistribution of wealth with refusing to address themselves to a question which Mr. Buckley himself italicizes: *"Is what most Americans want sound economics?"*

The concept of "sound economics" is hard to fit in with the categorical dichotomy of fact and policy, for "sound economics" simply means "sound economic policies," and what makes such policies sound can only be some relation they bear to economic fact, which is not borne by policies declared unsound. In effect, a sound economic policy is another way of speaking about a "true" or "valid" economic policy with an implicit comparative judgment intended concerning other proposed policies.

Other passages in Mr. Buckley's book confirm the suspicion that he cannot abide by his own distinction. He often speaks about the necessity of embracing and propagating values "after thoughtful examination" of their alternatives. He even asks the question whether a "wrong value" can be embraced and he answers: "Unquestionably. Wrong values have been embraced in the past by men of profound vision and noble intent. It will happen again. But hazard of error cannot be used as an argument against thoughtful action." (p. 177.)

How can a value be wrong unless there is some method of determining its wrongness or rightness aside from the fact that we desire it? How can there be "hazard of error" unless there is also a "probability of truth"? And if an action or examination is thoughtful, surely it must be because such examination or action proceeds according to some objective discipline which makes it possible for us to say that an action or examination is more or less thoughtful. And in every such case the degree of thoughtfulness will depend upon the variety, intensity, and comprehensiveness of our reference to the facts in the case.

It is not surprising therefore to find Mr. Buckley arguing that the value orthodoxies he is concerned to have the colleges inculcate in students are actually "truer" than their alternatives. Of Christianity as well as of individualism, he asserts that "we are entitled to say" of them that they are "if not truth, the nearest thing we have to truth, no closer thing to truth in the field of social relations having appeared on the horizon." (p. 151.) But if this is so, why cannot that conclusion be established in the procedure of fair and open inquiry, similar to the type of inquiry we pursue in other fields? Why is inculcation, indoctrination, or a fixed value orthodoxy necessary? There is hardly a scientific discipline in which the leading practitioners will claim for the very latest discovery the accolade of "the truth." They are much more likely to say that it is the nearest they can come, for the moment, to truth. The approximation is sufficient, particularly when we have a method of making our claims *more* approximate.

Indeed, Mr. Buckley at times writes as if he himself did not believe in inculcation and indoctrination of values but in reflective choice of values. "I cannot sufficiently stress the responsibility of the faculty to insist upon student examination of other and even unfriendly creeds . . ." (p. 180). And further: "Ultimately, of course, the student must decide for himself. If he chooses to repudiate the values of his instructor, he is free— and ought to be free—to do so. No coercion of any sort whether through low examination grades, ridicule, or academic bullying, would be tolerable. The teacher must rest his case after he has done his best to show why one value is better than another. He can do no more. The institution can do no more. Neither should try to do more. Both have discharged their responsibilities to steer the student toward the truth as they see it." (p. 181.)

So long as it is not demanded of teachers that they have only one point of view, each teacher can and should proceed as Mr. Buckley describes. He need not be neutral. He may take a stand on any issue relevant to his subject, no matter how controversial. All that is required of him is that he consider with scholarly objectivity alternatives to his own position, and that he try to show the rational and evidential grounds on the basis of which he espouses any particular policy.

The Case for Academic Freedom

The teacher then finds his freedom within the compulsions of the evidence, and especially of the method by which the evidence is gathered, weighed and interpreted. In the light of his own admissions and abandonment of the sharp dichotomy between fact and policy, Mr. Buckley is profoundly mistaken in his assertion that the only kind of academic freedom which is not a superstition is "the freedom of men and women to supervise the educational activities and aims of the schools they oversee and support." The truth may not be the only, or the most powerful, authority in the world: but in respect to academic life *the quest for truth* is the only appropriate authority. Most of Mr. Buckley's own theories would be proscribed under the system of academic freedom he defends.

Mr. Buckley believes that the schools and colleges in a democracy must bar from teaching the Plato of the *Republic* and the Santayana of *Dominion and Powers* as well as the Hitlers and Stalins, since they are totalitarians in their social thought. But there is another conception of academic freedom in a democracy which would accept the challenge of any idea critical of, or incompatible with, the belief in democracy, provided certain minimum intellectual conditions are met. To this we shall presently turn.

Philosophically more basic to Mr. Buckley's position is the view that, since in a democracy each citizen has the right to choose his political course, therefore every man is as competent an authority as any other on what is good, better or best in a definite situation. This is comparable to saying that because every man has a right to eat what he pleases, therefore he is as good an authority on food values as any other, and that it is undemocratic to recognize experts. Of course we have nowhere near the same knowledge about "human values" as we have about food values, but some knowledge of the former exists and not all human beings share it equally. Everybody has a right to discuss foreign policy, and help indirectly in determining what our foreign policy should be. But not everybody is equally versed in the complex of historical, economic, ethnic and political facts, knowledge of which is so important for the formulation of a wise foreign policy.

From the acknowledgment that there are experts, it does not follow that we should permit ourselves to be ruled by experts. But because we should not permit ourselves to be ruled by experts, it does not follow that there are no experts, or that we are all equally expert, or that we are educationally justified in telling the expert "where to get off," or what he is to teach. Mr. Buckley, and not only he, acts as if our only alternative was a choice between the Platonic conception of democracy—undisciplined, unintelligent, decisions by the mob—and the Platonic conception of the just society—the rule of the expert, of those who not only know better than we about the ways of things, nations and men but profess to know what our interests are better than we know ourselves.

IV

Since a democratic community is dedicated to the value of freedom, and since it is justified in expecting its institutions of learning to strengthen the sense of the value of freedom in its citizens, why should it tolerate among its teachers those who reach conclusions that are favorable to dictatorship and despotism? Why should it give freedom and economic security, ultimately at the cost of the public purse, to individuals who hold and defend Fascist or Communist *ideas* or *heresies?* (This question must not be confused with one about the advisability of the employment of *members* of Fascist and Communist organizations.)

The answer to this is that the democratic commitment to the value of freedom is not irrational or arbitrary but grounded in a critical evaluation of the consequences of alternative values especially those embodied in the authoritarian way of life. Another way of saying this is that the commitment of democracy is not merely to freedom, but to the method of *intelligence* in social and political affairs. It is confident that in the honest give

The Case for Academic Freedom

and take of discussion and inquiry, the validity of democratic values as compared with conflicting values will sustain itself. The assumption behind the tolerance extended to the teacher who expresses Fascist or Communist views is that he is an *honest* inquirer, that he, too, is in quest of the truth, and that he is not an indoctrinator of precommitted beliefs which he has pledged himself to put over, by fair means or foul, in the classroom, *i.e.,* that he is not a member of a Fascist or Communist organization. This assumption may be hard to make but there is reason to believe it is sometimes true. Where it is not true, then the teacher has disqualified himself in virtue of his intellectual dishonesty, not in virtue of his conclusions. But where it is true, we may learn from his criticisms of democracy, just as he may learn from the criticisms of his colleagues. What is decisive is not the fact that any individual teacher expresses agreement with a Fascist or Communist conclusion but how he reaches it, the quality of his thinking, the nature of the evidence he presents. We shall later on consider some of the practical problems which flow from the distinctions we are making between a member of the Communist Party and one who defends Communist ideas.

What I am concerned with at the moment is to justify the educational tolerance which democracy extends to its own intellectually honest critics, even to those who would deny tolerance to democrats. This tolerance testifies not to the weakness but the strength of its faith. I do not believe I can improve upon the way I stated this point in a previous writing, and I take the liberty of quoting some relevant paragraphs:

> The belief that faith in democracy can be instilled by the same methods as faith in other forms of society overlooks the distinctive character of the democratic faith. This lies in its assumption that the reasonableness of the democratic way of life may be established by open, critical inquiry of its consequences. The initial loyalty to democracy, like the initial loyalty to anything else, arises from social atmosphere and practice. *Rational* loyalty results from a

critical consideration of the claims, achievements and shortcomings of democracy compared with those of its rivals. The
practice of democracy comes first in the order of time; the
justification of democracy comes first in the order of logic.
By training its students to think critically, a democracy
gives them the power and the right to evaluate democracy,
confident that its claims will withstand the analysis—that
initial loyalties will become transformed into rational loyalties. No other form of society dares to chance this.

This means that ultimately a democracy is committed to
facing the truth about itself. Preaching and edification have
their holiday uses but they do not inspire initial loyalty—
only practice does—nor do they sustain loyalty against critical
doubts, for they present no rational grounds. It is in the very
process of public, critical thinking that the democratic
community and scientific community meet. Whoever introduces a breach in this process offends against both. Scientific skepticism in any specific situation flowers from a seed
which is love of truth. A democracy is the only society
which in principle believes that men can accept the truth in
every realm of thought, and live with it.

Education for Modern Man, p. 118-9. New York, 1946.

V

This volume consists of variations on the theme that a democracy must defend the right of heresy even as it moves to expose
and destroy conspiracy. Educational conspiracy I shall discuss
at length in subsequent chapters. Nothing I say here should be
interpreted as advocacy of limitation upon the right to educational heresy. I find that most people's attitude towards heresy
depends upon the nature of the heresy, and who holds it. Some
will call for immediate action against a teacher who concludes
that there are inherent racial differences, and the Negroes or
Chinese are inherently inferior to the Caucasian race, but will
defend the right of a teacher to assert that the Soviet Union,
despite its concentration camps and periodic purges, is a "higher"
type of democracy than the capitalist democracies of the West.

The Case for Academic Freedom

Others will agitate for the expulsion of teachers who reach conclusions similar to the sentiments expressed by the teacher friendly to the Soviet regime but will defend the right of a teacher to assert that Hitler, despite *his* concentration camps and wide practice of genocide, was acting as the savior of Western civilization against the Bolshevik tide. Each group has its own pet aversion and reverses its judgment from issue to issue, or person to person.

Here I am making a plea for tolerance, *within the limits of competence,* of all heresies.

This open house to heresy must not be interpreted to mean that a university or college is a community of the fey, the eccentric, or slightly mad vying with each other in exhibitionistic glee to see who can believe more impossible things or make the more outrageous remarks. The ordinary canons of selection weed out the obsessed incompetents who father most of the panaceas and cure-all world machines. The normal run of mediocrity fears the glare of attention which focuses upon the heretic. The less it achieves, the more it congratulates itself that its ideas are sane and safe. Indeed, it is arguable that we suffer more from a dearth of heretics, taking them as an unsorted, undifferentiated mass, than from a plethora of them.

The academic community in one essential respect is, or should be, like the scientific community. It should be open to anyone to make a contribution. But he must play according to the rules— the laws of confirmation and evidence in the one case, and the principles of intellectual integrity in the other. A man with a private sense of evidence does not belong in a scientific community; a man who has sworn or pledged himself to follow a party line through thick and thin and insofar abandoned his freedom to think, to choose and act, does not belong in the academic community. It is not only as inquirers into truth that such men forfeit their privileges as members of the academic community but as teachers, too. This brings us to a consideration of educational conspiracy.

Chapter 9

COMMUNISM AND ACADEMIC FREEDOM

The defence of academic freedom for even the extremest kind of heresy by those who have been certified as competent by their professional peers or betters rests on the assumption that the teacher's primary loyalty is to the ethics and logic of reasoned inquiry or to those processes which constitute intellectual freedom. In consequence, any doctrinal impositions or organizational controls which dictate what he should do in the classroom or lay down doctrinal limits beyond which he cannot go in investigation, affect him both as a scholar and teacher and citizen of a democratic community.

As a scholar, he loses professional standing in the intellectual community if it is suspected that his findings must fit the predetermined conclusions and prejudices of those whose loyalties are not to the objective methods of seeking the truth. As a teacher he cannot engage in the honest presentation and reasoned investigation of all relevant *alternatives* to the theories and policies he is considering. He runs the risk of forfeiting the respect of his students, who look to him for candid evaluation and intellectual stimulus, if they believe that he is time-serving or prudent beyond the call of scientific evidence or a mere instrument of another's will. As a citizen he is undermining the faith and hope of a democratic community in the processes of an education which aims to develop free minds and free men on the basis of the truth about nature, society, and the human spirit. "If a nation expects to be ignorant and free in a state of civilization," wrote Jefferson, "it expects what never was and what never will be."

The teacher is therefore in a position of threefold trust from which we can derive the duties and responsibilities that are correlative with the rights of academic freedom. No teacher can violate them under the plea or pretext that he is exercising his freedom. For their violation constitutes an abrogation of academic freedom. Until recently the notion that members of a university faculty could themselves be guilty of violating the principles of academic freedom, and therefore of conduct unbecoming a teacher, would have been dismissed as a wild paradox. Attacks on academic freedom until our own time came from groups which sought to set limits to instruction and research only from the outside. The emergence of a group which organized individuals *within* the university to implement external control is a new historical phenomenon in American education bound up with the rise of modern totalitarianism. It was not recognized by the academic community generally until the University of Washington case exploded into the headlines with the news that three members of the faculty, two of whom were proved members of the Communist Party, had been dismissed on the grounds that they had been guilty of a violation of the principles of academic freedom.

Very few persons in the academic community of the thirties realized that the operations of modern totalitarianism posed problems about academic freedom that could not be so easily settled as the case, say, of selfish dairy interests moving to discipline a professor in an agricultural college who proclaimed that oleomargarine is as nutritious as butter. Among them were members of the Graduate Faculty of the New School for Social Research, made up largely of refugees from Nazi Germany, who declared

OUR SCHOOL AND THE WORLD

Issued by the New York University Unit of the Communist Party of the United States

Vol. I, No. 2   NOVEMBER, 1938

p. 3

Communist Literature for the Professor

From time to time American readers are confronted with startling announcements in the press that Communist aims, organizations, and propaganda agencies have been "revealed" or "discovered"— presumably in dark and secret places. Yet the Communist Party is not a conspiratorial club; it works in full view of the public. Anyone can buy its literature in open, legal shops and newsstands. It possesses a number of press organs which report on all its activities. The same literature which it constantly urges its members to read and study is available to the public. Some of it is presented in popular and simple form; other publications of a more theoretical and scholarly nature contribute information which non-Communist intellectuals find valuable as source material or criticism.

The Communist is such an organ. It is a magazine of the theory and practice of Marxism-Leninism, and is published monthly by the Communist Party of the U.S.A. Members of the National Committee, including Earl Browder, are its editors. It interprets the important political, economic and cultural developments in the United States in relation to the progressive forces which can influence these movements towards the construction of a better world. One of the features of *The Communist* is the "Review of the Month," a penetrating analysis of activities in our national life which are the concern of every American. Recently the "Review" has considered such topics as "Prospects for Temporary Business Improvement—How to Insure Its Realization and Prevent Subsequent Slump; Housing, Railroads, Banking; How to Make the New Deal Work Better; Farmers and Middle Classes."

William Z. Foster's article in the August *Communist* on "The American Federation of Labor and Trade Union Progress" is a clear description of the role of the Communist Party in the trade unions. Here is source material which no teacher interested in the development of American civilization can afford to miss. The man of judgment, abhorring the slanderous sensationalism of the Dies Committee and eager to discover the truth at first hand, would do well to turn to the sober, responsible discussions of the Party's leading members. An article in the September issue discusses the role of the professional in the Communist Party and answers the question why an increasing number of teachers, doctors, actors and lawyers are joining the ranks of the Communist Party to share its struggles for peace and democracy.

Communist cell paper at New York University cites authoritative literature on party's theory and practice

THE CITY COLLEGE TEACHER and WORKER

"The freest government cannot long endure when the tendency of the law is to create a rapid accumulation of property in the hands of a few, and to render the masses poor and dependent."—DANIEL WEBSTER.

PRICE: 5c

"Labor is prior to and independent of capital. Capital is only the fruit of labor, could never have existed if labor had not first existed. Labor is the superior of capital, and deserves much the higher consideration." ABRAHAM LINCOLN.

ISSUED MONTHLY BY THE COMMUNIST PARTY UNIT OF THE CITY COLLEGE

Vol. 1, No. 7   SEPTEMBER, 1935

7th CONGRESS STIRS WORLD

Dimitroff, New C. I. Chairman, Calls for United Anti-Facist Front

Because the Seventh World Congress of the Communist International (C. I.) placed the question of the United Front against Fascism in the forefront of its deliberations and because it defined the struggle for the United Front as the chief and most urgent task of Communists, the ...

Setback Shows ISA Needs Teacher Unity, Mass Action

As Teacher & Worker predicted in June, the incorrect policies of the ISA Administration have led to a defeat. The new By-Laws of the Board of Higher Education, embodying new salary schedules, new requirements for appointment, advancement, and promotion are the climax to these policies, a climax which brings to a close a certain period in the history of ISA affairs. Three years of briefs, of accepting evasions and delays, of counting on the good-will of the Board, or of ...

COLUMBIAN STUDENTS STRIKE

(Special Cable to the New York Times)

BOGOTA, Colombia, Aug. 28.—The entire student body of the Medical College of the National University struck ...

Typical page from cell paper of Communist Party unit of City College, New York that in the interests of academic freedom "no member of the faculty can be a member of any political party or group which asserts the right to dictate in matters of science or scientific opinion." A few years ago the General Faculty of the New School, when it became a degree granting institution, incorporated the same provision with its own academic rules, so that it now reads:

> The New School knows that no man can teach well, nor should he be permitted to teach at all, unless he is prepared "to follow the truth of scholarship wherever it may lead." No inquiry is ever made as to whether a lecturer's private views are conservative, liberal, or radical; orthodox or agnostic; views of the aristocrat or commoner. Jealously safeguarding this precious principle, the New School stoutly affirms that a member of any political party or group which asserts the right to dictate in matters of science or scientific opinion is not free to teach the truth and thereby is disqualified as a teacher.

But all this, and its significance, remained unnoticed until the University of Washington case broke. Since then the issue has become focal in American higher education and remains unresolved.

To the discussion of this issue I now turn.

I

Should members of the Communist Party, or those under its discipline, even if they do not carry membership cards, be employed in the American school system? This is a complex question since we shall have to consider certain distinctions between the public schools, elementary and high, the colleges and the universities. We shall have to consider the distinction between employing and retaining, "hiring" and "firing." We shall finally have to consider the distinction between teaching and research. All of these subsidiary questions will be examined but I wish first to present some material which bears on what is true for all members of the Communist Party, especially in view of the character of the arguments made that membership in the Communist Party should be considered as no more relevant than membership in any other political party. For if these arguments were sound, they would support the same policy of occupational toleration of members of the Communist Party in respect to appointment and dismissal, both in elementary schools and in universities.

It does not follow, however, that a policy of exclusion justified in *making* appointments is justified in *terminating* them; nor that a policy justified for the lower schools, is also justified for the universities; and that what will be an acceptable conclusion for teachers will hold for research workers.

Finally, even if we reach the conclusion that members of the Communist Party are unfit to teach at any time and at any level, we shall have to consider the possibility that any attempt to bar them may be more likely to imperil the integrity of the educational process than suffering them to carry on as usual. But we must not confuse these issues. There are some who say with a bluff coarseness which begs all the questions: "It is not necessary to burn down the barn to destroy the rats," and therefore conclude that there is no *other* way of ridding ourselves of them. They sometimes end up by maintaining that there are only love birds in the barn.

The first point I wish to make is that fitness or unfitness to teach is a question that must be decided primarily on educational rather than political grounds. The introduction of the political angle, *before* the exact nature of the Communist Party is understood, is apt to create confusion. For some have argued from the fact that the Communist Party is a legal party, the inadmissibility of making membership within it a bar to the rights enjoyed by all citizens. This is correct in so far as political rights are concerned; the right to vote, nominate and elect candidates, and so on, but it does not hold for non-political privileges. To teach is a privilege won by indications given of intellectual capacity and integrity. It is neither a civic nor a political right. Although an individual has a political right to join or organize a party, the nature and activities of such a party may render him unfit for certain types of activity or employment. If say during Prohibition days a political party had been formed whose members were pledged to fanatical advocacy of the violation of the Prohibition laws, and not merely their abolition, it is not likely that any member of such a party, who was refused employment in the enforcement authority, would have complained that his *civil* rights were being violated.

Once we concentrate on the issue of professional competence, of professional ethics and responsibility, it is not difficult to reach an answer to our first question. A sober evaluation of the evidence will reveal that in theory and practice members of the Communist Party are committed to grave and systematic violation of their three-fold educational trust. For their responsibility to help their students to mature intellectually and emotionally, for their responsibility to their colleagues in the quest for truth, and for their responsibility to the democratic community to develop free men, they have substituted a blind and partisan loyalty to the objectives of the Communist Party. Their act of membership in the Communist Party is comparable to the action of a physician who has banded himself together with others for the express violation of his Hippocratic oath. Indeed, the concluding sentence of the public pledge, now formally discontinued for reasons of safety, which the member inducted into the Communist Party used to take reads: "I pledge myself to remain at all times a vigilant and firm defender of the Leninist line of the party, the only line that insures the triumph of Soviet Power in the United States." (*Daily Worker*, April 2, 1936.)

The evidence of the Communist Party teacher's professional unfitness falls under three heads: (a) teaching (b) other campus activities (c) research.

Communism and Academic Freedom

II

Hardly anything is more damaging to the cause of the Communist teacher in the eyes of parents and educators than the *official* instructions he receives from the Communist Party on how to behave in the classroom. I have italicized *official* instructions because members of the Communist Party themselves in the literature they distribute to their colleagues ask us not to judge the Communist Party by what others say about it but what it says about itself. We should, of course, do both.

Here are some instructions from the official organ of the Communist Party: (*The Communist,* May 1937).

> Party and Y.C.L. (Young Communist League) fractions set up within classes and departments must supplement and combat by means of discussions, brochures, etc., bourgeois omissions and distortions in the regular curriculum . . . *Marxist-Leninist analysis must be injected into every class.*
> *Communist teachers must take advantage of their positions, without exposing themselves,* to give their students to the best of their ability workingclass education.
> To enable the teachers in the party to do the latter, the party must take careful steps to see that all teacher comrades are given thorough education in the teaching of Marxism-Leninism. Only when teachers have really mastered Marxism-Leninism will they be able skillfully to inject it into their teaching *at the least risk of exposure* and at the same time conduct struggles around the schools in a truly Bolshevik manner. (My italics.)

Two things are significant here. The first is the injunction to cooperate with Communist Party fractions among students in order—I am still quoting from official sources—"to guide and direct that spirit of rebelliousness which already exists." The practice, many years ago, was to organize Communist students and teachers in the same cells. It was the rare student whose self esteem was not flattered, first by his teacher's special interest in him, and then by his sense of equal status as a "professional revolutionist." But since this led to exposure when students dropped out, teachers and students were organized into separate fractions which met only through carefully selected committees. The teacher would usually cultivate and sometimes recruit the student but the formal act of induction was carried out by the student Communist group properly briefed.

The second noteworthy thing is strikingly apparent in the sentences I have italicized. The Communist Party teachers are fearful of exposure. They are quite aware that their practices violate accepted notions of academic freedom and responsibility. They are playing outside the rules of the game, prepared, according to the lessons driven home by Lenin, to use deceit and stratagem, outright lies or lying evasions, to achieve their ends.

This may be the official doctrine. But how do we know that members of the Communist Party are aware of it? Professor Kirkland, a former President of the American Association of University Professors, in an article in the *Key Reporter* * of the Phi Beta Kappa asserts that these and similar instructions were "addressed to an inner circle." The truth is that they were addressed to the general membership in the teaching profession. *They have never been modified, repudiated, or withdrawn;* they are implicitly reaffirmed in the continuing instructions as to how to apply Marxism-Leninism-Stalinism in the party study groups which all recruits must attend. The new recruit will be told again and again what was declared in one of the Resolutions of the Ninth Convention of the Communist Party of the U.S.A. "In order to carry through their work effectively . . . all Communists must *at all times* take a position *on every question* that is in line with the policies of the Party. . . ." **

If members of the Communist Party are aware of their instructions how do we know that they carry them out or attempt

---

* Vol. XV, No. 2, Spring 1950, p. 3.
** *Resolution of the Ninth Convention of the C. P. of the U. S. A.*, Workers Library Publishers, 1936, p. 63, my italics.

Communism and Academic Freedom

to carry them out? The answer to this question indicates the ways in which the Communist Party differs from other political parties. First, recruiting is selective. William Z. Foster, one time secretary of the Party, in an important article on "The Communist Party and the Professionals" describes the care with which members are selected and the criteria of the selections. "In drawing professionals into the Party care should be taken to select *only* those individuals who show by practical work that they definitely understand the Party line, are prepared to put it into effect, and *especially* display a thorough readiness to accept Party discipline" (*The Communist,* Sept. 1938, p. 808, my italics). Second, the statutes of membership define a party member as one who not only "accepts the party program, attends the regular meetings of the membership branch of his place of work" (in the case of the Communist Party teacher this is the school "cell") and "who is *active* in party work." Inactivity, unless it is a directed inactivity, *reculer pour mieux sauter,* as well as disagreement with the decisions of any party organization or committee are grounds for expulsion. Third, the Communist Party weeds its ranks carefully by purge and re-registration and other forms of control. As we have already seen, there exists a Central Control Commission whose task it is to check on all members.

It should now be clear that the Communist Party is not an ordinary political party. It is not a tea-drinking, merely dues-paying society. It is in reality a para-military organization. Not everyone who applies for membership is selected. Not everyone is retained after he is selected. Inactive members are excluded. "Bad" Communists are excluded. There is an overwhelming presumption of an empirical kind that a member in *continued* good standing is a good Communist—unless he is an F.B.I. undercover agent who can survive only by exemplary activity. The Communist Party member may be efficient or inefficient, clever or inept, but to remain in the party he must convince it that he is at work on his Communist tasks. The longer he is in the Party the greater the likelihood that his work has been satisfactory to the

Heresy, Yes—Conspiracy, No

Party in carrying out its directives. There is every reason to have more confidence in the ability of the Communist Party to detect a "bad" Communist, in virtue of its mechanisms of control, than in the ability of outsiders.

Is there any other evidence that members of the Communist Party indoctrinate? The evidence, for reasons which will soon be discussed, rarely comes from the students themselves. We have some testimony from former members of the Communist Party who assert that the question of classroom indoctrination is one of the standing problems of the Communist Party unit. One such meeting is described in the following transcript of a hearing before the Rapp-Coudert Committee.

> Q. Do you remember the discussion, the nature of the discussion? A. I remember highlights of it, of course.
>
> Q. Will you state them? A. The main thing I recall is that various people got up to testify, you might call it, as to their effectiveness and success; and one of these was my colleague, Ingram Bander, and he was quite proud of his success as a Communist teacher, and recited an experience he had just had, apparently a week or so before this meeting.
>
> He called upon the students to write on a little slip of paper criticisms of his course. This was a course in Modern European History, and he was elated, he told us—
>
> Q. Delighted? A. Delighted and elated that some of these slips said, 'I wish Mr. Bander, that you would not use the words, 'dialectical materialism' so much, and the word 'proletariat' and the words 'Soviet Democracy,' and so on—a long list; and Mr. Bander told us that this proved to his satisfaction—that he had been eminently successful in implanting these ideas, or at least the ideas that these words signified in the minds of the students.
>
> Q. In other words, the complaint of the students to him that he was using these Communist terms and Communist terminology he took as a compliment to himself? A. He did, yes.
>
> Q. And as evidence of his skill as a teacher of communism or skill in indoctrinating? A. Right.

Communism and Academic Freedom

Q. What did the comrades think about that report? A. Well, what happened reminded me quite a bit of Mr. Mintus' experience in issuing a report which he thought was adequate. Mr. Bander was severely rebuked by all of the leading Communists, all of whom got up and—

Q. Let us see. Was that a cell meeting, or a unit meeting? A. A full meeting of the unit; not exactly a plenary session, because a plenary session was a term used only for meetings at the terminals of the term, the beginning and the end.

Q. But this was a full— A. Full unit meeting and the criticism that Mr. Schappes had, that Mr. Copstein had, that Mr. Shukotoff had, was that rather than being evidence of his excellence as a Communist teacher, this was evidence of his great lack of skill; that he had wearied the students; that he had been clumsy in giving these ideas to the students; and that he hadn't exercised the proper subtlety; that he hadn't woven his message into the very fabric of the course, you see. It was too glaring and too gross a method of propaganda.

Q. So Comrades Schappes and Shukotoff and Copstein— A. Several others, of course.

Q. They rebuked Comrade Bander? A. Everyone laughed and poor Bander felt quite embarrassed at this *faux pas*.

Q. They didn't rebuke him because he had used his position to indoctrinate the students? A. Oh, of course not.

Q. It was simply that his technique was clumsy? A. Yes, clumsy and futile.

Q. And that he should have done this without the students knowing it was being done? A. Of course.

Q. That was it? A. Of course, following that various models to follow were presented to Mr. Bander. He was advised how he could improve his technique." *

Other former members of the Communist Party have similarly testified.

* State of New York, Legislative Document (1942) No. 49, *Report of the Subcommittee of the Joint Legislative Committee to Investigate Procedure and Methods of Allocating State Moneys for Public School Purposes and Subversive Activities*, pp. 265-267. *The witness was Mr. William Canning.*

Heresy, Yes—Conspiracy, No

Testimony of this sort is dismissed by some liberals as invalid. For example, Dean L. H. Chamberlain flatly characterizes it, "as largely derived and hearsay in character." Although the witness gave concrete examples of how indoctrination could be carried on, "he could not testify that he had actually seen it done because he had not attended the classes himself." * Dean Chamberlain must have a delicious sense of humor. The witness was a former Communist teacher who taught classes at C.C.N.Y. and it is not customary for teachers at that or other institutions to take one another's courses. He did testify that he himself indoctrinated but in the nature of the case can only describe the cell meeting's discussions of the proper techniques of indoctrination. The variety of the subjects and techniques discussed shows how unplausible it is, to anyone acquainted with communist theory and practice, that the witness was inventing his facts. Given the official instructions of the Communist Party to indoctrinate, and the self-incriminating testimony of some Communists, and their report of meetings of this kind with other Communists who lie about their membership, it is certainly overwhelmingly probable that members of the Communist Party attempted to indoctrinate whenever they could do so. Dean Chamberlain, however, asserts in a rather unusual usage of the term that all this is *"a priori"* (p. 127). He demands evidence in each case that the indoctrination was actually carried out in the classroom.

But what would constitute such evidence?

This raises a key point which invariably comes to the fore in every discussion of the place of Communist Party teachers in the schools. Someone is sure to ask: Why not judge members of the Communist Party by their performance in class? To be sure, they may be under official instructions "to take advantage of their position" to indoctrinate, but this is tantamount only to a declaration of intent. The intent to do something wrong, and the commission of the wrong, are two different things.

* L. H. Chamberlain, *Loyalty and Legislative Action,* Cornell University Press, 1951, p. 123.

186

Communism and Academic Freedom

It may be granted that there is a distinction between the intent to perform an action, and its actual performance, but this is relevant in distinguishing between criminal or legal guilt and moral guilt. Intent to commit a wrong may be sufficient evidence of moral guilt which would justify us in denying an individual the vocational opportunity to carry it out.

Let us examine a few situations in which common sense distinctions of this character are easily recognized. An individual is employed in a position where financial probity is a qualification. It is subsequently discovered that he is waiting for an appropriate moment to steal. His intent is not legally punishable. But would we not be justified in asking him to work elsewhere?

Even where no legal questions arise, the same distinction is recognized. I sit down to play a game of cards with an individual. After some time I discover that he has come prepared to cheat, although I have not detected him in the act of cheating. If I refuse to play with him on the ground that he has declared his intent to cheat in virtue of the props he has brought with him or the cards secreted on his person, am I doing him an injustice?

Consider, finally, in order to bring home the force of the argument as it concerns Communist Party members in schools, an analogous situation which involves a position of personal trust instead of public trust. I engage someone to work for me in my home. I discover subsequently that this individual is a present and active member of a group whose officially expressed policy is to take advantage of his position in my home to further some cause, either by ransacking my private papers, spreading slander, indoctrinating my children or by some other kind of dishonest or malicious conduct. After confirming the fact of his membership in such a group, I discharge the individual from my employment. Whereupon he insists that I have judged him guilty by association, that I have no moral right to discharge him because an intention is not an action, because he has not been detected in *flagrante delicto*, because his outside activities are irrelevant to the duties he has been employed to fill.

187

Heresy, Yes — Conspiracy, No

The obvious and commonsensical retort to such a plea is this: why should I wait until you have done your damage before protecting myself? Why should I take all the time and trouble involved in watching you? Your act of voluntary membership in a group which officially instructs you to betray your trust is an indication of professional unfitness to carry out this trust.

As we have seen, teaching the young is a *public* trust—a great public trust. It is not because of his political ideas but because of his membership in an organization which instructs him to violate his trust that the Communist is guilty of *conduct* unbecoming a teacher. In view of the documentary evidence of the Communist Party instructions on this and similar subjects, any member who professed unawareness of its stand would be guilty of *ignorance* unbecoming a teacher. Or, it is more likely, he would be resorting to the typical Communist strategy of deceit.

Let us assume, however, that the above considerations are not decisive, and that we actually tried to detect whether or not a teacher who is a member of the Communist Party, or is suspected of being one, is carrying out his instructions to indoctrinate in class.

How shall we find out? Shall we observe him in class? No one indoctrinates when he is under observation. Here we reach a very crucial point and one difficult for educational laymen to grasp. Episodic inspection in the classroom can enable one to tell something about the pedagogic *techniques* of the teacher, his skill in motivating and keeping attention, the adequacy of his use of available teaching materials, his ability to evoke class participation, the organization of his subject matter, and similar things. But the *content* of his teaching, its direction, emphasis, selective bias, and cumulative force as it is slowly built up over a period of time, cannot be observed by periodic inspection. An individual may be a skillful teacher technically speaking and yet be all the worse a propagandist in virtue of the very expertness of his skills. No matter how blatantly one-sided a certain presen-

Communism and Academic Freedom

tation may appear to be, the teacher can always say, *because sometimes it is actually true,* that he is building up a position in order subsequently to refute it or that he is giving the position in the terms of its own advocate so that students can more readily understand it.

Our conclusion is that, except in its crudest forms, indoctrination in the classroom can rarely be detected save by a critically trained observer who is almost *continuously* present. This is not only undesirable but for all practical purposes impossible. The difficulty is compounded by the fact that although he knows he is doing what the ethics of the profession forbids and therefore takes appropriate precautions not to be caught, he is subjectively convinced that his action is justified by his higher loyalty to the Communist cause, and that his very partisanship is closer to the truth than the objectivity and impartiality of allegedly classless scientific inquiry. What is a little deceit in the interest of *the* truth—and humanity, too? To a Communist this is a rhetorical question.

If we cannot detect a teacher engaged in skillful indoctrination by classroom visits, can't we determine whether he is indoctrinating by questioning his students from time to time and putting them on guard on what to observe? Even if we could rely on students to do this, it would be a sad day in the history of American education if we used students in this way or encouraged them to stoop to the techniques of a police state. Far better to leave Communist Party teachers to do as they please than to degrade their students by impressing them into the kind of service made so notorious in countries behind the Iron Curtain. My own view is that what goes on in the classroom of the qualified teacher should be considered privileged, particularly expression of opinion by students as they grope their way to understanding and self-consciousness in exchanges with the teacher and other students.

But as a matter of fact, even if we wished to do so, we could not rely on students to detect and report indoctrination—especially skillful indoctrination. Students who have been indoctri-

189

nated are not aware they are indoctrinated. Together with their teacher, they are convinced that they have been taught the truth. Where the indoctrination has not taken, as in the case that Mr. Canning reported, students may still not recognize that an intellectually dishonest attempt to win them over to a certain point of view has been made. The teacher believes one thing, they believe another—so it appears to them. It is easy to flatter students about their perceptiveness but they are disadvantaged in the hands of an unscrupulous and intelligent teacher. And even in the cases where students know or suspect what is going on in the classroom of an indoctrinating teacher, they are as a rule naturally and rightfully loath to carry tales. Students may gripe but they shrink from publicly testifying against a teacher if this means imperilling his or her job. The few sophisticated socialist or liberal students who are both aware and indignant when a Communist Party teacher is indoctrinating would hesitate, even if they felt minded to make public protest, to submit themselves to the taunts, jeers and personal abuse to which they would be subjected even by non-Communists.

Dean Chamberlain's demand that the students testify to indoctrination by members of the Communist Party before he will believe it, seems to show no familiarity with the mores which prevail among students or with the mechanisms of the youthful mind. The individual student does not like to be an informer particularly when he has no personal animus against the teacher. The way Dean Chamberlain uses the term "informer" suggests that he himself dislikes them and would tend to disbelieve or discount what they say in advance.

Nor can any experienced teacher be taken in by the fact that some individuals of a class taught by a teacher discovered to be a member of the Communist Party will come forward to testify that he did not corrupt or indoctrinate *them*. No one can indoctrinate everybody, those who are indoctrinated are not recruited in class, and those who are recruited by a teacher will rarely testify against him, even when they have lapsed from the faith.

Communism and Academic Freedom

For all their pose of being hard-boiled, students are generous, even sentimental, and it would be a pity if they were otherwise. I have known students to write petitions in a body to retain a teacher in a course which privately they were not enthusiastic about. Let the rumor get around that any teacher, threatened with dismissal for any cause, except some criminal offence, has a dependent wife and child, and overnight most students will convince themselves that he was an able teacher. The popularity of a teacher among students is not a reliable index of his competence as a teacher; the unpopularity of a teacher is a much better index of his incompetence, for students who learn something from a severe taskmaster will not judge him as incompetent even if they regard him as an "old sourpuss." Unfavorable judgments are usually expressed anonymously, and therefore must be very gingerly interpreted but the main point is that such judgments are not very reliable in determining whether a teacher has been guilty of indoctrination because, as we have seen, a technically "good" teacher, who is a party member, may be also doing a very good job of Communist indoctrination.

Consequently, in view of the explicit instructions of the Communist Party to its members to indoctrinate, in the face of the self-incriminating character of the testimony of former Communists that they have indoctrinated and worked together with other members on the problem of how best to indoctrinate, and in the light of the easy conscience with which members of the Communist Party demonstrably lie about their activities, the fact that an individual student testifies that "X," a teacher identified as a member of the Communist Party, did not indoctrinate while he was in class, is hardly as decisive as Dean Chamberlain believes. At best such a student may have the status of a character witness whose testimony even if accepted on its face value would not enable us to tell whether *other* students had been indoctrinated in the past, or to predict whether still others would be indoctrinated in the future.

One of the most eloquent statements ever penned of the disintegrating consequences of attempt to check up on a teacher's loyalty or his fulfillment of his obligations in the classroom is contained in the dissenting opinion of Justice Douglas in the Feinberg Law—an ill-considered and unenforceable piece of legislation. Justice Douglas rings all the variations on the charge that the close supervision of teachers required by the Feinberg Law "inevitably turns the school system into a spying project."

And this is certainly something we must avoid. But then he adds:

"Of course the school systems of the country need not become cells for Communist activities; and the classrooms need not become forums for propagandizing the Marxist creed. But the guilt of the teacher should turn on overt acts."

In other words only if the member of the Communist Party is detected in the act of propagandizing for the Marxist creed should he be dismissed. Suppose we identify a teacher as a member of the Communist Party. Since we know what his instructions are it is reasonable to try to find out, on Justice Douglas' view, whether he is carrying them out. But how can we do this without resorting to the very techniques which Justice Douglas denounces in such unmeasured terms? By insisting that we judge members of the Communist Party by their performance in class, Justice Douglas is inviting the very activities he deplores. He has in effect justified turning the school system into a spying project in order to find evidence of overt or covert indoctrination in class.

For all of these reasons it seems to me incontestable that the best safeguard against indoctrination and related dishonorable practices is not prying supervision of teachers, subtle interrogation of students, foolish and needless imposition of loyalty oaths, but the recruiting of competent men and women sufficiently dedicated to the ideas of teaching and scholarship to recognize that such practices are incompatible with professional integrity. Once we have found such teachers we should have implicit faith in them and not swoop or hover over them to determine *what* they are teaching as distinct from *how* they are teaching, in the event that friendly visits to help improve instruction at the beginning of their careers is deemed necessary.

III

The second line of evidence bearing on the fitness of members of the Communist Party to teach is derived from activities outside the classroom, but on the premises of their place of employment. Their tasks are several: recruiting among colleagues and students for party and youth organizations; setting up "party fractions" within departments, and where administrative regulations make it possible, control of new appointments, influence on recommendations for promotions and salary increases and election of sympathetic chairman; the dissemination of party literature; and wherever it exists, the publication and distribution of the party-fraction newsletter or bulletin. All of these activities, leaving aside the special tasks of Communist Party teachers in science departments and laboratories, are directly or indirectly designed to convert students to communism or to influence their thinking along communist lines. As one of the most widely distributed party-bulletins expressed it: "We cannot afford to forget the words of Earl Browder, General Secretary of the Communist Party of the United States: 'Who wins the youth, wins the future of America.' " (*Teacher-Worker*, February 1938, Vol. IV, No. 5, p. 5).

No one who has not examined these anonymously issued campus shop papers can understand the ways in which members of the Communist Party operate and their morality on the job. These publications are variously named: *The Staff, Teacher and Worker, The Spark*—after Lenin's *Iskra*—, *Our School and the World*. They are put into the hands of colleagues and students either through first-class mail or, when this is too expensive, by furtive stuffing of lockers and post-office boxes. For purposes of mutal protection every member of the party fraction is required to do something for the paper; if not in the preparation of copy, then at least in folding and distribution. It is a genuine collective project. And it is financed out of the members' dues.

The purpose of these papers is not to rehash the political line of the party, which is available in the *Daily Worker,* but to apply it to campus issues, to consolidate the influence of the cell and win sympathizers, and to expose those members of the faculty or administration who are "enemies of the working class" or the Communist Party. In pursuit of the latter goal, there are no limits of scurrility to which these anonymous sheets will not go. Those who have run afoul for any reason of the Communist Party are libelled and slandered, branded as plagiarists and thieves, accused of diverting college property to their own use and padding payrolls. In one case indirect responsibility for death was charged to college authorities. And all this is coupled with the most opprobrious epithets from the communist litany of denunciation like "spy," "Fascist," "anti-semite." Rumor is printed as fact, and students are invited to send in anonymous reports.

Made without the cloak of anonymity, some of these charges would lay those responsible for them open to criminal prosecution. For they are not merely politically subversive but subversive of the basic decencies of any educational system. The enormity of this practice, however, from the educational point of view does not lie in the injustice done to individuals by these methods of character assassination but in the fact that, persisted in, it can destroy the morale of the staff, keep an institution in ferment, and make teaching and learning more difficult.

Before citing some evidence to justify my characterization of these shop papers, I wish to present a radically different description of them. The reader will then be in a better position to check on the validity of the account here presented. The different description is presented by Dean Chamberlain of Columbia College, and is fairly typical of one type of liberal thinking about Communist teachers in schools.

Communism and Academic Freedom

Writing of the *Teacher-Worker*, Dean Chamberlain says:

These papers have been termed vicious, scurrilous, libellous. The question arises: What constitutes subversion in a newspaper? Does its anonymous character automatically make it subversive? If the answer to this question is affirmative, nothing remains to be considered. If a periodical circulated anonymously contained only noncontroversial matters to which no one could take exception, would it still be classified as subversive because of the hidden identity of its author? If the answer in this case is negative, then the question of subversion apparently depends more upon what the paper says than upon its underground character. Let us apply this test to the *Teacher-Worker*.

From a careful and thorough sampling of the various issues of the *Teacher-Worker* throughout the more than four years of its publication, the following observations seem warranted: The tone of the paper was invariably critical, militantly opposed to capitalism, the vested interests, the college administration; in its effort to be the outspoken advocate of the teacher's interests, the paper was sometimes insolent; it frequently exaggerated and was not above twisting the facts in a particular situation for the sake of embellishing a good tale. On the other hand, it did not incite to violence; it did print corrections and retractions when individuals indicated that it had misrepresented them. Finally, the paper stated plainly on its masthead that it was published by the Communist unit on the campus and thus put its readers on notice as to the kind of paper it was. No one was compelled to read it; there was no compulsion to believe its contents. It is difficult to see how, under these circumstances, the paper could be taken seriously enough to be regarded as subversive.

op. cit. pp. 120-121, quoted with permission from the Cornell University Press.

I shall now cite some passages from the *Teacher-Worker* using initials instead of the full names of the persons mentioned.

Heresy, Yes—Conspiracy, No

H. an Anti-Semite

The B— of the Bronx is H.E.H., the notorious Tammany politician, whose change of religion facilitated his advance in the school system, and who is now under surveillance of the Commissioner of Accounts' office for possible fraud . . . (He once sent a circular notice to his high school department chairmen asking them not to hire Jewish teachers if they could help it).

Teacher-Worker, December 1937, p. 3.

H., New Prexy stooge . . . Apparently Prof. H. has decided to take the cue from his colleague Professor W., who by dint of loyalty to his President has risen to a professorship despite his limitations as a scholar in Mathematics . . . A certain W.S., a stooge of H., who as an alumnus illegally participated in Student Council activities has already reaped the harvest of his pro-administration stand. He has been appointed as a personnel director.

Ibid, March 1936, p. 4.

$20,000 (of College money) squandered by Dean M. He has attempted to have people spy on one another and on the students . . . To cap his record M. is a poorly concealed anti-Semite . . .

Ibid, October 1935, p. 1.

Teacher and Worker exposes P. as charlatan, Ruthless Exploiter . . . Dr. P. also stands indicted on many other charges. He has appropriated Prof. M's Personality Rating Scale, changed the name of the Scale to Index, and 'neglected' to mention in his publication of the scale that Index was Prof. M.'s Personality Rating Scale with Prof. M.'s name omitted. He has had mimeographed, on college supplies by college employees at the expense of the college, a great deal of material which he has been using, for his private practice . . . A perusal of some of Dr. P.'s contributions to the pseudo-psychological magazines such as *Modern Psychology* justifies the nomination of him by prominent scientific psychologists as Public Charlatan No. 1 . . .

Ibid, December 1935, p. 3.

196

Communism and Academic Freedom

. . . But Dr. N., Associate Librarian, who receives over $4,000 per year, also 'earns' $4.00 per hour in the evenings, for merely sitting in the office reading books, when he should be in the Circulation Library working. Or perhaps he gets paid for taking photographs of students at meetings and demonstrations? Perhaps if he does a good job as a boot-licker for President Robinson he may make his job good for the next 99 years.

Ibid, September 1935, p. 3.

The corrupt P. must go!

Ibid, January 1937, p. 4.

W., who won a startling increase in salary, at a time (odd coincidence!) when he showed great diligence in copying down student's names, at student demonstrations . . .

Ibid, March 1936, p. 5.

Prof. P. . . . we charge you with maintaining a blacklist and using the technique of blacklisting on students and staff members . . .

Ibid, April 1936, p. 5.

. . . We think the conclusion may fairly be drawn that anti-Semitism has been an important influence in shaping the growth and organization of the Biology Dept.

Ibid, February 1938, p. 4.

. . . But 'cutting costs' doesn't prevent I.M., who loves to call himself "Co-Director" of the Evening Session, from getting a nice fat salary for not doing a damned thing. As one of President Robinson's trained noodles, he merely struts around . . .

. . . according to the regulations, nobody in the Evening Session office is supposed to get less than 50¢ per hour. To overcome this difficulty, Professor G. himself fills out time-cards of his workers and credits them with fewer hours than they really worked with the result that the workers actually receive 35¢ per hour . . ."

from any anonymous letter, *Ibid*, April 1935, p. 3.

Heresy, Yes—Conspiracy, No

Passages of this kind appear in almost each issue. They are characteristic not only of the *Teacher and Worker* but of other shop papers.

The reader is now in a position to determine for himself whether these papers are as innocent as Dean Chamberlain seems to believe or whether they contain "vicious, scurrilous and libellous" material. One way of finding out is to substitute one's own name for the names cited in the passages above. Dean Chamberlain might very well ask himself whether if similar characterizations were made about *him,* and distributed anonymously to his colleagues and students at Columbia College, he would dismiss these vile slanders so airily. In extenuation of his refusal to condemn these papers he remarks that they printed "corrections and retractions when individuals indicated that it had misrepresented them." Certainly, it is hardly any satisfaction to an individual who has been anonymously slandered as a thief to have his statement printed that he is not a thief. All the more so because the obvious tactic of the Communist cell papers to build up circulation was to have its contemptible remarks taken notice of. The fact that no one was compelled to read or believe the contents of the papers hardly exonerates the writers or alters the fact that their statements were libellous, and anonymously such. Indeed, it is difficult to see what could be more educationally subversive than the consistent character assassination expressed through its purported facts and rumors.

Perhaps the most despicable of the practices of the Communist Party cell paper which left Dean Chamberlain's moral withers unwrung was its publication of anonymous criminal charges— diversion of city property—against specifically named persons, even when such charges were admittedly based on "gossip" and "rumor."

The following item is taken from an anonymous letter (December 1935, p. 4.) :

I offer you the following items of gossip which you may be able to check up. The Hygiene Department once ordered a truck. One of the limousines [dating] from Walker's administration was assigned to be renovated with a truck body. But Prexy got hold of it instead because his own car was pretty well shot. The car is now washed and serviced by the workers in the Tech School. Prexy used a Tech School carpenter to make fancy furniture for his own house. And [he] changed an order for an angle-bending machine to get a new refrigerator for his private use.

Dean S . . . uses City College manual workers for private construction work. I understand that he doesn't pay them much if at all.

The following Editorial Comment appeared immediately after the letter:

> *Teacher and Worker* has found itself unable to investigate these rumors. It is hoped, however, that making them public will discourage the widespread practice at the College of impressing manual workers such as mechanics, cleaners, etc., into the private (and unpaid) service of the 'higher-ups.'

The editors unable to investigate what they recognize as "rumors" nonetheless assume the general truth of the rumors! Whenever they wished to print a slander they could easily cite "rumor" as authority even if *they* were the source of the rumor. Rumor was even cited as authority for "facts." In an earlier issue, we read *"Rumor now has it* that at least three men, possibly four, are involved in this case (History Department dismissals) . . . *According to the present rumor* . . . the explanation seems rather peculiar. In any event, *these facts, as rumor now has them,* point more definitely to a policy of rotation than *the fact* we cited in our leaflet." (March 1935, p. 4, my italics) In the light of Dean Chamberlain's remarks about the *Teacher and Worker,* one must reluctantly conclude either that his research was incomplete (far from "thorough" and "careful"), or that like some other liberals he applies different and lower moral standards to Communists than to other teachers.

Heresy, Yes—Conspiracy, No

The situation is still graver if Dean Chamberlain bases his remarks on the politically subversive character of the *Teacher and Worker*. Dean Chamberlain cites a relatively innocuous passage which compares the Soviet students' educational advantages with our own. He refers to it as an extreme example with the result that the reader naturally smiles and wonders what's all the "subversive" stuff about. Unfortunately Dean Chamberlain does not cite the actually subversive passages from the *Teacher and Worker,* passages whose presence is as plain as a pikestaff to anyone who actually has read through its issues. Even if he missed them in the *Teacher and Worker,* Dean Chamberlain could hardly have missed them in the very Report of the *Rapp-Coudert Committee* from which he takes the innocuous passage.

Here is the passage which Dean Chamberlain quotes as an extreme illustration of the allegedly subversive character of the *Teacher and Worker:*

> How dare Robinson slander the Soviet Union, where every student is paid a salary as a "worker in training," and is sure of a position when he is graduated! The Soviet plans for 1936 call for more than 4,000 new schools and a 20 per cent increase of students in pedagogical schools. Why can we not "plan" for obviously necessary expansion here at City College? Is it not because the only planning done here is to increase the flow of profits to the bankers? How else was our City budget planned? And all of Robinson's planning now is how to fit the College budget to the banker's requirements, not to educational ones. Such is free higher education under capitalism.
>
> *Teacher-Worker,* March 1936, Vol. I, No. 12, p. 4.

Here are the subversive passages which Dean Chamberlain seems to have overlooked:

> We cannot be 'against class war,' we can merely take one side or the other *in* it. There is one sense in which one can, however, be intelligently against the class war, but it is not the pacifist sense. It is the Communist sense of using the

class war to destroy capitalist power, to transfer it to the proletariat, which, as Soviet Russia is showing can in a relatively short time wipe out class distinctions and conflicts. The Communisty Party, therefore, believes in fighting imperialist war before it begins; if it begins (and unless the anti-war forces are strong enough it will begin) then the Communist Party will organize opposition against the American capitalist class and its state in the form of strikes, demonstrations, general strikes and revolutionary work within the armed forces. *The Communist Party will strive to lead the American masses to battle against the American capitalists, who sent them to war to turn the imperialist war into a civil war and a proletarian victory.*

April 1935, p. 2, last italics mine.

And again:

"Further, we believe that in the struggle to preserve democracy under capitalism through trade union struggle, through the establishment of a People's Party our fellow Americans will learn that the only way out for them is the Communist way, *the establishment of socialism through the dictatorship of the proletariat.*"

Summer Session, 1937, p. 4, my italics.

Dean Chamberlain is free to evaluate the significance of the evidence of Communist subversivness as he pleases. He is not free to disregard the evidence. The reader may determine for himself whether anonymous publication of this type of literature, distributed to students and faculty, constitutes conduct unbecoming a teacher.

IV

The third line of evidence is derived from the activity of members of the Communist Party doing research and scholarship. There is a party line for every field of knowledge from art to zoology presumably deduced from the principles of dialectical materialism but actually laid down in accordance with the shifting political exigencies of the Soviet Union and the Communist Party. With the rare exception of some prominent individual whose reputation is exploited for party purposes, no individual who is known to hold views incompatible with the party line is accepted as a member. For example, if he is an historian he cannot become a member if he teaches that the economic factor is not the most decisive factor in history. (Scott Nearing's difficulties which terminated in his exclusion from the Communist Party began when he referred to ancient "imperialism" in a sense which the pundits of the Central Committee held was applicable only to modern states.) He is likewise barred if he holds that the state is not the executive committee of the ruling class or that the Soviet Union is not a democracy. Individuals have been denied membership for denying the esoteric doctrine that "dialectics" apply to nature as well as history.

Once in the Communist Party, as William Z. Foster points out, the teacher-member must do his best to rewrite the textbooks in his field from the Communist Party point of view, win students and colleagues to this point of view, and mercilessly criticize opponents of Communist doctrine including his own past views. If a philosopher, to cite some actual instances, has accepted the theories of Mach or Carnap or Husserl or Alexander or T. H. Green or Whitehead or Dewey or G. E. Moore, upon joining the Communist Party he will criticize the philosophical doctrines he had previously held. He will never criticize the philosophy of dialectical materialism or the theories of Lenin and Stalin whom he now regards as sacred philosophical authorities. If a physicist or mathematician becomes a member of the Communist Party he is required, wherever it is possible for him to do so, to relate his subject to the growth of technology, its impact upon social and class divisions, the class uses to which the discovery is put, and the liberating role it can play in a Communist economy. The general theme is: science under capitalism makes for poverty, war and death; under communism, science makes for peace and abundance. Whatever his private beliefs may be, he cannot proclaim that there are any objective universal truths independent of country, class or even party, without running foul of the party line.

The party line, however, is not constant in all fields. It changes with political exigencies. The life of a Communist Party teacher, therefore, is not a happy one, since he may have to prove the opposite of what he once so fervently taught. His difficulties are mitigated by the fact that in different terms he faces different students whose memories are apt to be short in any event. But English teachers who have been members of the Communist Party during the last few years have had to reverse their judgments about the same novelists, and sometimes even about the same books, e.g., Malraux's *Man's Fate,* Dos Passos' *U.S.A.,* Wright's *Native Son.* A Communist Party teacher offering a course in literary criticism will now regard Hemingway, Sinclair and other novelists who have incurred the wrath of the Party quite differently from the way he would have done during the period of the Popular Front. Nor will any teacher who adheres to the Communist Party position comment *today*, as one of them did during the sectarian Third Period which preceded the Popular Front, on the lines of Stephen Spender greeting the Russian Revolution:

> *through torn-down portions of old fabrics let their eyes*
> *watch the admiring dawn explode like a shell around us,*
> *dazing us with its light like snow.*

Said this critic—a grown man at the time and a professor!—
"The passive position of watching the dawn is hardly fitting to the revolutionary, nor should the dawn daze like snow those who under self-discipline have known what to expect and are ready for the next move." (Edwin Berry Burgum, in the *New Masses,* July 3, 1934, p. 34)

In the social sciences, Communist Party teachers taught in 1934 that Roosevelt was a fascist; in 1936, during the period of the Popular Front, a progressive; in 1940, during the Nazi-

Heresy, Yes—Conspiracy, No

Stalin Pact, a war-monger and imperialist; in 1941, after Hitler invaded the Soviet Union, a leader of the oppressed peoples of the world.

Whether with respect to specific issues Communist teachers have been right or wrong in these kaleidoscopic changes is not the relevant question. What is relevant is that their conclusions are not reached by free inquiry into the evidence. To remain in the Communist Party, they must believe and teach what the party line decrees. At the very least, they must keep a discreet public silence about what they may privately or mentally disapprove. Dramatic evidence of this was provided by Granville Hicks in his public letter of resignation from the Communist Party. Hicks resigned because he was refused even the right to *suspend judgment* on the Nazi-Stalin pact. "If the party," he writes, "had left any room for doubt, I could go along with it . . . But they made it clear that if I eventually found it impossible to defend the pact, and defend it in their terms, there was nothing for me to do but resign." (*New Republic*, October 4, 1939.)

The fact that a teacher goes along with the Communist Party despite its intellectual somersaults on subjects in which he himself is presumed to have intellectual competence indicates that he has voluntarily placed allegiance to a political party above allegiance to the quest for truth. In one sense his betrayal of the methods of scholarship and science is graver than that of members of the Communist Party in the Soviet Union who recant out of fear of loss of their job if not of their life. This probably explains the case of Professor Zhebrak who publicly proclaimed (*Pravda,* August 15, 1948.) :

> As long as both trends in Soviet genetics were recognized by our party and the disputes between these trends were regarded as creative discussions on theoretical questions of contemporary science, helping to find the truth, I persistently defended my views, which in individual questions differed from the views of Academician Lysenko. But now that it has become clear to me that the basic theses of the Michurin

(Lysenko) trend in Soviet genetics are approved by the Central Committee of the CPSU, as a member of the Party I do not consider that I can adhere to positions which have been acknowledged false by the Central Committee of the Party.

Quoted by Counts and Lodge, *The Country of the Blind,* New York, 1949, p. 211.

A member of the American Communist Party who clings to it like a burr despite every zig and zag in its dizzy turns cannot plead in extenuation as Professor Zhebrak might, that his life or freedom or job are at stake. At most he faces severe personal or social pressures, and occasionally threat of denunciation as a party member. It is a more reasonable assumption that by remaining within the Communist Party he has made the supreme sacrifice to the cause—the sacrifice of professional integrity.

V

There is another and more unsavory aspect of the problem created by the presence of members of the Communist Party in science departments, research centers and laboratories. This follows from the way in which the Communist Party is organized, its primary loyalty to the Soviet Union, and what we know about the role of members of the Communist Party in espionage rings.

On the Political Committee of every Communist Party of the world, affiliated with the Kremlin, there is one member who is liaison officer with the Foreign Branch of the Soviet M.V.D. or Secret Police, which interlocks at the top with the Foreign Intelligence Service of the Red Army. All members of the Communist Party are screened by him for their potential serviceability in the extremely ramified espionage nets which the Communist movement has woven throughout the country. All members of the Communist Party in science departments or on science projects are sooner or later requested to report on new work, particularly on inventions and discoveries, to a party functionary or special agent who transmits it to the national liaison officer of the M.V.D. or someone else delegated by him. An elaborate system has been devised to funnel this information to the Kremlin. The roles of Drs. Allen Nun May, Klaus Fuchs, Clarence Hiskey, Raymond Boyer and others in the Soviet Canadian espionage ring and the U.S. Soviet espionage ring have been incontestably documented. Since in actuality no hard and fast lines exist between secret and non-secret scientific information, it is difficult to see how members of the Communist Party can be safely entrusted with the run of American laboratories. No matter what security regulations exist, no matter how tightly restricted certain information is—and some restrictions are hurtful to research —where members of the Communist Party are regarded as bona fide members of the scientific community and mingle and converse freely with their fellows, it is humanly impossible to prevent them from acquiring restricted information or knowledge which transmitted to enemy agents in an emergency can be used to further Communist sabotage or damage the interests of the nation.

VI

To these considerations must be added a powerful argument advanced in different form by several writers but most persuasively by Professor Arthur O. Lovejoy, one of the original organizers of the American Association of University Professors and its first Secretary, and now notoriously at odds with its present position. This argument may be recapitulated in three propositions:

a—"freedom of inquiry and teaching is essential to the proper exercise of the scholar's function."

b—The political program of the Communist Party calls for a one party dictatorship which abolishes completely freedom of inquiry inside or outside the universities and substitutes for the authority of intelligence, reason or scientific method

in every field the authority of the Political Committee of
the Communist Party.

c—Therefore any member of the Communist Party by virtue
of the varied activities which flow from his membership,
propagandistic, pecuniary, and otherwise, is contributing to
the victory of an international organization which has already destroyed academic freedom wherever it has come to
power, and which will destroy it anywhere else it triumphs.

Consequently any member of the Communist Party, whose
knowledge of these facts can be assumed, is unfit to be a member
of a university. He is violating the presupposition of honest
teaching.*

VII

Those who defend the privileges of members of the Communist
Party to teach on the same terms as members of other political
parties do not, of course, demand that the former be put in a
position where they threaten national security. They maintain,
however, that there is no mischief members of the Communist
Party can do in colleges and universities which is even remotely
comparable to the mischief that may result from their presence
in atomic energy plants. We shall see below that there is weighty
authority to contest this statement.

Even admitting it is true, if we had to wait to move against
unprincipled malefactors until they threatened to be as dangerous
to the community as espionage agents in atomic plants, we would
simply be inviting evils, injustices and tragedies that could be
avoided by some judicious pinches of common sense. To the
parents whose son's or daughter's life has been transformed by
conversion to the Communist Party, it is small consolation to
hear that the community as a whole is not imperiled thereby.
The young men or women who retrospectively look back on a
broken career must blame themselves but this does not absolve

* *Cf. Journal of Philosophy,* February 14, 1952.

those who may have recruited them. It is one thing to be converted by an idea, to play with an hypothesis, as one is maturing. For these ideas must withstand open criticism and confrontation by alternative views in and through an open society. It is another thing entirely to be converted to a conspiratorial movement, where it is only the first step that costs, in which resignation is not formally permitted, and in which one is gradually entangled in a mesh of duplicities until it almost seems easier to go along when doubts arise than to risk denunciation and social boycott.

There are to be sure normal chances and risks that all growing minds run. One student loses faith, another gains it, a third sees a vision which sets him afire, a fourth becomes worldly wise and spiritually dead. To add to this process of change and chance, the needless risk of entrapment into a Communist group which leaves its dark mark even on those who have broken their association with it, seems needlessly to complicate the educational situation. It is not a question of exposure to Communist *ideas*—every student should be exposed through study to Communist and Fascist ideas and to their democratic criticism—but a question of organizational affiliation. Some argue that the normal risk of growing up should include the risk of being gently pressured into Communist cells by teachers commissioned to perform that task. Their logic is hardly different from those who say that because every young man and woman risks seduction as part of their normal growing up—which is undoubtedly true—that therefore one should not worry about the presence of white slavers in their society.

We do not have to go as far as Henry Adams who remarked that: "A teacher affects eternity; he can never tell where his influence stops," to recognize that a teacher may often be more influential than a parent. There is hardly an individual come to maturity who will not testify that in the course of his life some teacher played a special role in influencing his development. Children in elementary school are more impressionable emotion-

Communism and Academic Freedom

ally than students at college but until an individual is an adult the teacher stands in a special relation of counselor, guide, friend, and authority to him.

The number of teachers who are members of the Communist Party cannot be regarded as the main point when the question of principle is raised, since the issues can be stated in a general way and may have to be applied to new situations tomorrow. Nonetheless the number of such teachers is relevant in that it shows that the situation is not merely hypothetical or trivial as it would be if only a bare handful were involved. Some disturbing testimony on this point has been presented by Dr. Bella Dodd, former member of the National Executive Committee of the Communist Party, and quondam legislative representative of the Communist dominated Teachers Union of New York which was expelled as a captive Communist union both by the A.F. of L. and the C.I.O. Dr. Dodd testified that at one time a thousand members of the New York City teaching staff were members of the Communist Party—most of them in the high schools and colleges.*

How many students were exposed to skillful indoctrination by these enemies of freedom? Allowing for overlapping, even if each teacher, on a conservative estimate, taught only a hundred students in the course of a year this would mean that every year one hundred thousand students in New York City alone would be subject to educationally pernicious indoctrination. Of these it would be safe to say that, directly and indirectly, scores, and in some years, hundreds would have been influenced by their teachers to join the Communist youth organizations from which the Communist movement draws its most fanatical followers. According to Dr. Dodd, Communist Party teachers practice strategic infiltration into posts where they can influence the greatest numbers, particularly university schools of education, where "they affect the philosophy of education and teach other teach-

* *New York Times,* September 9, 1952.

ers." Class size, or teaching loads, must be greater in such schools than in the estimate above, because the account reads "She said one Communist teacher might influence 300 future teachers in a single term." On the basis of her own personal knowledge as a Communist Party functionary, Dr. Dodd named the following colleges and universites as having had units of three or more Communist Party staff members: Columbia, Long Island, City College, Brooklyn, Queens, Hunter, New York, Vassar, Wellesley, Smith, Harvard, M.I.T., Chicago, Michigan, Northwestern, Howard, California and Minnesota. Some of these units were quite large. Evidence exists that units functioned at some other colleges.

VIII

The fifth and final line of argument is political. The courts have held that the Communist Party advocates the overthrow of constitutional democratic government by force and violence and the establishment of a dictatorship based upon the destruction of the whole structure of democratic freedom. Members of such an organization cannot therefore be trusted to carry out their responsibility as educators in a democratic society. They cannot be trusted to develop in the lower schools habits of critical thought and aversion to cruelty, fraud and violence; and in higher institutions to consider honestly the case for the free mind in a free society.

The cumulative force of the evidence and arguments so far adduced justify a policy of exclusion of members of the Communist Party and similar groups. Only powerful counter-considerations should induce us to tolerate the presence of members of the Communist Party in our schools on the same terms as all other teachers. To some of these considerations we shall presently turn. Until we have discussed them, the answers to some of the problems posed at the beginning of this chapter cannot be clearly made.

Communism and Academic Freedom

APPENDIX

These letters are typical of a number I have received since the theme of communism in education became a topic of public discussion. Because they are *ex parte* I have omitted the names of the teachers mentioned—as well as of the writers of the letters. Were any particular individual publicly accused, it would be impermissible, of course, to leave them unsignatured. I present these letters because one represents an extreme case, and the other a run of the mine case, of crudely attempted Communist indoctrination. One can easily conceive of a smoother and more sophisticated indoctrination which would not only be far more effective but far less likely to be detected by students.

PROFESSOR SIDNEY HOOK
NEW YORK UNIVERSITY
NEW YORK CITY

DEAR PROFESSOR:

In connection with your recent article which appeared in last Sunday's *Times* discussing the desirability of Communists as instructors, I feel that the following information might be of some little use to you.

The other day in discussing the English statesman and orator, Edmund Burke, I suddenly discovered how many misconceptions and untruths I had carried away from a basic College Composition Course. I referred to Burke as a "fascistic sycophant" and was astounded to discover how wrong I had been. After I had devoured the evidence on the subject of Burke and came to a rational conclusion, I wondered what other thoughts and fallacies I had carried away from that class.

Burke was "fascistic" because he opposed the French revolution. General Marshall's "Report to the Nation" was a "fabrication and a pack of lies" because he had failed to give Russia its proper place in the winning of the war. These are only two of the subjects I remember which were discussed and analyzed from the Instructor's viewpoint. This viewpoint seems to me now as decidedly biased.

It is true that we discussed the styles of the writing of the men involved but when we came to the context of their writings or political convictions, we were presented distorted versions from the Instructor's Party Line leanings. The remarkable aspect of these teachings was that the Instructor had such an engaging personality and warm sense of humor that those few members of the class who saw fit to disagree with his contentions and assumption, found themselves disagreeing not only with him but with the majority of the entire class. His subtle misrepresentations of certain facts, his personal, colored interpretations of the material under discussion were so forceful and effective that I went out of the course believing many things to be true which were actually false. I assume from class discussion that many others were similarly impressed.

During the course of that term, at the suggestion of the Instructor, I wrote a paper on the topic, "Idealism Verses Materialism." Looking back now I realize how ridiculous an essay this really was, but at the time, under the influence of this man, and helped by a suggested reference, Stalin's *Historical and Dialectical Materialism*. I attacked the problem crudely but enthusiastically. The result was a hodgepodge of adolescent gibberish.

Another memory which I carry with me as a result of this Freshman Course is a rather unpleasant one. One evening, during a class discussion, members of the class (apparently with the permission of the Instructor—because he did not object), circulated an enrollment petition for an organization which stated as its purpose support for Civil Rights, Price Controls, Veteran's Housing and an imposing list of similar benefits. The name of the organization was the "American Youth for Democracy." I signed the membership list. This group, as we now know, was later revealed to be a front for the Communist Party. Due to my ignorance and gullibility, today my name is contained on the

Communism and Academic Freedom

scrolls along with those of the other one-time members of this organization, and although I never attended any meetings— never was active in *any* sense of the word, if this knowledge comes into the hands of future employers, my position might be jeopardized. I wonder how many others were duped in the same manner? I say duped, because I have never seen that procedure carried out in any other classroom.

Fortunately, in the course of my education, I came in contact with other instructors as a result of accident who not only weren't dogmatic but who gave me the necessary techniques and methods for approaching problems myself—rationally and intelligently. And so I have been able to overcome the disadvantage of this first impression, which, although it wasn't etched in my mind was nonetheless effective for a time. I wonder if the other students were as "accidentally" fortunate as I was. If their education had been devoid of these instructors, then they probably still hold these same biased and untruthful ideas. I fervently hope that the young, pliable students who were like me, quite definitely swayed, have also learned how to think for themselves. That, I feel, should be the prime purpose of an education which has for its basis, academic freedom.

Sincerely yours,
(Signed) ———

MEMORANDUM TO PROFESSOR HOOK

X was explaining that Russia has "economic democracy," a condition that no other nation can lay claim to. This exposition was during a course in modern philosophy given by X at "Y" University in the summer of 1942. Quite earnestly, I, a student, asked X a few probing questions about Russia. He answered with standard apologetics and evasions and concluded by rattling off a string of "important" names [of those] who buttressed his own beneficent view of Russia. Among the names I recall were Haldane and Levy, the latter considered the greatest living philosopher by X. I rejoined by saying that names were irrelevant to the argument, but added that I too could cite names [of those] who support a view of Russia that conflicts with his. With that I mentioned Dewey, Russell, Hook, Eastman and some others.

As though the mere mention of these names was an assault on his faith, X's personality [was] transformed completely. He hurled his pencil to the floor savagely and glared at me. For a moment I feared he would attack me physically. Then, after a moment of silence, he turned to the class and very emotionally said: "Ladies and gentlemen . . . I am afraid that for the rest of the term we shall have to be in the same room with a Trot-skyist. I'm sorry, but there's nothing I can do about it." He spoke as though I were some loathsome disease. The class was as stunned as I was and some of them later expressed sympathy with me because of the tantrum of X. What was a humorous aftermath, some of the students later approached me and wanted to know what "Trotskyist" means.

At the end of the class I went into X's office for a clarification. He was a totally changed and chastened person. He cringed and was almost cowardly. I said that he uses labels recklessly and tried to get an apology from him but didn't.

Earlier in the term I cited a pertinent viewpoint from Sidney Hook's *Reason, Social Myths, and Democracy*. He charged that Hook was a Fascist. I took objection, said I was familiar with Hook's views, and added that as a matter of fact, Hook attacks fascism in that very book. After an exchange of views, X re-treated to the viewpoint that Hook was a "psychological Fascist."

(Signed)——

Chapter 10

REJOINDERS AND COMPLEXITIES

The argument that members of the Communist Party are unfit to teach on professional grounds, when propounded a few years ago, struck the academic community, or its more articulate groups, as a violent paradox. It provoked after the first gasp of surprise some reasoned replies which sought to evaluate the evidence and the principles on which the policy of exclusion rested. But these replies were surprisingly few, and were outnumbered by vehement denunciations in which life-long adherents of academic freedom, some of them veterans of outstanding battles, were roundly abused.*

Another surprising feature was the number of educational administrators, presidents of universities and deans of colleges, who came to the defense of the right of Communist Party teachers to hold their teaching posts on the same terms as any other groups. Some scholarly publications expressed strong opinions

* Perhaps the most vituperative of these criticisms took the form of an implicit comparison of "some teachers and philosophers," who adopted the position taken in this book with the position of Hitler. *Cf.* Negley, *Journal of Higher Education,* March 1952, pp. 121-2, and my rejoinder, "Academic Manners and Morals" in the June issue, pp. 323-327.

along similar lines and a number of professional associations adopted resolutions which insisted that classroom performances be the *sole* criterion of employability. No, it cannot be said that the rights of Communist Party members to teach lacked many and eloquent supporters.

Many of the arguments advanced in the discussion stubbornly confuse the question of holding *beliefs* that may be called Communist or Fascist with the question of membership in the Communist and Fascist organizations. I shall consider here only the weightiest or most frequently expressed arguments which recognize this distinction, but nonetheless reject any policy of exclusion.

Before doing so it is necessary to say something about the charge that the whole discussion about Communists in education is part of a campaign which has been whipped up by reactionaries who wish to destroy every vestige of liberal ideas, undermine the public school system, and introduce thought control.

There may be some individuals of whom this is true just as there may be some individuals who defend the right of members of the Communist Party to teach in order to better destroy democracy. But directed against those who have presented a reasoned case, such charges are conceived in ignorance, nourished by resentment of the very reasonableness of their case, and born of impotent rage.

For the truth is fatal to such charges. The first group which put itself on record against the employment of members of the Communist Party as teachers was the National Commission on Educational Reconstruction of the American Federation of Teachers, an affiliate of the A.F. of L., and this, by a unanimous vote in 1948 before the decision was made in the University of Washington case. The first institution which officially barred from its faculty members of groups like the Communist Party was the Graduate School of the New School for Social Research in 1935. The first political party which recognized that the right to teach in public schools was not a civil right like joining a

Rejoinders and Complexities

legal political party, was the Socialist Party at its National Executive Committee meeting at Reading in July, 1949. In this it agreed with Norman Thomas, the foremost socialist libertarian in America, who believes that "proved communists have no place on the teaching staffs of our public schools."

"The Socialist Party," declares the opening paragraph of the resolution, "recognizes the right and duty of public authorities to protect our schools against Fascists, the Ku Klux Klan or Communists who would subvert our democracy. The right to teach in public schools, charged with education in democracy, is not a civil liberty on a par with the right to speak or write one's opinions or to join a political party of one's choice." (*The Call*, July 22, 1949.)

Finally, the largest organization of teachers in the country with a direct membership of a half million, and an affiliated membership of almost a million, the National Education Association, which has opposed special loyalty oaths for teachers, witch hunts and classroom snooping, and enjoys a splendid record of militant struggle for academic freedom, approved at its Eighty-Seventh Annual Meeting in 1949 a ban against members of the Communist Party in the schools of the nation. They dotted the *i*'s of their resolution by banning them from membership in the N.E.A., too.*

---

* The position of John Dewey on the employment of Communist Party teachers has sometimes been misunderstood. In a letter to the *New York Times,* he took exception to the position that members of the Communist Party should be automatically dismissed without consideration of specific conditions in which such decisions were made. After an exchange of letters with the author, he expressed himself as follows on the author's article in the *Saturday Evening Post,* Sept. 10, 1949, which substantially expresses the same position taken in Chapter 12 of this book. I quote the relevant paragraph:

Sept. 18, 1949

Dear Sidney:

 Robby brought home from town—we are several miles from any stores, being quite in the woods—a copy of *Sat. Eve. Post* with your article in it. I was glad to be assured again that there was no real difference between us. But quite aside from that fact, I think your treatment is a model in both content and form of the way the subject should be discussed, the fact

Heresy, Yes—Conspiracy, No

All this, however, does not add one iota to the weight of the arguments which have been advanced for exclusion. All of the organizations cited above, as well as all the persons on the roster of liberal thinkers who agree with them, may be wrong. But the fact that they do hold the position should make it impossible for ritualistic liberals to denounce it as a reactionary plot. It should induce them to entertain the possibility that the position may be sound. At the very least, it should move them to reconsider the position on proper grounds, and leave the attribution of ulterior motives to creatures of the intellectual underworld.

I return now to the counter-arguments presented against the position defended in Chapter 9.

1. It is sometimes asserted that the best teacher despite himself falls short of objectivity, that "almost all minds are considerably unfree and unobjective," that professors are crochety and fanatical on all sorts of subjects, and that therefore members of the Communist Party are not unique in their behavior to the extent that they carry out their instructions to indoctrinate.

It is, of course, true that no one is an ideal teacher. On occasion, guard against it as we may, bias and distortion may creep into teaching. But surely there is all the moral difference in the world between an involuntary lapse from an ideal to which we firmly subscribe, and deliberate, systematic violation of that ideal. To fail to distinguish the case of a teacher who sometimes unwisely

---

that you recognize that exceptions are possible to the application of the general principle is in line with the point I tried to make in the *New York Times* letter—it is quite likely that the exceptions in my view would carry further than on yours, but that there are cases in which specific conditions should be taken into acct. was the point of my letter. . . ."

John Dewey

On the subsequent occasion of an interview with Mr. Benjamin Fine in connection with Mr. Dewey's ninetieth anniversary celebration, the latter said: "I do not think Communists should be permitted to teach. I know from personal experience how difficult it is to conduct a teachers' group if you have to deal with Communists. But in getting rid of Communists we must not destroy the morale of the teaching profession."

New York Times, Oct. 19, 1949

"sounds off" on his own from the case of teachers who are instructed deliberately to turn their backs on the ideal of objectivity, and to avoid the counter-revolutionary deviation of "objectivism" like the very plague, has as much sense as saying that because many men unwittingly make mistakes in arithmetic there is no moral difference between them and professional short-change artists. We are all fallible creatures. Therefore there is no significant difference between cheats and honest men! By the same logic because no community is a perfect or complete democracy there is no significant political difference between the imperfect democratic West and Soviet despotism.

2. Another type of objection recognizes the legitimacy of barring members of the Communist Party from the schools but argues that consistency demands that the same principles be extended to those who hold membership in similar organizations; and that these organizations would include not merely the Ku Klux Klan, Nazi and Fascist groups but the Roman Catholic Church. Since this would mean too extensive a purge of colleges and universities, it would be most sensible to drop the whole matter.

Certainly, what is wrong for one group to do cannot be right for another. Were the Catholic Church like the Communist Party in the respects relevant for the present discussion, and were Catholic teachers organized like Communist teachers and for similar purposes in the schools, obviously what held for one would hold for the other. But the doctrine and practices of the Catholic Church differ significantly from those of the Communist Party in communities and countries in which the Catholics constitute a minority group. In such situations Catholics have justification under papal encyclicals to live under, and even enforce, certain laws which run counter to Catholic dogma. When they are a minority, and where violation of their conscience is not involved, they are permitted to accept and fulfill the obligations of office in a community, and to practice the "sufferance of liberties" of which they religiously disapprove, as part of their duties of good citizenship.

Heresy, Yes—Conspiracy, No

For example, judges who are members of the Catholic Church grant divorces to Catholic petitioners, and with the sanction of Papal authority recognize that they have a duty both to the standards of their profession and to the laws of the state, even when it is not a Catholic law or Catholic state under which they live. The same rule applies to Catholic teachers *insofar as they are members of non-Catholic educational institutions.* They are expected to fulfill honorably their obligations and duties as members of the inclusive academic community and not surreptitiously to take advantage of their position in the classroom or on the campus to proselytize for the Church. Catholic teachers in secular institutions prescribe books which are on the Catholic Index of Prohibited Books for their students, even when their students are Catholic. For example, Dean Harry Carman, of Columbia College, who is a good Catholic, used to take great pride in the Columbia Contemporary Civilization and Humanities courses, in which students read many works on the Catholic Index. Of course in Catholic institutions, the Church dogma is the decisive matter. There is no academic freedom in Catholic colleges and were the Catholics to constitute a majority of the population, education would in all likelihood lose its secular character. But since we are discussing secular schools, the comparison between Communist and Catholic teachers must be rejected. One might add in addition that there has never been any evidence of the operation of Catholic cells in nonsectarian universities which impose a party line in all the arts and sciences that must be followed by Catholic teachers on pain of excommunication. The threats which emanate from certain quarters to the autonomy of the secular educational enterprise are not attributable to Catholic teachers in secular schools but to clerical influences, and not only Catholic, working outside the school.

3. A very plausible argument against the policy of exclusion is that it judges members of the Communist Party by what they say, by the Party program, that it overlooks the possibility that there may be a "bad" Communist. Those who would exclude

Rejoinders and Complexities

members of the Communist Party—so the argument runs—are thinking about Communist Party members who are perfect *by definition*. But flesh and blood creatures are never perfect specimens. And some may be so imperfect as to warrant our employing them.

I quote from an article sharply criticizing the position of the author:

> The most frequent argument for his exclusion from the teaching profession runs: Professor X is a Communist; a Communist has no respect for freedom of inquiry or for objectivity in teaching; to put it positively, he indoctrinates for the party line and the Soviet dictatorship; therefore X is not fit to be a professor. The logical subject of the second premise is the perfect or complete Communist, while the victim of the Conclusion is Professor X.
>
> Lowe, *Journal of Philosophy*, 1951, p. 438.

The actual argument of which the foregoing is a caricature reads:

> Professor X is a Communist. Communists are voluntary members of an organization which gives them explicit instructions to indoctrinate, lie, and commit perjury, if necessary, and to act always in the interests of the Soviet Union. We also know that Communists have been convicted of perjury again and again, that they organize secretly, and act in manifold ways unbecoming intellectually honest men. In addition we have evidence that the Communist Party has efficient mechanisms by which it purges its ranks of members who disagree with or disobey, or are inactive in carrying out, its instructions. Therefore we are justified in refusing X access to, or tenure in, a post which requires moral and intellectual integrity.

Note carefully that the argument does not assume that Professor X is a "perfect or complete" Communist. Nor does the Communist Party assume this. Its instructions hold for ordinary mortals. Not even Stalin was a perfect or complete Communist, although sufficiently untrustworthy as an imperfect and incomplete one.

What the above criticism ignores is that the argument for a policy of exclusion of Communist Party teachers rests not only on the specific behavior of this specific Communist here and now but on the weight we should give to various kinds of evidence we possess about the clearly expressed intentions of this party and its related activities—past and threatened. A man who joins a group of assassins is not always an assassin. But if I know he is a member of such a group, and know the purposes of the group, am I not justified in denying him—I do not say his freedom or his life—but access to a position in which he has a good chance to kill me? One may be killed by an imperfect assassin.

This is not, of course, to accuse members of the Communist Party who are not a part of its underground liquidation squads of being assassins or of planning assassination. I make the comparison to show that one can be dangerous, sometimes lethal, even if imperfect. But I do charge all members of the Communist Party who are teachers in our schools with an intent to commit those practices which, however *they* justify them, would in the eyes of non-Communists demoralize and corrupt the minds of their students. Such practices do not have to be perfect and complete to be vicious and undesirable.

We are concerned with formulating a just policy about a troublesome class of cases, and with the relation of the policy to the specific case when it is encountered. We are not concerned with making an infallible prediction about how closely the specific case will approximate the ideal or perfect case. A policy may be sound and reasonable even if we do not enforce it in some special situation.

Our critic's confusion between the relation of specific fact to generalization and the relation of policy to specific fact is quite general and extends to natural as well as human affairs. It may therefore be instructive to examine the logic of the issue in terms of the fallacy which is allegedly here being committed by

Rejoinders and Complexities

the advocates of a policy of exclusion. "It would be an obvious instance of vicious intellectualism," he writes, "to say that what flows from the faucet can not contain chlorine because *we know* that water is H_2O. But we do not hesitate to say that the man who holds a party card can not be other than a pure propagandist" (*loc. cit.*, p. 444).

Of course water may contain chlorine, but if I am looking for a disinfectant shall I go to the water tap instead of the medicine cabinet on the chance that water *may* contain chlorine? If I need gasoline, should I pour water into my tank on the ground that it is not purely water, or only water, and that it may even contain a tincture of gasoline? Of course, no one is a pure propagandist, or only a propagandist, but the question is: should I hire or retain a man, if I do *not* want a propagandist, who is a member of a group which instructs him to propagandize and commit other actions incompatible with his duties as a teacher?

Our critic shakes his head sadly over the defection from empiricism of those he criticizes. But all he has established is that they wish to use relevant knowledge and experience in making decisions of policy, and to render his own empiricism suspect. Empiricism is not going from case to case—*von Fall zu Fall* as the Germans suggestively put it—but learning from a case, in the light of some general knowledge, what is probably true of other cases *before* experiencing them, and arranging our actions accordingly. The function of knowledge is in part to avoid unpleasant surprises in the world, and to do so we have to learn from the experiences of others as much as, if not more than, from our own. Because we can not be certain that a generalization which we have good reason to believe true for a kind is true for any particular instance of that kind, it does not follow that we are without justification for treating the instance on the basis of the knowledge we already have *without the necessity of further investigation of the instance*. We may decide to investigate but we are under no compelling necessity to do so in order to be either reasonable or just.

223

Heresy, Yes—Conspiracy, No

To assume otherwise is to be guilty of what may be called the converse fallacy of vicious intellectualism: because any two instances of a kind differ in some respect, it is never reasonable to assume that a particular instance will exhibit the generic trait of the kind. If this is empiricism, it would be hard to find any empiricists among reasonable men—or even among living men, for they all would have died off because of avoidable mishaps in this dangerous world. It is one thing to say: Marsh water into which sewage empties is usually polluted; this is marsh water; therefore it certainly is polluted and should not be drunk—which is what we are accused of saying. It is quite another to say: Marsh water into which sewage enters is usually polluted; this is marsh water; therefore it is reasonable not to drink it. This is what we are actually saying, with the addendum that if, out of theoretical curiosity, we wish to find out whether any particular specimen is polluted, it is not necessary to take it (read Communist Party teachers) into our system (read school).

We assuredly are aware that "the behavior of humans is not so uniform as that of sticks and stones"; but in certain contexts the behavior of humans, despite differences, shows reliable uniformities, and in *political* contexts, as Communists understand that word, the behavior of members of the Communist Party, despite *their* differences, is more uniform than the behavior of members of nontotalitarian political parties. However, Mr. Lowe gives his argument a completely general form by claiming that any policy towards specific individuals based on knowledge of their membership in a class *as such* is "vicious intellectualism." I shall now consider a crucial case in which policy is based on the type of procedure denounced by Lowe as "vicious," as not "civilized [or] open-minded," but which all, save those who are sympathetic to Soviet Communism, would regard as sensible.

Should members of the Communist Party *as such* be barred from access to restricted data in atomic energy plans? There is not a single argument used by Mr. Lowe which does not equally apply to this situation. No one is a "perfect" Communist. Because

Rejoinders and Complexities

the Party expects its members to engage in espionage and sabotage, if they are strategically placed, it does not follow that this particular member "will follow its instructions perfectly." Judge him by his behavior as a particular person, just like everyone else, not by what his party stands for. If he is found guilty of espionage or sabotage exclude him; but it is vicious intellectualism to exclude him on the ground of his membership as such, for this would be "to predict a man's behavior from his isms and his party [and] forget the great fact of human variation."

Indeed, since fewer Communist members are likely to engage in espionage than to violate their academic trust, and since the punishment for espionage may be imprisonment and death but for academic subversion only dismissal, there is even a stronger case on Mr. Lowe's logic for *not* barring members of the Communist Party as such from restricted atomic data than for *not* barring them from teaching.

Nonetheless, every sensible person would regard a conclusion that Communist Party members as such should not be barred from access to these data, as a *reductio ad absurdum* of the position from which it was drawn. Nor are we arguing in *a priori* fashion when we bar Scientist X about whom we know nothing more than his membership in the Party. For we know from the evidence revealed in the report of the Canadian Royal Commission on Communist espionage, in the writings of Alexander Foote and Walter Krivitsky, and in the Fuchs and other cases, that the local Communist Parties are chiefly responsible for the amazing successes of Soviet espionage, and that every member of the Communist Party in a strategic position is carefully appraised for his potentialities as an espionage agent.*

But even without this particular evidence, there was the record

---

* I have discussed the mechanism of Soviet espionage and its ideological motivation in the *Sunday Times Magazine* of November 26, 1950. Foote was one of the leading figures in the key Soviet espionage ring in Europe during World War II; Krivitsky was Chief of Soviet Intelligence in Europe before World War II.

of instructions by the Kremlin to affiliated Communist Parties throughout the world, spelled out in the most explicit way, to infiltrate into key positions in trade-unions, government bureaus, army, police, and other social and cultural institutions. (Some of these instructions are cited in our first chapter.) Together with other evidence of Communist Party directives and activities, its encouragement of perjury in the party cause when under investigation, all this would have been sufficient in the eyes of an intelligent democrat to bar members of the Communist Party as such from some types of employment before some of them were caught. Whenever such a policy is adopted, no judgment is passed on how close to, or far from, perfection any particular member of the Communist Party is whom that policy affects. What is being said, and it requires considerable philosophical sophistication not to see it, is that it is unsafe to trust him, unwise needlessly to take chances on him.

The justification of a policy rests not only on its supporting generalizations but on the purpose to which it is oriented. Without reference to purpose we can not tell which among an indefinite number of true generalizations to select and weigh. *The purpose of barring members of the Communist Party from certain kinds of employment is not punishment for acts committed but prevention of acts threatened.* Mr. Lowe overlooks this and disastrously misunderstands the position of those criticized. He seems to believe that barring an individual from a post on grounds of his membership in the Communist Party is like convicting him of a crime or imprisoning him without a fair trial. Such a suggestion is preposterous, if we remember that the actual purpose of the policy is merely to prevent him from carrying out his instructions by depriving him of the opportunity to do so. Fair rules of evidence apply of course to determining whether an individual *is* a member of the Communist Party. But the moral responsibility for his action in joining and *remaining* in an organization of this character is his alone. That is why, when the consequences of refusing employment to a Communist Party member or dismissing him are experienced as punishment, they cannot justly be interpreted as deliberate imposition of punishment for a specific offence for which the individual has been neither charged nor tried. If a man intends to make his living by joining a gang of card-sharpers, pledged to deceit without exposing themselves, my refusal to play with him based on my knowledge of his membership *as such* may result in economic hardship for him. But unless he studied philosophy, he is not likely to accuse me of vicious intellectualism because there are card-sharpers and card-sharpers, none of them perfect, and because until I catch him in the act of cheating, I can not know that he *will* certainly cheat merely on the ground of his intention.

I believe it is fairly clear that a reasonable *policy* can be based on membership *as such* in some situations without being guilty of the uncivilized, categorized, and un-openminded thinking which marks "vicious rationalism." Teaching and research in schools obviously pose different situations from filling sensitive posts in government, although in places the problems they involve overlap. What may be a justified policy in the first type of situation may not be so in the second. That will depend upon the series of valid generalizations relevant to the class which is affected by the policy, the relative weights we give them, and the purposes the policy is designed to achieve.

In the above argument I have taken for granted that if members of the Communist Party were to be successful in carrying out, even in a small degree, their declared intentions they would be exercising a pernicious influence on the minds, character and possibly the whole tenor the lives of students whom they managed to indoctrinate or enroll in the Communist Party. This, apparently, is not sufficient to justify our action in the eyes of some innocents. Before we bar a Communist teacher we must show that there is a dangerous risk involved in employing him comparable to a risk which might result in a national disaster. Replying to the above, Mr. Lowe states:

"Mr. Hook should have shown that in judging whether a Communist is sufficiently trustworthy to be a professor we must first attend to factors of extraordinary risk comparable to the risks of catastrophe in judging the trustworthiness of a physicist in an atomic weapons laboratory." * This is a preposterous request. There are few situations in which any action would have consequences comparable to those of a "Fuchs-like act." Intelligent evaluation of risk must be commensurate to specific positions, purposes, and responsibilities.

There are some individuals who have been in a position to evaluate the degrees of risk involved in employing soldiers, scientists, and teachers in the current ideological war of communism against democracy, who disagree sharply with Mr. Lowe's estimate. Shortly after resigning as President of Columbia University to become President of the nation, Dwight Eisenhower proclaimed: "No man flying a war plane, no man with a defensive gun in his hand, can possibly be more important than the teacher."

(The *New York Times,* January 17, 1953.)

One need not be unmindful of the respective differences in danger that flow from the presence of C. P. members in restricted science projects and in schools. But from the point of view of parents who do not want their sons and daughters (or educators their students) inducted into the Communist Party, or subjected to calculatedly dishonest teaching, or recruited to fight in a Communist battalion, or indoctrinated to a point where they lend themselves to the stratagems of a Communist espionage ring, there is educational risk enough. Many illustrations can be given of lives blasted by early Communist indoctrination and enrollment in the Party. It has also been established that Communist members of espionage groups have taught in our educational institutions.**

* *Journal of Philosophy,* 1952, p. 109. The reader is urged to consult the whole of Mr. Lowe's reply and my rejoinder, *loc. cit.*

** The names and attendant circumstances are given in *The Shameful Years: Thirty Years of Soviet Espionage in the United States,* a report published December 30, 1951, by the House Committee on Un-American Activities.

Rejoinders and Complexities

4. Suppose a man is a good Communist but also a great painter like Picasso. Would we not permit Picasso to teach? The logic which uses border line cases to derive principles governing general policy is defective for many reasons. Its effect is to wipe out all distinctions in kind because of the existence of certain indeterminate zones or areas in which clarifications are difficult. Yet the existence of dawn and twilight does not prevent us from saying that two things are as different from each other as day and night: and the fact that no one can tell whether some organisms are living or non-living does not prevent us from burying a corpse after three days.

What makes Picasso a border line case is not any difficulty in determining whether he is a member of the Communist Party— which he avowedly and proudly is—but in determining whether the educational advantages to be derived from employing him as a teacher outweigh the evils that would result from his political propaganda for the Communist Party and the Soviet Union. Presumably the same problem would arise if an Ezra Pound, known to be a member of an anti-Semitic or Fascist group, were to apply for a teaching post. If there were no reason to believe the teaching capacities of either of these men was anything extraordinary, there would be no reason for breaching the general rule against employing members of the Communist Party or of similar Parties.

Let us assume, however, that the stimulus these men would provide would be extremely fruitful—and indeed, so fruitful as to outweigh the harm they would undoubtedly do. Then provided some educational measures were taken to counteract their political influence, they might very well be employed, particularly if there was no concealment on their part of their membership in the Communist Party or Fascist Party. We would regard their cases as exceptions and cheerfully make them, or consider making them, whenever a painter with the stature of Picasso or a poet like Pound were being considered.

5. Another plausible argument, already broached in another

connection, admits that members of the Communist Party need not be hired but pleads that, after they have already been hired, they should not be dismissed until they have been convicted of particular acts of educational wrongdoing. A member of the Communist Party who has taught five, ten or twenty years at an institution is discovered to be a member of the Communist Party. Should his record not count for something in considering his reliability in the future? If he has not indoctrinated, or carried out his party instructions in any way in the past, why assume he will do so in the future?

Obviously, if the evidence of unprofessional conduct can be easily obtained, there is no objection to proceeding on this basis. The question, however, is directed against the view that membership in the Communist Party, after long years of service, should *ever* be regarded as itself a sufficient ground for dismissal. Again what is overlooked is that the Communist Party is not an ordinary party, that no member can remain inactive in it and survive the warning, exposure, denunciation and ultimate expulsion which results from failure to conform with party instructions. It is warranted to assume that any member of long standing has in terms of Communist Party estimates represented a net profit to it, and therefore that it is much more probable that activities which have been profitable to the Communist Party have gone undetected than that he has consistently violated the Party's instructions. Further, if any individual originally acquired a post by concealing or lying about his Communist Party membership, when that fact is discovered, he must be held to account for practicing the original deception.

But the main point which this plausible objection overlooks is this: the very notion that a man could be a member of the Communist Party for many years and have a perfect record of non-cooperation with the Communist Party, although logically noncontradictory, is psychologically fantastic. Consider! Here is Professor X, a member of the Communist Party, who presumably does not accept any of its directives and has managed to evade searching detection by his comrades. Yet he knows that his continued membership in an organization whose directives he disobeys, and from whose watchdogs he must carefully conceal his honorable conduct, is presumptive evidence of lack of moral and intellectual integrity in the eyes of his colleagues. If discovered it probably will lead to dismissal. Why, then, does he remain in the Party? What masochistic compulsion prevents him from resigning? Why is he not content with the status of a sympathizer? It is so improbable that anyone like X exists that it would be taking a foolish educational risk to assume that he or any party member is as harmless as some of them may conceivably *appear* to be—and as, this objection would have us believe, some actually are.

Let us stretch our imagination and entertain the notion that such schizophrenic dissociation is not uncommon, and that these apparent cases of membership in the Communist Party and total non-compliance with regular Party duties are not using an academic career as cover for underground work. *Theoretically*, if we had a vast amount of time and energy at our disposal, it would not be impossible to get to the bottom of things in each case and discover who had been deceiving whom, and will *continue* to deceive. But we haven't the time and resources. And if we had, we are not morally obligated to do so—since (a) the teacher in question is free to resign from the party with whose instructions he disagrees, and since, as we have seen, (b) the processes of continued supervision of Communist Party teachers in the classrooms, laboratories, the quiet hours of library and office conferences, and the necessarily close interrogation of students and colleagues to check up on such teachers, would not only be morally stultifying but would poison the atmosphere of a decent academic community.

A great many of the objections interposed to the policy advocated in this book, judging by extensive discussion, consist in thinking up some extraordinary situations or some special kind of Communist Party member for whom we would be willing to

Heresy, Yes—Conspiracy, No

breach the rules. And into the breach ride all the members of the Communist Party! We should be glad to accept Vishinsky as a teacher of Soviet Law in some American university if only the Kremlin would permit Jerome Frank to lecture freely on Anglo-American Law at the University of Moscow; Mitin or Aleksandrov (provided the latter survived the last purge) in philosophy if only the Kremlin would take Curt Ducasse or C. I. Lewis or Ernest Nagel for a course of lectures in exchange. Perhaps it would be wise to take the Soviet Communist Party professors without an exchange for the sake of what we may learn from them, or in order to test our faith in the rationality of man. But this would have no bearing on our policy toward members of the American Communist Party.

Whatever exceptions we make to meet ingeniously contrived suppositions it is safe to say that most of them would be confined to the university where students are mature, full grown, and able to fend for themselves. As intellectually untrustworthy as members of the Communist Party are, a lone member or two may be conceivably tolerated on the post-graduate University level in non-science departments if they have openly admitted their membership and don't pose as Jeffersonian Democrats, La Follette Republicans or Christian Socialists. More than two on any campus will constitute themselves into a conspiratorial group in accordance with Party instructions.

6. Another objection to barring Communist Party teachers has been formulated by Arthur Garfield Hays who argues that since Communist theories and doctrines should be carefully studied in any modern educational institution, members of the Communist Party are the best qualified to teach it. As reported in the *New York Times* of June 21, 1949, Mr. Hays maintains that "if communism is to be taught, Communists should teach it." The odd thing about Mr. Hays' position is that he has never maintained that fascism should be taught by Fascists, the theory of racialism studied under Nazi or anti-Semitic teachers, or that the theory of plural marriages, religious or secular, should be

232

investigated under the educational leadership of polygamists. It is not difficult for a person who is not a member of the Communist Party to give an adequate and intellectually fair presentation of Communist theory using official Communist sources; for example, Mr. Hays himself. And that Communist theory should be a required study in all colleges is the contention of some of the staunchest proponents of the measure to bar members of the Communist Party from the teaching profession.

The notion that only members of the Communist Party are in a position to understand and expound Communist theory accurately is an obscurantist claim more in keeping with the pretensions of a mystical theology than with an avowedly scientific theory of nature, man and society. Why should membership *per se* bestow illumination? One can understand why the Communists should make such a claim, as absurd as it is, because the dogmas of orthodoxy are political weapons in factional struggles. Why should someone who is not a Communist make it? A practical difficulty in Mr. Hays' proposal is that either we should have to dismiss our Party-line Communist whenever he is purged, and hire one to profess the newer orthodoxy, or we would end up with a rather embarrassingly large collection of former orthodoxies of various models. But it usually requires a bourgeois objective scholar to sort out their conflicting claims and to tell who is lying about whom.

7. In his *Education Between Two Worlds*, Dr. Alexander Meiklejohn maintains that *"the purpose of all teaching is to express the cultural authority of the group by which the teaching is given"* (p. 91, italics in original) and explicitly asserts that teacher and pupil "are both agents of the state." These Hegelian notions seem to me incompatible with the educational philosophy of liberalism, but there is a certain piquancy to be found in the fact that despite these views Dr. Meiklejohn has forthrightly defended the rights of members of the Communist Party to teach in our schools on the same terms as anybody else. Since his posi-

tion is often cited in the literature on the question, I shall examine it in some detail.*

The nub of Dr. Meiklejohn's argument is that since "the primary task of education in our colleges and universities is the teaching of intellectual freedom, as the first principle of the democratic way of life," we would be interfering with "fair and unabridged discussion" if teachers were dismissed on grounds of membership in the Communist Party.

Dr. Meiklejohn does not feel called upon to explain how "fair and unabridged discussion" can be carried on by those who are under instruction to inject and indoctrinate party dogmas and who have clearly expressed their intention to do so by virtue of their membership in an organization which gives them these instructions and does not countenance refusal to abide by them. The only assumption on which this glaring inconsistency can be justified is that none but members of the Communist Party can give an adequate and fair statement of Communist theory and strategy. But this as we have previously seen is clearly absurd. If generalized, it would imply that objective teaching on any issue in dispute is impossible. If anything, members of the Communist Party are prepared to suppress evidence (*e.g*, in their denial of the existence of Lenin's testament, the denial of the role of Trotsky in the early history of the Red Army, etc.) in accordance with the exigencies of the Kremlin's policy. "Fair and unabridged discussion" by all means. But in matters of the class struggle, which according to party doctrine pervades every aspect of our culture, the ideal of "fair" discussion is considered in Communist theory as a bourgeois illusion. "Objectivism" is in fact one of the great heresies in the international Communist movement.

Even more startling is Dr. Meiklejohn's discovery that despite the fact that Communist Party members shift their ideas "as

* Dr. Meiklejohn's discussion appeared in the *New York Sunday Times Magazine* of March 27, 1949, as a presentation of a point of view different from the one expressed by the author in the issue of February 27, 1949.

the policies of the party shift," and despite the fact that they are under "an unusually rigid and severe discipline," the only explanation of their behavior is that in general they "are moved by a passionate determination to follow the truth where it seems to lead." Communist Party members must believe, then, if what Dr. Meiklejohn is saying is the case, that the shifts of the party line are also motivated by a passionate determination to follow the truth. Apparently they have somewhat mistaken the Politbureau for an Academy of Science.

But there is a simpler question still which stares out of Dr. Meiklejohn's words. If the explanation of Communist Party members' behavior is their search for the truth, then why the necessity of the "unusually rigid and severe discipline" he admits exists? The scientific *methods* by which the truth is reached, and the specific conclusions or pieces of knowledge won by these methods, are certainly sufficient discipline for democratic educators. Why then is there need for the *organizational* discipline of the Communist Party in respect to belief? Why is there need of the threat of expulsion of those who are critical of Soviet theory and practice?

It is at this point that Dr. Meiklejohn makes his most momentous discovery. The organizational discipline of the Communist Party is not really discipline, or is discipline only in a Pickwickian sense. According to him, members of the Communist Party are not required to believe anything. For their actions are voluntary. And then, in a sentence for which I predict immortality as an illustration of an obvious *non-sequitur* concealed by an equivocation, he adds: "If membership is free, then the beliefs are free." In other words, because an action is free, *i.e.*, voluntary —joining the Communist Party—the beliefs which are held in virtue of that membership are also free, *i.e*, a result of the quest for the truth.

Let us examine this. Suppose a teacher accepts money from the National Association of Manufacturers or from a foreign government on the understanding that he champion its side on any issue. I assume that in such a case Dr. Meiklejohn would grant that he has betrayed his trust and is unworthy to teach. I am also confident that Dr. Meiklejohn would say of such a person that he was under orders to reach predetermined conclusions, that he was bound by a discipline that was foreign to the scholar's proper objectivity. But note: the teacher's action is free, *i.e.*, voluntary. No one compelled him to accept the offer. He could take it or leave it. Were he to argue that because his action was free therefore his beliefs were free, *i.e.*, a result of the quest for the truth, Dr. Meiklejohn would be the first to expose the sophistical ambiguity by which he sought to gloss over his intellectual dishonesty. Two different senses of the word "free" are obviously being confused.

The fact that a man is paid to work for the NAM or a foreign government is irrelevant to the free or voluntary nature of his act. He might even believe in the program of the NAM or the goals of a foreign government and work for nothing. What makes him intellectually dishonest as a teacher is that by his action he has signified his willingness to teach *according to directives received* and not in accordance with objective methods of searching for the truth. If a scientist is paid money by an industrial firm to undertake research, that does not make him intellectually dishonest. If he is paid money on the understanding that his research will "prove" what the firm tells him to prove, he is intellectually dishonest.

Certainly, membership in the Communist Party or in the Ku Klux Klan is free. Even in the Soviet Union no one is compelled to join the party, so, on Dr. Meiklejohn's principle, no thought control exists there. But what he fails to see, despite mountains of evidence, is that the nature of a member's commitment to the Communist Party is incompatible with commitment to the scientific method of inquiry and honest teaching because of (a) his party pledge, (b) the party dogmas, and (c) clearly defined party duties as given in official instructions on how to behave in the classroom and on the campus.

Rejoinders and Complexities

In a certain sense one can speak of the "integrity" or the "courage" of a person who joins the Communist Party or the Ku Klux Klan openly. But so long as he remains in the organization —and the discussion is about present and active members—he is *not* free to profess only what he believes the scientific evidence warrants. Lenin made this crystal clear even before the October Revolution. He reversed Dr. Meiklejohn's argument and with better justification. *Just because* membership is voluntary, those who join the Communist Party must accept its intellectual discipline; they are not free to think and write as they please while they are in that organization. If this irks them, they can resign; if they remain, they are bound. A decade after the Revolution, Stalin drew the awful consequences for the whole field of human knowledge and art.

Obviously thousands upon thousands of individuals have left the Communist Party who have come to disagree with it. But the point is that so long as they *remain* in the organization, they are not free *publicly* to express any thoughts which are critical of Party dogma even when they believe such thoughts are true.

Dr. Meiklejohn is profoundly mistaken about what motivates the Communist Party member's beliefs. It is loyalty to the Soviet regime and its promise of salvation and not "a passionate determination to follow the truth" wherever it leads, which explains why the Communist Party member will teach any specific Communist doctrine on any specific point. His "integrity" is expressed only in his total commitment. This does not mean that he necessarily agrees with the truth, say, of a specific Communist characterization of Roosevelt or of the Marshall Plan at any time. It does mean that in so far as he is loyal to the Kremlin, in so far as he chooses freely to remain in the Communist Party, he is not free to be *publicly* critical of the Party line even if he privately disagrees with it. Usually, he squares this to himself with the reflection that the point on which he feels the Party line is wrong is comparatively unimportant. *But it is precisely this subordination to his total commitment, and his evaluation of*

what is important or unimportant in the light of a political ob-
jective, that makes it impossible for him to exercise the free
criticism he would engage in were he loyal to the principles of
scientific inquiry.

This is the crux of the matter and it bears repeating. The
residue of truth in Dr. Meiklejohn's position is that a member
of the Communist Party in the U.S.A. is freer to resign than his
comrade in the U.S.S.R. To that extent he is a freer person.
This by no means gainsays the fact that whenever the evidence
leads him to the belief that the Party or Stalin is clearly wrong,
he will *not* express that criticism publicly as a scholar and
teacher as his colleagues who are not members of the Party and
who will express such criticisms freely, forthrightly and as a
matter-of-course whenever they are relevant to the course of
study. At each occasion of doubt or disbelief, the Communist
teacher will first ask himself whether the promise of political
salvation which the Soviet Union holds out is sufficiently important to overweigh and override his duty as a scholar and
teacher to tell the truth. If it is not, he speaks up and is expelled
or resigns: if it is, he keeps silent or says publicly what he does
not believe, in either case betraying the truth. On each alternative,
his lack of intellectual freedom and professional integrity consists in the fact that he has made the *decisive* consideration something totally irrelevant to the processes of honest scholarship and
teaching.

What about the problem of the "fellow traveler"? Is his case
the same as that of the Communist Party member? We shall de-
vote the next chapter to this question and then present some
positive proposals for faculty procedures when membership in
the Communist Party is charged and/or admitted.

Chapter 11

ACADEMIC INTEGRITY AND
ACADEMIC FREEDOM

I

The current discussion of the question whether members of the Communist Party should be permitted to teach in our schools and colleges has been conducted in such a way that it has eclipsed much more important problems concerning the character and direction of American education. Granted that some defensive measures may be necessary to prevent the process of teaching and learning from being subverted by zealots of undemocratic political organizations. Such measures, however, can never be a substitute for the long-range educational philosophy and strategy that should have as one of its aims the intellectual sophistication which alone gives lasting immunity to infectious myth and dishonest argument.

Even if our schools and colleges were overnight to be liberated from every member of the Communist Party—the fundamental problem would remain of how to meet the challenge to the liberal temper which comes from the exploitation for totalitarian purposes, either deliberately or through misunderstanding, of liberal catch-words and slogans. Here no disciplinary measures, whether by administration or faculty, can or should be invoked. Here the struggle can only be waged in the educational arena with educational weapons. This struggle is particularly difficult to conduct, not merely because academic decorum must sometimes be sacrificed in the interests of academic integrity, but because the effective exercise of the critical function, without which education is lifeless, arrays all reactionary groups, irrespective of their labels, against the teacher as honest inquirer and scholar.

During the fifteen year period from 1934 to 1949—which roughly began with the Popular Front reorientation of the Communist Party in the United States and ended after the Communist coup in Czechoslovakia—there emerged on the campuses of the nation a complex of ideas, and a form of social action which had a profound influence on the attitudes of students. These ideas, generous in intention even if vague in expression, centered around the ideals of equality, freedom and peace. Their roots were not found in Marxist doctrine, which regards all such abstractions with suspicion, but in the traditional unanalyzed ideology of American democracy. Their dynamism was not the result of a calculated political tactic but a consequence of the fervors and moral idealism of youth.

Two things were characteristic of this awakened liberalism. As distinct from previous liberal movements, which ebbed and flowed spontaneously with student interest but had no cumulative force, it was carefully channeled in a definite political direction. Every large social action to which it led, turned out to be in behalf of a cause in which the Communist Party took leadership, either from the outset or by gradual organizational manipulation. No other political tendency offered competition, partly out of weakness but mainly because such competition entailed full-time activity and a sacrifice of academic for political life which few, except for the professionally dedicated, were prepared to make.

Secondly, the implications of these liberal ideas and ideals in their devastating critical impact upon Soviet culture in theory and practice were never drawn. Any attempt to do so provoked the most vehement denunciation from the leaders of social action on the campus. Thus the peace movements of the thirties among students, and the wholehearted support of the Spanish Loyalist government among both faculties and students, were either organized or soon captured by the Communist Party. The public evidence that this was so had little effect, even when the crassness of party control was revealed, as in the typically sudden transition from the pacifist "Oxford pledge" slogan among students in 1934 to the nationalist war cries required by the new party line. In further documentation, we need only cite the reaction in the universities to such liberal efforts as the organization of the Commission of Inquiry into the Moscow Trials, headed by John Dewey, in 1936, and to the launching of the Committee for Cultural Freedom, again under John Dewey's leadership, in 1939.*

The continuity of ideas and action which made almost every movement on the campus that called itself "progressive" or "radical" a recruiting ground for the Young Communist League and the Communist Party, was provided not by students but by members of the faculties, most of whom could, with clearer conscience than political understanding, deny that they were Communists. Statistical studies of the most influential Communist front organizations, conducted by the author from 1936 to the present, show that college and University teachers constituted the strongest and most influential group of Communist fellow travelers in the United States. And when I say this I am not speaking of disguised Communist Party members, non-party Bolsheviks, or even of theoretical "Marxists" of the Stalinist persuasion.

I am speaking of individuals who were members and supporters of Communist front organizations, who far from feeling it necessary to dissociate themselves from such organizations when they had a common cause for the moment, were willing to let their

* Part of the story will be found in my "Academic Freedom and 'the Trojan Horse' in American Education," *Bulletin of the American Association of University Professors,* 1940.

names, prestige, institutional connections, and their divers contributions of energy and money be exploited by groups that were Communist inspired, directed or controlled. Further, when I say that the largest and most influential group of fellow travelers were members of the academic community, I am *not* saying, as the President of Sarah Lawrence College interprets me, that the largest and most influential group in the academic community were fellow travelers. The rules of logic are no different for progressive educators than for conventional ones, and the fallacy of simple conversion is still a fallacy in any curriculum.

The vast majority of academic fellow travelers were *not* Marxists and held views in their own fields for which they would be "liquidated" or dismissed from their posts in the Soviet Union. Yet they constituted the most loyal battalion of that little army of "progressive" intellectuals who, until yesterday, were invariably found lending their names and prestige to Communist Party front organizations, championing the foreign policy of the Soviet Union, defending Communists against their liberal critics and never defending, or speaking for, the victims of Communism anywhere.

On any view of academic freedom these men and women had, and have, every right to be members of the academic community. They had not made the total commitment of membership in the Communist Party which compelled them to uphold or remain silent about distasteful party dogmas and Soviet actions in the interests of a fancied ultimate historical good. Nonetheless, because of their number and because of the passivity of their colleagues, they had, and still have here and there, far more influence upon students' political habits of thought than any other group—an influence which in its mildest form substitutes a "radical" philistinism for the conventional kind, and in its more vicious forms softens students up for participation and membership in the Communist movement and all that this implies.

These professionals of good will who play the role of ideological "typhus Marys" are not, I repeat, the concern of legislators and administrators. They are the concern of educators who must solve the problems of "totalitarian liberalism" within the framework of democratic education.

Political events since the invasion of Korea have given pause to all but the most blatant fellow travelers, and at the moment of writing their numbers are considerably diminished. The Soviet cries for peace have been revealed as hypocritical; grim signs of officially approved anti-Semitic agitation have appeared in the satellite countries; the shadows of all-out war lengthen behind the Iron Curtain as the Kremlin mobilizes its resources to ward off by familiar "defensive" offensives an encirclement which is not geographical but political. In consequence, many fellow travelers have awakened with a shock to discover how precious are the freedoms we and they can still lose. Others have become neutralists prepared to concede, with an air of making an over-generous admission, that the Soviet Union is *equally* at fault with the United States for the state of the world, and calmly asserting that what is happening in the United States is essentially not different from the cultural and political terror of Communist countries.* Still others have not altered their point of view.

From the point of view of the *present* activity of the fellow

* For example, commenting on the Prague purge trials with their brutal executions, the framed-up evidence, the forced confessions, the fantastic and incoherent testimony before a judge, prosecutor and defense lawyer who are part of the same government machine of terror, the *Nation* comments:

Americans should read the accounts of this trial with care, and having read them, should then reread the testimony of the professional informers and denouncers, the ex-traitors, the self-confessed perjurers and espionage agents who have testified before the various Congressional committees in this country to see if they can find a parallel or any similarity between the two witch hunts. Soviet criminal procedure has never excited our admiration; hence we were neither surprised nor disappointed—although we were dismayed—by the brutal cynicism of the Prague purge. We are disappointed, however, and will not cease to protest, *when American Congressional committees reproduce, even in milder form, procedures and pressure techniques that have become an established part of the Soviet sacrifice of individual rights in the struggle for power.* Hatred of such procedures could best be exhibited through denunciations, not only of Soviet justice, but of witch hunts wherever they take place. (December 6, 1952, my italics.)

traveler, the following pages of this chapter would hardly be justified. But the difficulty is that so long as there does not exist a basic comprehension of what Communist theory, practice, organization, and strategy are, the education of the fellow traveler is not complete. He guides himself by the political events of the moment, but he does not understand them. Should Stalin's successor make one friendly or genuinely peaceful move, and all the old illusions will arise again in the minds and breast of the fellow travelers, and with it the kind of activities associated with this illusion. There is warrant for skepticism concerning the power of historical events to teach those who approach them with deep emotions but shallow and uninformed minds. For we have gone through a phase of this kind before.

The Nazi-Soviet Pact of 1939, the Soviet invasion of Finland, the material support of fascism, including the return by Stalin to Hitler of German-Jewish Communists, also had a disillusioning effect on the academic fellow travelers. But no sooner did Stalin say a few words that might be interpreted as democratic than the Soviet stock rose among American liberals and a veritable hegira towards Communist dominated organizations began, even among those who had gotten off the bandwagon in 1939. The glorification of Stalin and the Soviet Union reached its apogee shortly before the end of the Second World War both in government circles and academic circles.

The only American liberals who refused to swallow the new crop of illusions, who fought steadfastly against them, often at the cost of calumny, were those who understood something about the nature of Leninism and Stalinism and did not wait to be taught by the historical events. Anyone can have twenty-twenty hindsight but it is one of the great merits of John Dewey that already in the early months of 1942 he was warning, on the basis of his knowledge of Soviet theory and practice, against the consequences of the uncritical attitude towards Stalin and the Soviet Union. I quote a few paragraphs from a long letter which John Dewey wrote at the time.

Academic Integrity and Academic Freedom

Dr. — cannot say too much, or say it too emphatically, about the importance of Russia in the after-war situation, including relations between that country, Great Britain and ourselves. It is just this importance which makes the present build-up of Stalin and *Stalin's* Russia dangerous. The build-up is no less sinister in its consequences when engaged in by weak-kneed liberals, "hard-headed" men for reasons of short range expediency and under the standard of patriotism, than when it is a campaign of propaganda maintained by those who were sure the war was a strictly imperialist one as long as Stalin was safely out of it and who carried on active defense of the alliance between the two totalitarian powers as long as both dictators found it to their interests to keep it up.

Danger is imminent. Anyone who reads between the lines of the statements that are already appearing in the newspapers is aware that negotiations are going on to which Great Britain is an active party, and to which for all we know the United States is at least a passive party, for the sacrifice of the Baltic states and of Poland. That the resistance Russia has put up makes it possible for Stalin to exact a high price for staying in the war after the time arrives when Hitler is ready for another deal is no less a fact because we are all happy that German power has received a check for the first time since the war began. Do we want what in effect are secret treaties, like those of the World War, to predetermine final terms of peace and to plant, as happened in the case of the last war, the seeds of another war? . . .

What is now needed is a sane, realistic appraisal by the men in this country who know the facts about Stalin's Russia of those conditions of both the war and the peace settlement which will eliminate the dangers inhering in Stalinist supremacy, and establish the basis for helpful relations after the peace between a Russia freed from totalitarian menace and Great Britain and this country: relations in which we can learn from whatever of good Russia has accomplished and that country can be assisted forward on a genuinely democratic path. When Stalin needs our help is the time to start setting up these conditions; when we need him more than he needs us is the worst time. So I repeat, first things first.

All this was lost on the academic fellow traveler. There is no evidence that those who are shocked are altogether cured of their illusions. That is why I continue the discussion about him.

Three general questions must be raised about this type of academic fellow traveler. What are his most easily identifiable intellectual habits? What are the causes of his fellow traveling? What can be done about him?

Perhaps the most depressing feature of the habits of the fellow traveler is the completely unscrupulous character of his intellectual procedures as soon as he discusses a political question which concerns Communists or the Soviet Union. A man who would rather starve than misreport the evidence of an experiment, who would sooner sacrifice popularity and preferment than risk making a snap judgment about a manuscript, feels not the slightest compunction, once his political *sympathies* take on a Communist tinge, about inventing his facts as he goes along, or refusing to investigate and verify evidence crucial to his arguments. I am not now referring to deliberate duplicity, which is rare and which, because it is conscious, covers its tracks so carefully that it is difficult to expose except by experts. I am referring to the half-conscious belief, born of political euphoria, that everything goes because one knows in one's heart that it is all in a good cause, and that in the interests of human welfare it is not necessary to put too fine a point on truth. Especially when one is dealing with the "enemy"—the enemy being anyone who disagrees on a matter of political importance. Intellectual integrity thus becomes the first victim of political enthusiasm.

Another characteristic feature of the non-party worker in the academic vineyard is his refusal to be bound by consistent standards of judgment. Absolute consistency, of course, is not always possible or desirable, but the departure from it in apparently similar cases always requires explanation or justification. Otherwise judgment has no rational basis and words become systematically ambiguous, no more than a cloak for political hypocrisy. Of myriads of possible illustrations of this attitude, I select a few for brief mention.

After the publication of the photostatic copies of the checks issued by the so-called Anti-Fascist Refugee Committee to Gerhard Eisler, accused by former leading Communists of serving as the chief Cominform representative in the United States, a government agency demanded that the books and records of the Committee be submitted for inspection. Refusal was adjudged as contempt and punishment upheld by the courts. Whereupon an intense campaign against the alleged violation of the civil rights of the responsible officials of this notorious Communist-front organization was conducted in the colleges and on the campuses of the country, spearheaded by fellow travelers. (Incidentally, none of the defenders of this organization showed the slightest qualms about the ethics of raising money for the "orphans and widows of anti-Fascist refugees" and diverting the funds, at least in part, to the support of Communist Party functionaries.) Let us assume that the point at issue is at least debatable and that the Supreme Court, which in the Terminiello and other cases has not betrayed an illiberal spirit in interpreting civil rights, was mistaken in refusing to set the conviction aside.

Some years ago the director of the Ku Klux Klan of the state of Alabama was sentenced to jail for contempt for refusing to produce Klan records of membership before a grand jury. He pleaded that he was bound by a sacred oath of secrecy and that revelation of the names of the Klansmen would be an act of betrayal and prejudicial to the interests of his fellow members. Not a single one of the staunch defenders of the refusal of the Communist front organization to submit its records, or of the Hollywood "ten" to answer questions concerning their membership in the Communist Party, so much as raised a murmur against the conviction of the Klan leader. It is a safe guess to say that they applauded it but not for the same reasons as every genuine liberal did. But no one vouchsafed an explanation of why it was wrong to withhold evidence of membership in the Ku Klux Klan but right to withhold evidence of membership in the Communist Party.

A second illustration is provided by the denazification procedures in occupied Germany. Anybody who has been on the scene knows that with all its limitations the American denazification policy has been the most stringent of all. This has not prevented the academic fellow traveler from bitterly complaining that the United States was giving aid and comfort to former Nazis. But when Walter Ulbricht, the leading German lieutenant of the Kremlin, openly proclaimed in the Russian-licensed *Nacht-Express* that formerly active Nazis were welcomed to leading posts in the new Germany, it evoked no similar response. And yet the motivation of the Kremlin in wooing these formerly active Nazis is transparently clear. "Even if they have not completed their conversion," says Ulbricht, "they clearly realize now that the aggressive forces in the United States aim at the destruction of the German nation."

Another illustration is provided by the so-called Scientific and Cultural Conference for World Peace at the Waldorf Astoria in New York in 1949. Called ostensibly to promote the cause of peace, it was actually designed to mobilize public support for the foreign policy of the Kremlin, then conducting a savage campaign against the Marshall Plan and the North Atlantic Defense Pact. It was sponsored by the National Council of the Arts, Sciences and Professions, the successor to the Independent Citizens Committee of Arts, Sciences and Professions, whose Chairman, Harold Ickes, resigned with a ringing denunciation of the organization as a Communist Front in 1946.

The New York meeting was an outgrowth of the Communist World Congress of Intellectuals at Wroclaw (Breslau), Poland, in 1948 and was followed by the Communist World Peace Conference in Paris in 1950. Of its 560 sponsors, approximately

Academic Integrity and Academic Freedom

twenty per cent were academic persons, the largest single professional group. They were circularized by the liberal, anti-Communist "Americans for Intellectual Freedom" and presented with evidence that the Conference was Communist-controlled, the program rigged to forestall criticism of Soviet cultural and scientific repression, and to pillory the United States as a warlike aggressor against the peaceful Soviet Union. Typical of the situation was the fact that Professor H. J. Muller, Nobel prize winner in genetics, was denied an invitation to appear on the program but that A. I. Oparin, the man who moved Muller's expulsion from the Academy of Sciences of the U.S.S.R. because of his criticisms of Lysenko, was brought all the way from Moscow to discuss science and culture.

Although there was an official Program Committee, it never met. The actual details were planned by a small, behind-the-scenes group. Some of the members of the official Program Committee, however, aware of the mounting criticism, sent suggestions to Dr. Harlow Shapley, Chairman of the Conference, recommending that certain individuals, critical of the foreign policy of the Kremlin and of the Communist cultural line taken at Wroclaw, be put on the program. Dr. Shapley denied that these letters were written or received by him, although copies of the letters sent him by members of the Program Committee were subsequently made available to the press. With the exception of one speaker introduced as a concession to public criticism, the Conference, as anticipated, followed the line of the Kremlin.

The significant point here is that hardly any of the academic sponsors, who had courageously lent their names and prestige to this event, protested the duplicity being practiced on the American public by the declaration that the Conference would permit free and fair discussion, or withdrew their support of the organization. To be sure, they were genuinely interested in peace. And so they were ten years earlier, too. But if at that time, the Nazi-American Bund had invited them to sponsor a

Peace Conference, to a man, indeed, to the very last pacifist, they would have scornfully refused their collaboration.

One can cite case after case of intellectual double-dealing and moral inconsistency, from condemnation of the Reichstag Fire Trial, despite van der Lubbe's confession, to support of the infamous Moscow Trials because of the confessions; from protest against Rakosi's imprisonment in pre-World War II Hungary to silence about, and sometimes defence of, the imprisonment of Cardinals Mindszenty and Stepinac, and the hanging of Petkov; from protest against internment by the Greek government of Communist military insurrectionists, to silence about Greek children, torn out of their parents' hands and kidnapped by Soviet satellite powers.

What explains this calamitous lapse from elementary justice on the part of men and women who in their own fields are so circumspect about intellectual consistency and moral decency? Many things, not the least of which are justifiable indignation against official stupidities and injustices in our own country, and occasional outrageous acts of vigilantism. But most of it can be traced to an assumption deeply held, even when it is unspoken, that the Communist movement is an integral element in a wider movement of progress and enlightenment. Communists, it is held, are people of "the left," uncouth perhaps, but undoubtedly sincere. Despite our legitimate criticisms of their amusing ideological crotchets, they are after all, people "on our side." Whoever criticizes them too severely or refuses to work with them in a common enterprise "breaks the unity of all progressive forces." Besides, the Communists are not always wrong, while our own government is often and clearly wrong. Even those academic fellow travelers who are in no sense revolutionaries themselves could be heard to say, "The Socialists just talk, but the Communists mean it," as if this were a point in the latter's favor. And then there is the Communist rhetoric about democracy. Communists are staunch and aggressive fighters, we are told, but after all they are for peace; they lie, but in the interests of a higher truth;

250

they may seem to be disloyal to this country, but it is out of loyalty to the Soviet Union, which in turn identifies loyalty to it with loyalty to humanity; they seem to be opposed to democracy but they only have a different conception of it—as if that made their views and practices less democratic.

How can intelligent men and women believe such nonsense? Here again there is a baffling inconsistency about the academic fellow traveler. He knows there is no transference of training from one field to another, and he doesn't know it, and he applies this alternating skepticism and faith with a characteristic selective bias. When he reads that a Nobel Prize winner in science has come out for free enterprise or the immortality of the soul, he murmurs: "Another smug scientist pontificating in a field in which he knows nothing." But let the same Nobel Prize winner say that the United States constitutes a greater threat to peace than the Soviet Union or that our supply of atomic bombs should be turned over to the U.N., and he will quote these opinions as authoritative.

Intelligence may be a native power but political intelligence is something that is slowly acquired, and only by hard study. The study, however, must not be confined merely to official documents but must be guided by a leading principle, which Marx himself formulated almost a century ago when he declared that we should not judge a class by what it says of itself any more than we judge an individual. This sounds elementary enough but is something that was never learned by that professor of political science who once argued that the Comintern had nothing to do with the Soviet regime because there was no mention of its existence in the constitution of the Soviet Union.

The best method—although not infallible—of aquiring political intelligence about political realities, is political experience. It is an interesting fact that the vast majority of academic persons who have had any experience in political activity or in the genuine labor movement, in the course of which they had to deal with members of the Communist Party, rapidly learn the truth about them. But since such interests must be peripheral for most scholars and teachers, the absolute number of the politically sophisticated about the Communist conspiracy is small.

Short of actual experience, a close study of Communist theory and *practice* is indispensable to developing a minimal awareness of the situation in the world today. This brings us to the question of what can be done to meet the challenge of the academic fellow traveller.

II

A few things by this time should be clear. First, the general situation is such that it cannot and should not be met by administrative measures. Even when justified against out-and-out party members such administrative measures, *unless authorized and implemented by the teachers themselves,* are apt to worsen the situation. Nor are loyalty oaths of the slightest aid in restoring intellectual integrity where it has been undermined, or in preventing the academic fellow traveler—and for that matter even the party member—from battling for the party line. For many years in the State of New York all teachers have been required during the course of their careers to take an oath pledging themselves to support the Constitution. No one has ever refused to take such an oath; no one has ever been punished for violating it. It is an empty gesture, recognized even by those who administer it as pointless.

Not pointless but dangerous is the directive by the New York State Board of Regents to all public school authorities under the Feinberg Law to report on the measures undertaken to enforce its provisions, which call for the dismissal of all subversive teachers. For the main issue, even as far as Communist Party members are concerned, is *not* one of political subversion but of professional ethics, about which the teachers themselves are the best judges. What makes the Feinberg Law pointedly dangerous is that a report is required of all teachers which in the nature of the case cannot be honestly made. It can only give them a feeling of not being trusted and intensify intellectual timidity and whatever tendencies exist to play safe. Further, one mistaken application of its provisions can easily create an incident which the Communist party will exploit to the utmost, swelling the ranks of the fellow travelers and imbuing them with crusading self-righteousness. If such an incident is not created by some zealously reactionary superintendent, we can be certain that the Communist party, which did not hesitate to denounce its political opponents, especially on the Left, to the Gestapo as secret Communists, will do its best to create one.

Since government intervention is inadvisable even in treating the problem created by members of the Communist party, *a fortiori* it should never be invoked in the struggle for intellectual integrity against the careless, the irresponsible, and the half-witting accomplices of the party line. In the interest of honest dissent, there must be no legal proscriptions of doctrines of any kind.

What then should be done? Until the threat to the democratic culture of the West disappears, the theory and practice of official Communism should be made a required study in the curriculum of all colleges. It is the great merit of President Conant to have realized the importance of this. We can expect Mr. Hutchins to denounce the proposal as a concession to temporalism, and to interpret the temporal as the immediate, and the immediate as the instantaneous. But as anyone knows who has even a bowing acquaintance with Communism, the issues it raises are not only immediate—they involve the foundations of belief for our age, and, according to Communist claims, for all recorded history and class societies. There is plenty of meat in a curriculum so expanded. But we must hasten to add—to safeguard against misunderstanding—that it cannot be the only subject of curricular emphasis. More important still, democracy is to be studied not as a conflicting ideology in a cold war or hot war but as a way of life to be independently explored, developed, and criticized in relation to the problems of contemporary society.

What good will such a study accomplish? The good not only

of understanding the enemy but of recognizing what must be done in the reconstruction of our own culture to realize the promise of democratic life. As a by-product, it will no longer be possible—let us hope—for so many college-trained persons, not to mention their teachers, to believe that the Bolsheviks overthrew the Czar rather than a political system which Lenin himself had characterized as the freest in the world. Using official Communist sources, students will become acquainted, at least as an hypothesis, with the view that the official Communist parties in all countries are organizational tools of the Soviet regime, employed for every purpose including espionage, and not at all an integral section of the indigenous "Left" movement. They will perhaps begin to understand what a politics based on a *Weltanschauung* involves, and the far-reaching consequences of a movement which openly declares that *any means* is justified to achieve the victory of the proletariat, whose dictatorship is "substantially" identified with the dictatorship of the Communist party.

The end of such instruction should be not only to clarify the issues between democracy and communism but to make all persons aware of what they are doing when they reject, accept, or travel along with the Communist Party and its organizational fronts. The age of political innocence in the colleges and universities will come to an end. It will not be possible for a man in the position of Mr. Hutchins, then Chancellor of the University of Chicago, in answer to a question whether he recognized that the U.S. Communist Party was not merely a political party but part of an international conspiratorial movement working in the interest of the U.S.S.R., to blandly reply that he had no knowledge on this subject. And this after the first Hiss trial! Instruction properly given will also make clear how one kind of reaction helps another, and that just as Communist attacks on "Fascists" are often the prelude to the extirpation of democracy (as in Czechoslovakia), so Fascist attacks on "Communists" may (as in Spain) be aimed at all liberals and democrats. At the same time it is to be hoped that the fashionable and undiscriminating trend against the welfare state and welfare economy as an expression of "statism," as a forerunner if not a weaker version of totalitarianism on the Soviet model, will be halted, and the arguments for all sorts of alternative systems of planning, from the New Deal to democratic socialism, will be considered on their merits.

There is something more, in addition to revising the curriculum, that American educators can do to improve the quality and accuracy of political discussion in academic circles. That is to break with the genteel tradition of suffering intolerance, disingenuousness, and intellectual dishonesty in silence. One of the most amazing expressions of liberal sentimentalism and muddled thinking is the view that we cannot be intolerant of those who preach and practice intolerance, that if we oppose fanaticism we cannot ever do so passionately, and that forthright exposure of dishonesty and dangerous ignorance is somehow a betrayal of the intellectual process. This overlooks the truth that ideas can corrupt as well as power; and that ignorance, especially when it is cultivated, can be deadly. Liberalism as a temper of mind is the sworn foe of all absolutes of doctrine and program; but only because it is pledged to a self-critical and self-corrective exercise of the processes of intelligence.

Some individuals who do not like to be exposed for their gullibility in being taken in by Communist fronts occasionally criticize liberals who passionately combat communism as temperamentally of the same kin as Communists. They equate passion for freedom with the totalitarian's passionate sadism in the hope of winning immunity from liberal criticism by discrediting its fervor as a psychologically totalitarian obsession. It is noteworthy that passionate liberal criticism of fascism never provoked this kind of retort. It is not a retort which requires an extensive answer. If those who love freedom do not fight for it passionately, do not make it their ultimate concern, those who have passion for power, for domination over others, will win their war against freedom.

A scholar who propounds anti-Semitic or racist views should be criticized vigorously even when we grant his constitutional and academic right (provided he is not a member of the Klan, a Fascist party, or similar organization) to hold and express such views. Catholic professors, wherever they are, who proclaim that secularism *must* lead to communism or fascism, whose fantastic attacks on the philosophies of men like John Dewey and Bertrand Russell show that they are more fearful of *their* ideas than those of the totalitarian rival power of communism, should be given public lessons in logic and history. The record of Catholic collaboration with Franco, Mussolini, Salazar, Tiso, Dollfuss, and others should be brought vigorously to their attention. A sociologist who defends concentration camps in the Soviet Union as a model of corrective prison labor in the face of books like Gliksman's *Tell the West* should not be administratively curbed but he should be called publicly to account by his colleagues. A fellow traveler who justifies his refusal to protest outrages against civil liberties in countries under Communist rule on the ground that we must clean our own doorstep, when he has been active on every committee organized by the Communist Party to protest lack of civil rights in Germany, China, Argentina and Spain, should be exposed as a political hypocrite.

An astronomer who couples the Soviet purge of scientists with the unenforced laws against the teaching of evolution in our three Southern states as equally bad, when he refrained from mentioning these laws in his denunciation of the Nazis purge of scientists, should be challenged to defend his discriminatory judgments. A literary critic who tells us that if he were in France he would be a Communist and who denies the facts about the suppression of civil liberties and academic rights in satellite countries should not be permitted to pose as a lover of freedom by his colleagues. *This means challenge and criticism, not expulsion.*

A political scientist who writes that the Communist International was organized to defend the Soviet Union against invasion, when its existence was actually planned even before the October Revolution, or who invents a legend about there being two General Vlassovs in order to uphold the fiction that all the Russians rallied to Stalin's regime after Hitler's invasion, or who affirms that Trotsky was a Fascist whose dealings with the Nazis were proved, and that he was assassinated by a bona fide member of his own organization who objected to his plotting with Martin Dies to overthrow the American government—such a man should have his credentials to competent scholarship openly questioned by his peers. Finally, anyone who professes to be appalled at Stalin's regime of terror but who claims that the reports of Hitler's atrocities were exaggerated and either justifies or is evasive about the brutal suppression of all democratic opposition in Spain should be subjected to the same critical exposure.

It is not the fact that these men lack imagination to comprehend the sufferings of the victims of totalitarian oppression, or the compassion to feel akin to the innocent and unjustly accused, or the courage to make an open and total commitment to a new political religion, which chiefly evidences their absence of academic integrity. Whatever failings they reveal on this score are the failings of human beings no matter what their vocations. Scholars or shoemakers may be morally insensitive, cruel, mean, and cowardly, and still turn out competent books or well-made boots. What crucially defines the treason to *academic* integrity on the part of these non-party scholars I have described is not even their violations of the canons of inquiry, which may only be occasional. It is their defense of, or silent acquiescence in, the use of police methods against their colleagues abroad—and what police methods—to suppress ideas in any field not countenanced by party dogma, and their direct and indirect support in this country of a movement which wherever it comes to power aims to destroy every vestige of academic freedom. These "defenders" of academic freedom are its gravediggers.

Not even the most slippery apologist can deny that Communist regimes neither believe in nor practice academic freedom. It is no part of academic freedom for teachers anywhere to use the classroom as concealed members of a political party to "inject" party dogmas into teaching, and "to take advantage of their positions without exposing themselves"—as the Communist Party urges its members to do. The astronomers and geneticists, the artists and the historians who are purged in the Soviet Union are not punished for acting the way Communist Party teachers do in the West, but for holding "wrong" beliefs or for insufficient enthusiasm about "right" ones—"wrong" and "right" ultimately depending on the fiat of the Central Executive Committee of the Communist Party. It is certainly in order and quite understandable—although I believe mistaken—for an individual to argue that despite everything members of the Communist Party who are teaching in our schools and colleges should be tolerated and defended. But when this is coupled with an ambiguous attitude toward the elimination not only of the academic freedom of teachers but often of their persons in Soviet Russia and other countries, what can this betoken but an utter lack of academic integrity? And we may include those in this judgment who up to yesterday have refused to protest academic repressions in Communist countries but who now make brief and hasty references to the Soviet practice as a kind of rhetorical strategy in their campaign for the retention of Communist Party members in the school system of this country.

Public criticism of the academic fellow traveler by the genuinely liberal will not be easy. Some totalitarian liberals who vehemently oppose the loyalty program lock, stock and barrel and urge that all issues be settled in the free market-place of criticism are the first to utter shrill cries of "Red-baiter!" as soon as their ideas are exposed at their true value in this market-place. What they really desire is complete *immunity* from criticism.

They are tremendously helped by the irresponsible criticisms of the cultural vigilantes. Demagogues and reactionaries who attack fellow travelers on false grounds with false charges and false argument strengthen their position and make it all the more difficult for a liberal to win a hearing when he seeks to answer

Academic Integrity and Academic Freedom

the fellow traveler. Every time a false and unwarranted attack is made against a fellow traveler the more sympathy he wins, and the more difficult it is to illumine the issue with the relevant truths.

Whether we are aware of it or not, whether we like it or not, the groves of the academy—but let us hope, not the classrooms—have become one of the battlefields in the current struggle for freedom whose outcome will determine the pattern of culture for centuries to come. Whatever may be true for other battlefields, in the academy we must see to it that the struggle is fought under the same rules of the game which in the past have led in so many fields to clarification and new knowledge. But no one has a right to invoke the rules of the game as protection when he is detected violating them.

The man of academic integrity is prepared to learn from anyone. As a scholar he recognizes no doctrines as subversive. For him doctrines are only valid or invalid in the light of objective evidence and logical inference. That is why he is responsible for keeping the sources of knowledge free from contamination by secret political storm troopers—Communist or others. That is why he must be prepared to take up the struggle, without the help of the state or the regents or the administration, against the obscurantists and professional innocents who would destroy the condition of honest intellectual inquiry. He will have to fight on many fronts—against misguided patriots, clerical Fascists, and those who are maddened by Communist intrigue into foolishness that may be harmful to free institutions.

It is a pity that so much intellectual energy must go into the defense of values which in happier times were taken for granted as integral to the life of scholarship. But it is precisely these values which are today under attack. If they die, academic integrity dies, and with it academic freedom.

This is only the lesser part of the task. The other is to find the constructive devices and solutions to meet the recurrent problems which we face as long as we live. Men live by habit more than they do by thought. In settled times, habit provides security enough. Today we must have the courage to think, and to trust our thought, in order to survive, and possibly continue as a free culture.

It is not the McCarthys and McCarrens and their allies who can lead the struggle for a free culture against its enemies. For they have a distrust of freedom of thought and therefore of thought itself. Nor can such leadership be entrusted to ritualistic liberals who stupidly equate "terroristic McCarthyism" with "terroristic Communism." They think they are thinking when they are only reacting with their viscera. Thinking is making relevant discrimination in judgment in assessing goods and evils, proposed solutions of problems, and their consequences.

Chapter 12

SOME POSITIVE PROPOSALS

Perhaps the most difficult of all problems is how the rule against employment of members of the Communist Party (or any other group organized for purposes of professional misconduct) should be enforced.

Certain procedures are undesirable and likely to produce more harm than good. Among them are loyalty oaths which all members of the Communist Party scrupulously take but to which many non-Communists have conscientious objections. We have already seen that loyalty to democratic institutions cannot be tested by a form of words. The University of California case is a classic illustration of the insistence upon this unnecessary, and foolish, ritualism.

The basic issue in that controversy was not communism but the right of the faculty to determine the professional qualifications of its own members. By an overwhelming majority, the faculty of the University of California voted that members of the Communist Party by reason of their "commitments to that Party are not acceptable members of the faculty." It set up its own mechanism of enforcement but a handful of stubborn men on the State Board of Regents—a bare majority—insisted that all faculty members sign a contract which was equivalent to the oath-test that had been abandoned.

Legislative investigating committees, whether of the Congress or of the States, as a rule are both ineffective and unnecessary. I am not now referring to an investigation of individual members of a college staff who are involved in some private or public organizational activity into which the government has a right to inquire. I am referring to investigations specifically directed to what is going on at a particular campus to determine whether professional misconduct has taken place. Where a faculty is properly aware of its responsibilities, there is no need or justification of legislative invasion. Where it is indifferent or lax in upholding its standards, legislative investigation may still be undesirable but in time it becomes inescapable.

As a first and foremost step in procedure, every faculty ought to adopt rules to which the widest publicity should be given, on the rights and responsibilities of members of the teaching staff. This would correspond somewhat to the Hippocratic credo of the medical profession. These rules should declare that membership in organizations which order their members to indoctrinate for some predetermined "line," or dictate to them which positions they must believe and teach in the fields of scholarship and science, is *ipso facto* a ground for dismissal. No person who subsequently is discovered to be a member of such an organization would be able to plead ignorance of the rule. In this connection the graduate faculty of the New School has given the lead to the entire country.

It will not do to straddle this point as some institutions seem inclined to do even though it leaves them firmly impaled on a contradiction. For example, here is a statement adopted by one Eastern college after the issue of communism arose:

> Commitments of any kind which interfere with an individual's free and unbiased pursuit of truth and understanding are incompatible with the objectives of academic freedom, and no person so committed may, therefore, enjoy its rights.

Some Positive Proposals

This is straightforward enough and sufficient evidence has been offered to show that membership in the Communist Party is a commitment which emphatically interferes with free and unbiased pursuit of truth as well as of honest teaching. But immediately after this sentence, we read:

> Nevertheless, association with, or membership in, any group or organization shall not itself constitute *prima facie* disqualification from participation in free and unbiased pursuit of truth and understanding, and consequently shall not itself constitute sufficient grounds for disqualification from membership in an academic community.

This obviously negates the preceding sentence, for if that first sentence is sincerely meant, membership in the Communist Party should constitute, at the very least, *prima facie* evidence of unfitness and disqualification.

A similar ambiguity is found in the statement drafted for public distribution by the Executive Committee of the Board of Trustees of Sarah Lawrence College on January 22, 1952. I italicize the ambiguous phrases in the key sentences:

> Teachers who meet the test of candor, honesty, and scholarly integrity may not be deprived of any rights they hold as citizens of this country, *including the right to belong to any legal political organization* of their own choosing.

Leaving aside the superrogative declaration that the College may not deprive its faculty members of any rights they hold as citizens—for obviously the College cannot do something which is beyond its legal province—this seems perfectly clear. Any faculty member who belongs to the Communist Party, which is a legal political organization, will be judged strictly by performance like everybody else. This is the traditional position which we have found clearly wanting.

And in an apparent effort to strengthen it, the following two concluding sentences appear.

Heresy, Yes—Conspiracy, No

It is a principle accepted by the Faculty, the President, and Trustees alike that there is to be no indoctrination of students with a political, philosophical, or religious dogma. No person, therefore, who takes his intellectual orders from an outside authority, whether communist or other, *could be given or could retain* the responsibility of membership in the Sarah Lawrence faculty.

Why couldn't they? Because if they took their orders from the outside, it would be discovered by their practices in the classroom? Then this does not add anything essential to what has already been expressed before.

If instead of "no person . . . *could* be given or *could* retain" is really meant "no person . . . *will* be given or *will be permitted* to retain the responsibility of membership in the Sarah Lawrence faculty," then obviously membership in at least one legal political party, the Communist Party, is declared to be *ipso facto* incompatible with teaching at Sarah Lawrence.

Sad to say it is the first interpretation which expresses the real intentions of the drafters of the statement, for in explanation it is stated that "prejudiced or politically inspired teaching would quickly reveal itself, and would be rejected by the students and by the whole College." I am not concerned here with the reiterated assumption of President Harold Taylor that college students are too bright ever to be taken in by indoctrinating teachers, an extraordinarily barefaced piece of flattery, and at odds with the facts. What I wish to point out is that the use of the words "No person could be given or could retain" instead of "No person will be given nor will he be permitted to retain" is either evidence of honest confusion or rhetorical disingenuousness. It *seems* to suggest that members of the Communist Party would neither be employed nor retained on the faculty of Sarah Lawrence College. But taken literally members of the legal Communist Party, if any, who have not been detected carrying out their instructions, could claim protection and tenure under this declaration.

To serve any useful purpose a faculty declaration of principles should be at least as explicit as that of the New School for Social Research and not lump together logically irreconcilable positions in an attempt to compromise basic differences.

The second step in procedure would be the election of a Faculty Committee on Professional Ethics. Its function would be to receive complaints either from the faculty or administration or both and conduct investigations. Its role would not necessarily be so passive. Wherever there was evidence that a Communist group was at work, or any other group organized for unprofessional practices, it would undertake investigation on its own initiative. The specific modes of procedure will vary from place to place and from faculty to faculty, but in all cases it will culminate in a fair hearing for any teacher charged with being a member of the Communist Party. Any teacher so charged would be suspended with pay until reinstated or dismissed by decision of the Faculty Committee or governing Board at the recommendation of the Faculty Committee. No publicity would be given to the suspension or to the hearing unless requested by the teacher. He would have the privileges of counsel.

Thirdly, admitted Communist Party membership, although *prima facie* evidence of unfitness and disqualification, will not *automatically* lead to dismissal without further consideration of the case and of the consequences of acting on it. There may be sufficient reason to forego taking disciplinary action against the teacher. That is to say, there may sometimes be valid grounds for retaining a person which are stronger than the valid grounds for dismissing him.* In such consideration the faculty committee *may* deem it advisable to investigate the individual behavior of the admitted Communist Party member but in contradistinction to the position of the American Association of University Professors, this type of individual investigation *will not* be mandatory. Each case and each situation will be considered in the light of

---

* *Cf.* my discussion of this type of situation in *Journal of Philosophy*, 1952, pp. 98ff.

the rule, and sometimes it will be sufficient to know that an individual is a member of the Communist Party to dismiss him, something which is never regarded as legitimate by the AAUP.

For example, suppose anonymous defamatory leaflets of the kind described in an earlier chapter have been distributed by the Communist Party. In the light of its knowledge of how the Communist Party is organized and functions, a Faculty Committee may be justified in dismissing all known or proven members of the Communist Party on the campus without the *necessity* of establishing who did what when. If an individual member of the Communist Party claimed he was the "bad" kind of Communist often postulated in argument, it would be up to him to prove it; it would not be required of the faculty committee to prove that any member of the Communist Party was a "good" Communist; and particularly important, such a faculty committee would not be required to prove that a member of the Party indoctrinated in class.

Finally, if membership in the Communist Party is denied and then proved by the evidence of inquiry, dismissal will be automatic, since unprofessional conduct will have therewith been established by the lies and deceptions practiced by the individual in question.

Because of the instructions they receive, it is to be expected that most members of the Communist Party will blithely lie about their affiliations and practices. It may be very difficult to uncover evidence of their organizational connections and educationally conspiratorial activities. Nonetheless, the undertakings of the Communist Party, although carefully concealed almost always leave some traces. There is a trail of expulsions, denunciations, publications, demonstrations, special types of organizational action which to the knowledgeable eye are reliable signs that Communists are at work.

It is not proposed to undertake a hunt to ferret out members of the Communist Party on campuses or for faculty members on the payroll of corporations pledged to propagandize for or against legislation in accordance with instructions received. The above proposals are in fact designed to prevent such hunts, to allay the fears and suspicions of many groups, aroused by some recent revelations about organized Communist penetration of schools, that colleges and universities are hotbeds of communism, by convincing them that educators have appropriate means to eliminate educational abuses whenever they are discovered; and that they can do this as educators without disturbing the enterprise of learning, and without the help of volunteer firemen. Nor are these proposals presented as a camouflage behind which to do nothing about some outrageous violations of the ethics of teaching and scholarship. Sensibly interpreted, faculty committees will move whenever some evidence manifests itself of Communist activity of sufficient importance to warrant investigation. And because they will be prepared to move, because they will have clearly stated the principles of professional integrity, and described the mechanisms in readiness to uphold them against violators, they can reasonably expect the public to support them in contesting the right of any lay group to interfere with colleges and universities.

It is true that *formal* membership in the Communist Party no longer exists for teachers in the sense that membership cards are no longer issued. Sometimes, membership will have to be construed from a complex pattern consisting of activities, participation in key front organizations, publication in party line organs, content-analysis of variations in position establishing close correlation with the official Communist Party line. Since it is to be expected that most members of the Communist Party, not faced by threat of prosecutions for perjury, will refuse to admit membership, and certainly not present membership, the problem will be to determine when an individual is lying and when he is telling the truth. The faculty committee will serve as a kind of academic jury. It will assess the weight of different kinds of testimony and evidence offered in the inquiry in the light of the particular context or situation obtaining on the campus. I do not believe that it is placing too great a reliance upon the judicial capacities of the best trained minds of the community, *when they make themselves familiar with the ways and doctrines of the Communist Party,* to expect that they will be able to distinguish between the educational heretic and the conspirator.

This is obviously not a panacea. It is not guaranteed to track down and eliminate every last conspirator or unworthy teacher from the faculties of our schools and colleges. It would be preferable to tolerate the presence of an occasional Communist Party member than to resort to the practices of detection which would necessarily be introduced if we sought to establish guilt *only* by classroom performance. But intelligently applied, the procedure recommended should do three things.

It should have an enormous educational and psychological effect in reaffirming the critical function of the teacher in a free society. Everyone entrusted with teaching our youth would become focally aware of the meaning of professional integrity, and resentful of threats to the independence of inquiry no matter what its source. Second, it should enable faculties to clear up educationally embarrassing situations in which some individuals are deliberately exploiting their institutional connections to propagandize and indoctrinate for the Communist Party line. There have been cases in which members of the Communist Party connected with colleges and universities have not scrupled to disseminate the most outrageous falsehoods at the behest of the agents of the Kremlin from the charge that John Dewey was a Fascist to the charge that the United States was conducting bacteriological warfare in Korea—charges to which no one would have paid the slightest attention if these individuals did not occupy college or university posts. Finally, I repeat because of its importance, this procedure would enable educators to keep Congressional and Legislative investigating committees off their campuses by building up public support for the reasonable proposition that the determination of educational fitness should be left to professional educators. There is some reason to hope, according to T. V. Smith, who is notable both for his professional and Con-

Some Positive Proposals

gressional experience, that legislatures themselves would refuse to authorize legislative investigations into colleges and universities, once the community became aware that the teachers themselves were exercising vigilance in respect to the fulfillment of professional obligations.

There is always a danger that if faculties begin to act, they may be stampeded into foolishness and hysteria, and that the situation may get out of hand. But there is just as great, if not greater, danger that the situation will get out of hand if faculties do not act in the face of Communist provocations or remain supine when standards of honest scholarship and teaching are being flouted. If reliable generalizations can be made about the state of American public opinion, it is safe to predict that it will not countenance an attitude that "anything goes" in the school until it is found out, and that declared conspirators are to be given an opportunity for their work of subversion, and rewarded until apprehended in their dishonorable actions.

Unfortunately, up to the present time the teaching faculties of our colleges and universities have shown very little disposition to enforce the proper standards of professional conduct in regard to actual conspirators, with the result that agencies less qualified have occasionally rushed in to fill the vacuum. The time is already late; and if the offensive of the Soviet Union against the security of the democratic West increases in scope and intensity, the state may intervene systematically instead of episodically to rectify abuses. As far as elementary and high schools and public colleges go, legislation like the Feinberg and Ober Laws show the extent to which unwisdom can be carried in some states. It is important to prevent similar legislation from being adopted which would apply to privately supported colleges and universities.

The prime responsibility for the failure of college faculties to undertake the task of stating and enforcing the proper standards, particularly with respect to the employment of members of the Communist Party, must be laid at the door of the American Association of University Professors.

Heresy, Yes — Conspiracy, No

We shall therefore close with a brief criticism of the position of the American Association of University Professors on the problem under discussion. This is all the more necessary because, despite the noteworthy work the A.A.U.P. has done in the past, today its position is being exploited by a few members of the Communist Party in the schools—declared enemies of academic freedom, democracy, and professional integrity—to build a protective bulwark around themselves behind which to continue their work of educational subversion, the sapping and mining of free institutions, and the corruption of free inquiry.

Needless to say this is not the intent of the officers of the A.A.U.P. but one of the consequences of their position. The Secretary of the A.A.U.P. has always insisted, in denying the right of the membership as a whole to determine the position of the A.A.U.P., that the position in question is only that of Committee A—its leading Committee on Academic Freedom and Tenure. And it is true that the forty thousand members of the A.A.U.P. have never had an opportunity to pass upon it, or to read dissenting views in its official organ, the *Bulletin*, where a virtual censorship of contributions on this theme is enforced, if they differ from the position of Committee A.*

Committee A interprets the general position adopted by the A.A.U.P. in 1915, 1925, and 1940 to specific situations and to some general problems. From the time it has considered the prob-

* Up to the time this is written no article critical of the position of Committee A has been accepted for publication by the editor of the *Bulletin* of the AAUP, although such articles have been submitted. No speaker critical of the position of the AAUP has been permitted to address the annual meetings. No announcement has ever been made that the position of Committee A would be discussed at annual meetings and members were surprised to read for the first time in the Spring 1952 *Bulletin* that the position of Committee A had been endorsed by the handful of uninstructed delegates and whatever other individual active members (usually from the local chapters of the city in which the annual meeting is held) were present at the Thirty-eighth Annual Meeting in 1952. The resolution submitted for endorsement was presented in the closing hours of the closing session as a routine matter. The number present at the time was not indicated nor whether there was provision for discussion or debate.

lem of tenure for members of the Communist Party, it has invariably held that there is no difference in principle between the rights and duties of members of the Communist Party in American colleges and universities, and members of other parties. It holds no brief, of course, for the views of members of the Communist Party but it is convinced that to bar individuals from the faculty who are members of a lawful group is to lapse into the belief that there is "guilt by association."

The report of Committee A for 1947 states explicitly the position from which there has been no deviation despite the reams of evidence about the conspiratorial character of the Communist Party: "So long as the Communist Party in the United States is a legal political party, affiliation with that Party in and of itself should not be regarded as a justifiable reason for exclusion from the academic profession."

It should be noted carefully that this applies only to members of the faculty who have tenure. Committee A does not expect members of the Communist Party to be *hired,* and on several occasions has stated that to employ them, when they apply, is undesirable.

It is quite certain that it would not take this position in respect to any other legal political party. Although it would not investigate or formally condemn a university for refusing to *hire* a member of the Republican, Democratic or Socialist Party, or for dismissing him before he acquired tenure, it certainly would criticize such actions as violating the very spirit of academic freedom. But refusal to employ a member of the Communist Party or dismissing him before he acquires tenure, it does not condemn. Why? Because, almost despite itself, it recognizes that there is an important difference between the Communist Party and all other political parties, that the Communist Party is something more, and something other than merely a legally recognized association.

Nonetheless, after tenure has been *won* by an individual, Committee A refuses to recognize this distinction. The refusal is unreasonable on its very face. For if one says a college is justified in refusing to employ an individual known as a Communist because he "would need too much watching," does it not follow that if a member of the Communist Party had fooled or deceived a college about his membership in the Communist Party, he would bear even more watching than one who was honest? And what if a man joins the Communist Party *after* he has acquired tenure? Does he bear less watching?

There is something here which requires clarification and one turns to the reports of Committee A in hopes of finding it.

The views of Committee A during the last decade have annually been restated by three of its former Chairmen, Professors Shannon, Kirkwood and Laprade with the close collaboration of the secretary, Dr. Himstead. What strikes one about their discussion of the whole subject of Communist Party teachers in education is first, the failure to come to grips with the arguments presented for exclusion by Professors Lovejoy, Smith, Childs, V. Thayer, Hildebrandt and many others. Second, the Committee evinces no familiarity with the history, structure, and mode of operation of the Communist Party as a conspiratorial underground organization. Third, there is almost a willful confusion of the issues involved. In the annual reports of Committee A the position of those who desire to liberate the faculties of American colleges and universities from a few faithless individuals on grounds that they have violated their *professional* trust is equated with the position of the Communists, themselves, who wish to destroy all academic freedom by repressing scientific heresies. No distinction is made between a heresy and a conspiracy.

A few illustrations of the points made above will suffice. No matter what the Communist Party is, and no matter how it functioned, were Committee A consistent, it would still hold that these matters had no bearing upon the question of tenure for Communist Party teachers. But on occasion, Committee A has taken a position as to the relation of the Communist Party and Kremlin which is obviously mistaken. For example, Professor

Some Positive Proposals

Shannon in reporting for Committee A in 1948 wrote that "the evidence that the Communist Party in the United States is subservient to the dictates of international communism, which means the Communist Party of the Soviet Union, is not conclusive." (*Bulletin,* Spring 1948, p. 123.)

If this evidence is not conclusive to Committee A, no evidence on this matter or anything else will ever appear conclusive to it. The intent of Committee A's demurrer is not to assert that all empirical judgments are uncertain. It is specifically to leave it doubtful whether the American Communist Party owes its basic loyalty to the Soviet Union. Such a doubt would weaken the case of those who assert that fifth columnists, pledged to violate the ethics of their profession, have no place in the schools. Professor Shannon would have been better able to establish the inconclusive character of the assertion that the Communist Party is *completely* subservient to the dictates of the Communist Party of the Soviet Union, if he could point to a *single* instance in which the American Communist Party ever disagreed with, or criticized, any action or pronouncement on any subject at any time by the leadership of the Soviet Communist Party and the Soviet Union. Neither he nor anyone else is in a position to do so because there is no such instance.

One specially striking feature of Committee A's reports is their failure directly to discuss the significance of the empirical material about the educational activities of the Communist Party cited in this book, or to answer any of its explicit arguments. But Professor Kirkland, one of its chairmen, has on occasions made misleading references to this material of an oblique character, and attempted to answer one of the arguments. We have already seen that he has interpreted the instructions given to members of the Communist Party to indoctrinate, as "instructions to an inner group" when in actuality these instructions appear in the official organ of the Communist Party, which *all* members are expected to read.

Even more misleading, however, is his reference in the same

Heresy, Yes—Conspiracy, No

article * to the argument that no reasonable educator would turn loose a *present and active* member of the Ku Klux Klan upon students, and that what held for the Ku Klux Klan should also hold for the Communist Party.

He cites the case of someone who was a *past* member of the Ku Klux Klan and who repudiated his membership, in order to remind us that "if membership in the Ku Klux Klan automatically meant exclusion from the United States courts, the Supreme Court would have been deprived of the services of an associate justice who has been conspicuous in the support of freedom."

Surely Professor Kirkland cannot be unaware of the fact that the question is not about *past* members of the Communist Party but about present and active ones. Does he really believe that present and active members of the Ku Klux Klan are not, *per se,* objectionable candidates for our judiciary? If he does, further discussion is unnecessary. The Justice to whom Professor Kirkland refers went before the people to explain, and apologize for, his past membership in the Klan. Had he still been a Klan member, President Roosevelt would never have nominated him. Nor would the country have stood for it, if he had. A man may have a legal right to join the Klan, but this act disqualifies him from certain kinds of employment whose duties he has sworn to violate.

The logic behind the general principles which determine professional fitness for the judiciary applies to the question of professional fitness of teachers. It is extraordinary how sentimental liberalism can overlook the common sense of the matter.

This kind of sentimental liberalism becomes a dangerous weakness in dealing with hardened conspirators. Professor Kirkland adroitly refers to Communists not as Communists but as "radicals," leaving the implication that those who in the interest of honest heresy would bar conspiracy, are really seeking to punish Communist individuals for their beliefs. This is not sentimental-

* *The Key Reporter,* the Phi Beta Kappa news magazine, Vol. VI, No. 2, p. 3.

Some Positive Proposals

ism but malicious insinuation, aggravated by his reference in another article to "the loudest baying (*sic*!) against Communists on faculties arising from the ranks of American socialists . . ." (*Bulletin*, Autumn, 1950, p. 426)—without specifying that these socialists have carefully distinguished between heresy and conspiracy.

Polemical fervor sometimes carries scholars to strange lengths. One wonders whether Professor Kirkland, as a former President of the AAUP, was aware of the implications of the following passage in his address featured in the Association's *Bulletin* (*loc. cit.* p. 422.):

> In brief, we should exclude from the academic arena not only those who are incompetent and dishonest but those of such authoritarian mind that they do not believe in the practice of free inquiry and who, if they were in power, would deny its exercise to others, perhaps on the specious justification that error cannot be given the same opportunities as truth.

This goes farther than anything advocated in this book, is patently incompatible with the position of Committee A and makes heretical belief a bar to teaching. Yet Professor Kirkland ardently supports the rights of members of the Communist Party who have won tenure to teach on the same terms as all other teachers.

Professor Laprade is the author of most of the annual reports of Committee A in recent years. He, too, carefully avoids coming to grips with the evidence and arguments in behalf of the position advanced in this book to which, like all members of Committee A, his attention has often been called. Instead, he employs the method of amalgam and irrelevant reiteration of what is not in dispute, to conceal from himself or his readers his failure to meet the challenge to the ill-considered view of Committee A.

The method of Professor Laprade's amalgam consists in linking a position which he finds it difficult to assail with one which is not held, or is even actively opposed by those who hold the first position. By criticizing both positions with arguments relevant only to the second, the impression is given that the first position is being refuted when as a matter of fact it is not even being discussed.

"We cannot feel," writes Professor Laprade, in discussing the tenure rights of members of the Communist Party, "that a citizen of the United States who has long held a position of trust should be summarily dismissed from it solely because he has *at some time or other* been a member of an organization which contains *conspirators* and *dogmatists*." *

Notice the expression "some time or other," "conspirators and dogmatists." It implies that the position under discussion advocates the dismissal of someone who was *once* a member of the Communist Party, and had genuinely broken with it, or the dismissal of such a person who may have once been a member of a group of dogmatists. Surely Professor Laprade knows that the position he should criticize is that *present* members who are members of *conspiratorial* groups like the Communist Party should be barred. Conspirators may be dogmatists but not all dogmatists are conspirators. No one is proposing to dismiss a person for being a dogmatist, or a member of a group containing dogmatists. Members of many religious groups are dogmatists about some of their beliefs. But they are not under discussion unless they organize themselves into a presently active group of conspirators.

As we should expect, the consequence of this method of amalgam is to construe the recommendation to bar present members of the Communist conspiracy as if it meant the imposition of a political dogma. All it really means is that an individual is expected to live up to the minimum presuppositions of intellectual honesty and integrity which permits him to hold any principle in any field. But not to Professor Laprade. To bar members of an educational conspiracy is like killing scientific heretics in the

* *Bulletin of the A.A.U.P.*, Spring 1950, p. 42, my italics.

Soviet Union. "The imposition of dogma by authority," he gravely tells us, "whether in the field of genetics or politics, is fatal to scholarship."

Professor Laprade asserts again and again "that an individual ought to be blamed only for his own actions." Agreed. What he does not discuss is whether the *personal act* of joining the Communist Party, and whether the *continued acts of co-operation* with that Party, which, as we have seen, membership involves, is sufficiently blameworthy to make the individual unfit to teach in our schools and colleges. After all no one is compelled to join and stay in the Communist Party of the U.S.A. at the point of a gun!

I conclude with a challenge to Committee A and those who support its position to justify that position to its membership and the public generally by free and fair discussion. And the discussion can be carried on in terms of Committee A's own formulation. Professor Laprade asserts that once scholars and teachers have served their apprenticeship they should "thereafter be left secure and free to do their work *unless they are guilty of violating the mores of the profession or of society to an extent that renders them manifestly unfit for their task."* (*Bulletin,* 1951, p. 77, my italics)

In the light of our account of what the Communist Party is and how it functions in school and society, we ask: Is not the act of an individual who joins to help it achieve its conspiratorial purposes, a clear and manifest violation of both the mores of the profession and our society of sufficient gravity to render him unfit for his academic trust and task?

That is the question!

No matter how we answer it, let us be clear that it is not the first, second or third most important question in American education. Our schools suffer from many graver evils than that posed by the duplicity of a few Communist teachers. We must not lose perspective because the issue has been puffed up in discussion.

Heresy, Yes — Conspiracy, No

The discussion has been necessary if only because of the claim of ritualistic liberals that the exclusion of a few members of the Communist Party from our schools spells the end of freedom in American education. It has also been necessary in the interest of clarification in order to formulate an intelligent policy.

It is sad to observe the absence of sobriety not only in popular but academic discussions of the subject. After the University of Washington cases, which unfortunately were not handled according to a procedure which would make the decision of the faculty committee binding, it was widely predicted that an educational reign of terror would be unleashed at the university and that academic standards would deteriorate. It is almost five years now after the event and from the beginning these predictions proved entirely baseless. Without blinking an eyelash the same prophets prophesy in the same way whenever similar situations arise.

The chief evil from which the schools suffer is not communism but community neglect, and the failure to make the common and special needs of the individual personality their supreme concern. Whatever the responsibilities of the schools to a democratic society, the responsibilities of a democratic society to its schools are more basic and more numerous. These responsibilities have not been adequately discharged. The need for more schools and better schools, more teachers and better teachers and better-paid teachers, grows. The perennial need for educational thinking, for a consciously held philosophy of education, has become more acute in the long war for survival and freedom into which we have already entered. The task of American educators is to integrate the insights of liberal thinkers from Socrates to John Dewey, as well as the insights born of wider scientific knowledge, into a coherent philosophy to make the *practice* of education meaningful, excellent, joyful, and free.

INDEX

279

Index

Index

Index

Index

Vishinsky, Andrey, 232
Violence, advocated by Lenin, 24
Vocation of the teacher, Chapt. 7,
    passim

Ward, Harry, 51

Welfare State, 11
Whitehead, Alfred, 202
Webb, Sidney and Beatrice, 51
Wright, Richard, 202

Zehbrak, Professor, 204